Roman Conquests:
Egypt and Judaea

Roman Conquests: Egypt and Judaea

John D. Grainger

Pen & Sword
MILITARY

First published in Great Britain in 2013 by
PEN & SWORD MILITARY
an imprint of
Pen & Sword Books Ltd
47 Church Street
Barnsley
South Yorkshire
S70 2AS

ISBN 978-1-84884-823-8

Typeset by M. C. Bishop at The Armatura Press
Printed and bound in Great Britain by CPI Group (UK) Ltd, Croydon, CR0 4YY

Pen & Sword Books Ltd incorporates the Imprints of Pen & Sword Aviation, Pen & Sword Maritime, Pen & Sword Military, Wharncliffe Local History, Pen and Sword Select, Pen and Sword Military Classics, Leo Cooper, Remember When, Seaforth Publishing and Frontline Publishing.

For a complete list of Pen & Sword titles please contact
PEN & SWORD BOOKS LIMITED
47 Church Street, Barnsley, South Yorkshire, S70 2AS, England
E-mail: enquiries@pen-and-sword.co.uk
Website: www.pen-and-sword.co.uk

Contents

List of Illustrations

Maps

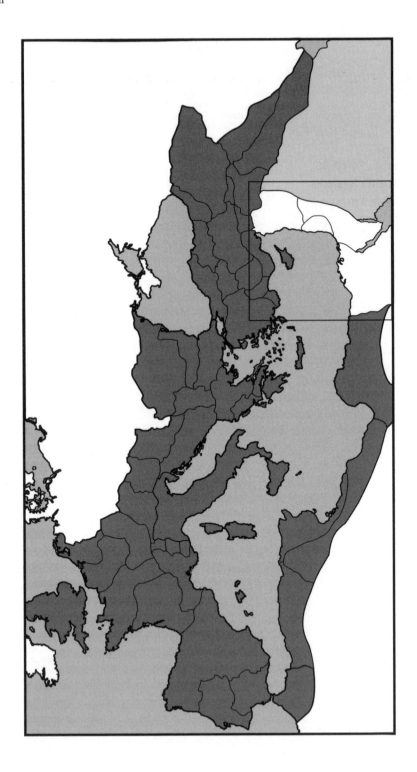

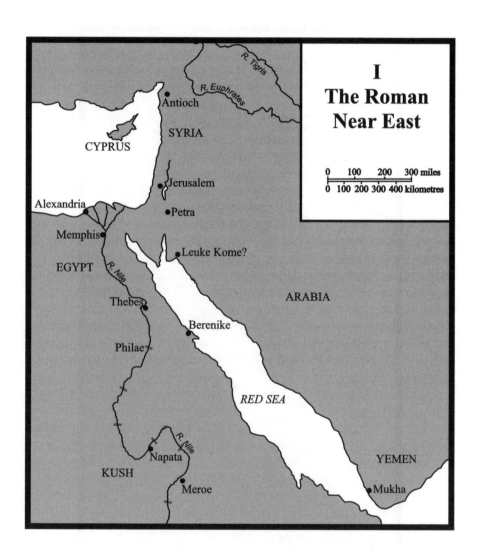

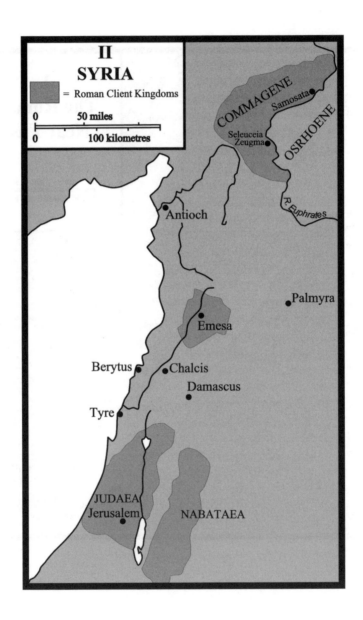

II
SYRIA

= Roman Client Kingdoms

0   50 miles

0   100 kilometres

COMMAGENE

Samosata

OSRHOENE

Seleuceia
Zeugma

R. Euphrates

Antioch

Palmyra

Emesa

Berytus   Chalcis

Damascus

Tyre

JUDAEA
Jerusalem   NABATAEA

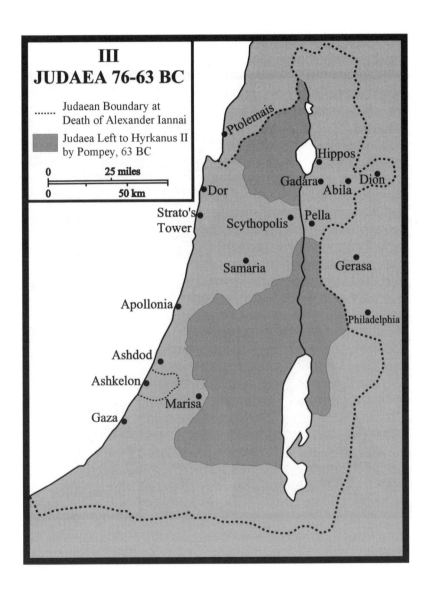

III
JUDAEA 76-63 BC

...... Judaean Boundary at
Death of Alexander Iannai

Judaea Left to Hyrkanus II
by Pompey, 63 BC

0   25 miles

0   50 km

Ptolemais

Hippos

Dor

Gadara   Dion
Abila

Strato's
Tower

Scythopolis   Pella

Samaria

Gerasa

Apollonia

Philadelphia

Ashdod

Ashkelon

Marisa

Gaza

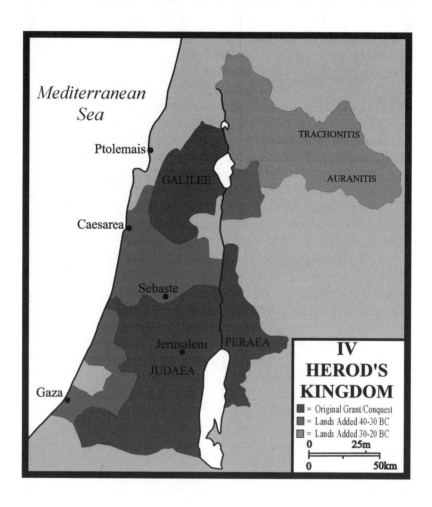

Mediterranean Sea

Ptolemais

GALILEE

Caesarea

Sebaste

Jerusalem   PERAEA

JUDAEA

Gaza

TRACHONITIS

AURANITIS

IV
HEROD'S
KINGDOM

■ = Original Grant/Conquest
■ = Lands Added 40-30 BC
■ = Lands Added 30-20 BC

0   25m

0   50km

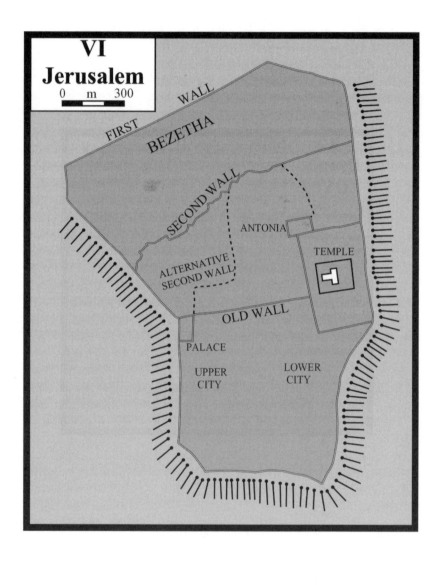

VII
ALEXANDRIA

H = Harbours   P = Palace Area
J = Jewish Quarter   W = City Wall
L = Lighthouse   S = Heptastadion

L

Pharos I.

H

H

S

P

J

W

W

Lake Mareotis

Genealogy of the Family of Herod

(Much simplified; dates are those of rulerships)

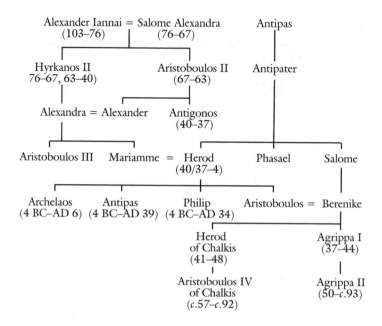

Alexander Iannai = Salome Alexandra   Antipas
(103–76)   (76–67)

Hyrkanos II   Aristoboulos II   Antipater
76–67, 63–40)   (67–63)

Alexandra = Alexander   Antigonos
(40–37)

Aristoboulos III   Mariamme = Herod   Phasael   Salome
(40/37–4)

Archelaos   Antipas   Philip   Aristoboulos = Berenike
(4 BC–AD 6)   (4 BC–AD 39)   (4 BC–AD 34)

Herod   Agrippa I
of Chalkis   (37–44)
(41–48)

Aristoboulos IV   Agrippa II
of Chalkis   (50–c.93)
(c.57–c.92)

Introduction

The lands of the eastern and south-eastern corner of the Mediterranean, Syria and Egypt had been the centres of power of two of the Great Powers of the ancient world since the days of Alexander the Great. But by 64 BC these lands had fallen on evil days, with no viable kingdom of Syria left, and misgovernment rife in Egypt. Syria had broken into a confusing medley of cities, kingdoms, tyrants, bandits, and rebels. And Rome, greedy for money and territory as always, was poised in the north to grab.

They may be geographical neighbours, but to link Judaea and Egypt into an account of their conquest by Rome is rather like yoking an ass and an ox in a ploughing contest. Egypt was conquered in a brief campaign of no more than a year; Judaea fought repeatedly to avoid such a fate, in wars lasting over a century. (This is an exaggeration, of course, and the conquest of Egypt took longer, though it was less violent than that of Judaea, and the Judaean wars were intermittent, but the contrast does exist.) Further, the two peoples did not particularly like each other, and their main rulers, Kleopatra and Herod, scarcely got on.

Nevertheless the link exists. Besides being neighbours, they were deeply involved in the final paroxysms of the Roman civil wars which destroyed the republic, as participants, exploiters, and eventually victims. The responses of the two were, however, different, the Egyptians submitting with scarcely a murmur, the Jews of Judaea fiercely and repeatedly resisting.

So, despite the obvious power of the Roman state, the elimination of the local rulers who occupied the land from the Taurus Mountains to the deserts of Egypt did not happen easily. It was already clear in 64 BC that Rome was capable of conquering all these places, probably in a single campaign, but instead it took 170 years to complete the task.

There are many reasons for this lethargy, partly Roman, partly local. Rome itself, of course, collapsed into a series of civil wars, which, at least in the east, delayed conquest. In the region itself there were unexpectedly stubborn resistances to conquest from a variety of groups, above all, but not only, from the Jews of Judaea. It did not help that a major and unconquerable power – Parthia – loomed nearby, equally willing to snap up bits of territory. Then there was Roman over-confidence, producing distant expeditions far beyond the empire's capabilities.

For the warfare in this corner of the Mediterranean extended over a much wider area than the two countries in the title. Roman aggression extended itself deep into Asia, Africa, and Arabia, and had done so even before the conquest of Syria had been completed. The continued existence of the Judaean state in a condition of semi-independence helped to maintain other Syrian kingdoms in the same condition, so that the destruction of Judaea was eventually accompanied by the final annexations of several of these other kingdoms.

It is thus a complicated tale, very different from the conquests achieved elsewhere, though the bit-by-bit acquisitions of Asia Minor and North Africa show similarities. The two countries which are here singled out for special treatment, Judaea and Egypt, merit it because their sources of information are rather better than other parts of the region, and this makes it possible to discuss what happened in those two countries in some detail. And yet, the geographical range cannot be confined to these two places. To understand the events it is also necessary to consider the rest of Syria, Arabia and Egypt's southern neighbour.

In the end, after much conflict, Rome ruled all Syria and Egypt, but in the process the imperial government discovered that there were areas which it was not able to reach. By 20 BC this had become clear and the expansion of Rome in the east effectively ended, except for mopping up several client states which Rome already dominated. Thirty years later, the same realization struck home in Germany, with the destruction of three legions by the Germans in the Teutoburg Forest in AD 9. Again, in Britain in the AD 80s, the same happened when Agricola failed to conquer Scotland. One might liken the Roman Empire to a caged bull, butting in all directions in frantic attempts to escape its imprisonment. It was in the East that the first check to this took place. It seems likely that by 20 BC Augustus had begun to formulate the policy which he eventually passed on as advice to his successor Tiberius: not to expand the empire further.

Chapter 1

Judaea: Pompey's Conquest

The Roman state reached Syria in 64 BC in the person of the General Cn. Pompeius Magnus ('Pompey'), his legates, and his army. Syria – taken to be all the land between the Taurus Mountains and Egypt – had, Pompey claimed, become Roman because he had defeated the Armenian King Tigranes, who in turn had more or less ruled it for the last few years. In fact, the land Pompey entered was in widespread political confusion. Whether he intended to annex it or not, declaring it to be annexed by Rome was a means of giving himself and Rome a free hand to sort things out.[1]

As an example of this process we have a notice in the Jewish historian Josephus. As Tigranes came south to tackle Ptolemais, which was on the northern Palestinian coast, the ruler of Judaea, Queen Salome Alexandra 'sent many valuable gifts and envoys to him'. That is, she submitted well before he could attack the kingdom. The message she sent was to ask him 'to grant favourable terms'. Tigranes 'gave them reason to hope for the best', and made a point of saying he accepted Judaea's 'homage'.[2] Salome was particularly prompt in her message, but, on a different timescale, this was how Tigranes established himself in his Syrian province.

The prospect of any further measures of control imposed by Tigranes evaporated along with his power when the news of Pompey's arrival in Syria came, but it was the political supremacy Tigranes had achieved which became the basis for Pompey's actions in Syria. He was, of course, much assisted by the extreme disintegration of Syria, and by the shallowness of the power of many of the rulers he encountered. Indeed, some of these rulers had only emerged since Tigranes withdrew; others had extended their reach in the power vacuum before Pompey arrived. But the subordination of the Syrians was, at least in Roman eyes, transferred to Rome as a result of Rome's defeat of their overlord Tigranes. At the same time it was evident almost from the first that Pompey was anxious to avoid much fighting. This enabled most of the Syrian states to make terms and survive.

On his way south from the Taurus passes and through Syria during 64, Pompey investigated the status of each community. Cities which were autonomous were generally left that way; cities subject to dictators were usually freed; monarchies might be abolished or preserved. The whole process was purely pragmatic, even erratic, but it was in its results just as superficial as Tigranes' measures. So the four great cities of northern Syria – Seleukeia, Antioch,

Laodikeia, Apamea – became autonomous cities in the new Roman province of Syria, as did a flock of smaller cities in the area. But Seleukeia-Zeugma, controlling the vital bridge over the Euphrates, which had been seized by the king of Kommagene, remained his, as did the small city of Doliche; he was a moderately powerful ruler at such a vital spot and this was a defensive necessity. He helped insulate Syria from Parthia to the east. The tyrants of Lysias and Tripolis, Silas the Jew and Dionysios, both very recent powers, were removed. The remaining Seleukid royal representatives, already driven out once by Tigranes were unceremoniously dismissed. Their pretensions, given even a foothold of power, would have caused continuous disruption as they attempted to recover their old power. Pompey merely confirmed Tigranes' action.[3]

As he came to central Syria, Pompey encountered a series of monarchies, all of which had established their rule over a number of Greek cities. The Hill Chieftain Kinyras had taken control of Byblos and Berytos and some smaller cities on the northern Lebanese coast; Pompey 'restored' the cities' 'freedom', which they celebrated by instigating a new dating era.[4] Several menacing hill forts were destroyed. Inland he found two monarchies, the Ituraean kingdom centred on the Bekaa Valley, and the Arab kingdom of Emesa, under Samsigeramos, in the upper valley of the Orontes River.[5] Both survived. The Ituraean ruler Ptolemy son of Mennaeus lost none of his territory, which included Chalkis and Baalbek, but he had to pay a thousand talents into Pompey's war chest.[6]

In all this Pompey showed a certain bias towards freeing cities from monarchic or tyrannical rule, but where stable monarchies existed they were allowed to continue. The Ituraean kingdom, for example, controlled an awkward area of mountain land as well as the southern Bekaa Valley and its two cities. Without a native ruler the region was likely to be turbulent and to require the repeated attentions of Roman troops and governors. Similarly the Emesan kings dominated a fairly remote area and a desert region which controlled a major desert route towards Babylonia by way of the oasis of Palmyra. It was economical to leave both of these kings in control. Beyond these kingdoms, the city of Damascus had long been the target of Ituraean and other rulers, was now firmly established as autonomous, with a Roman officer present from early on. On the coast, the old cities of Tyre and Sidon and others continued or revived in autonomy.

It seems that Pompey was able to deal with northern and central Syria relatively easily. There is no record of his forces having to fight anywhere, except in the suppression of some hill forts. The tyrants and kings who were dispatched apparently went quietly – though Dionysios of Tripolis and Kinyras were executed. The reason for the ease of the Roman takeover, of course, is that in most cases Pompey did not threaten anyone, and the Roman arrival, like that of Tigranes, meant the restoration of peace. Kings here and there may have had to give up a Greek city or two, but it was quickly understood that acquiescence to the new Roman power would bring confirmation of the king's position. Pompey's progress southwards was preceded by that of his legates, several of whom are known by name. He sent off these messengers in advance who researched the local situations, made clear the obligations Rome expected them to undertake, and produced draft agreements which Pompey would accept, modify and ratify on his arrival.

By late in 64, he arrived in Damascus. The city itself was not a problem. Two legates, L. Lollius and Q. Caecilius Metellus Nepos, had been in the city the year before, and no doubt had made it clear to the city's neighbours (and its council) that it was under Roman protection. In advance of Pompey, yet another legate, M. Aemilius Scaurus, reached the city, but this time his purpose was to assess the situation further south.[7]

Southern Syria consisted of two major kingdoms, Judaea and Nabataea, and a scatter of independent cities. Due south of Damascus, Ptolemy of Ituraea had conquered the rough basalt lands of Batanaea and Trachonitis, including some small cities.[8] His real aim had been to gain control of Damascus, but he was regularly thwarted, above all by the Damascenes who preferred to accept almost any master to the Ituraean. The arrival of the Romans was their definitive rescue. Beyond Batanaea was the kingdom of the Nabataeans, which included a series of desert or near-desert regions east of the Jordan Valley, and stretched south for 600 km into north Arabia. As a state it had emerged perhaps a century earlier and at one point its king controlled Damascus itself, though his rule had later been rejected by the Damascenes. Most of Nabataea's boundaries were vague and its true extent is difficult to discern. Its political and religious centre had long been the city of Petra, but as the kingdom had spread north, the better-watered lands of Auranitis (east of the Sea of Galilee) became more important; the later city of Bostra was developing even at this time. This northern part of the kingdom was more productive and more populous than the rest of the kingdom, hence its developing importance.[9]

The Nabataeans had gathered considerable wealth by trade, being the intermediaries between the rich cities of Syria and the land around the Mediterranean and the producers of spices and incenses in southern Arabia and India. Some of this wealth was spent on the elaboration of Petra, particularly its tomb architecture, and some went into the ingenious development of water conservation and desert agriculture; the land was not wholly dry, of course, much of it being steppe land. This pastureland was also the basis of the kingdom's military strength, which was largely in cavalry. The favourite fighting tactic of the Nabataeans was to retreat before an attacker into the desert, and then to harass him to destruction; the Nabataean armies had enjoyed considerable success using these methods.[10] Their kings were not overly aggressive, but had regularly defeated all attacks. Indeed the kingship had probably developed in reaction to attacks by neighbours, particularly Judaea.

Judaea was the only state in Syria at this time of whose internal affairs we have any detailed information.[11] In these internal affairs it was more fraught than in the other states, thanks to its curious history. The kingdom had developed from a religious rebellion, during which leaders had made themselves kings, a not unfamiliar process even now. There were still groups who were unwilling to accept a royal government, and hankered for a theocracy. Pharisees and Saducees were the main rival parties, but there were others. The kings had the task of balancing between these factions: Salome Alexandra, for example, tended to favour the Pharisees, who were more rigorous in the application of the Jewish law than the Saducees. The irony was that, despite owing its origin to a rebellion against Greek customs and religion, in order to survive the Judaean state had had to adopt many of the trappings of the surrounding Greek states, including the use of the Greek language. The Pharisees and others might see this as a betrayal of the revolutionary heritage.

By the time Scaurus arrived Salome Alexandra was dead (in 67), and her two sons had quarrelled over the succession. Hyrkanos II was already high priest by virtue of his birth as the eldest son, and had been made king as well before Salome died; the younger son, Aristoboulos II, had ousted him from that post, though Hyrkanos kept the position of high priest. Scaurus arrived as the fighting between the forces of the two brothers had become centred on the siege of the city of Jerusalem. Hyrkanos had made an alliance with the Nabataean King Aretas, and together they had shut Aristoboulos up in the fortified Jerusalem temple.[12]

The arrival of Roman authority, in the person of Scaurus, rapidly brought this confrontation to an end. On investigating the dispute Scaurus opted in favour of Aristoboulos as king. Josephus claims that this was because Aristoboulos offered the bigger bribe, but he also notes that he had been the more reasonable in his demands. Aristoboulos was also the more capable governor, and Scaurus clearly wanted to get Aretas away from Judaea and back into his own kingdom. The sheer power of the Roman state is demonstrated here, for Scaurus, who had no more than a personal guard with him, was able to impose terms on all three participants. Aretas withdrew with his forces, but Aristoboulos attacked his army as he went, winning a rather inconsequential victory. Scaurus returned to Damascus. Hyrkanos went off with Aretas.[13]

This was not the end of the matter. Scaurus' settlement was no more than an armistice. It was Pompey who would pronounce the final terms when he arrived. Therefore, when he reached Damascus, in early 63, he was confronted by the two claimants in person, and by a third group, claiming to speak for the 'people'.[14]

Pompey heard the arguments, but put off a decision. He had other matters to consider, and he must have been told by Scaurus of the size and bellicose nature of Judaea, and the strength of fortified Jerusalem. One of his problems was the Nabataeans, whose involvement in the Judaean crisis had brought them to Roman notice, perhaps for the first time. (It very much looks as though Pompey and the Romans generally had only the sketchiest knowledge of the political geography of Syria when he arrived; the legates' job was thus in part to scout out the various situations for him.) The arguments of the claimants to the Judaean kingship were complex and arcane, and he probably wanted to find out more about the two men before deciding.

The Roman force under Pompey's command marched south out of Damascus. He had Aristoboulos with him, and it seems he was inclining towards recognizing him as Judaean king. It is not clear where Hyrkanos was, but later he was with Pompey, together with Antipater, a rich Idumaean Jew who was advising him. Probably all three men were taken along with the Romans on the march. The Roman force was marching, says our only source (Josephus), 'against the Nabataeans'; it arrived at Dion, a Greek city which was under Judaean control, where the army was close to the boundary of the Judaean lands with the joint city-state of Philadelphia-Gerasa, which was sandwiched between the two kingdoms. Aristoboulos left the army and crossed the Jordan to the fortress of Alexandreion just south of the Auja River, the boundary of Judaea and the city of Skythopolis.[15]

These geographical details are important because they lead to an interpretation of these events which is different from that which Josephus has put forward. He claims that Aristoboulos left the Roman expedition without Pompey's permission, and that he did so intending to raise Judaea in rebellion against Rome. Certainly Pompey soon afterwards turned away from the march route he had been following and also crossed the Jordan, having apparently called up a larger force of 'auxiliaries from Damascus and the rest of Syria, as well as the Roman legions already at his disposal'. He then, says Josephus, 'marched against Aristoboulos'.[16]

Taking heed of the geography of these events, a different interpretation presents itself. The route of Pompey's march to Dion implies that he was aiming to attend to the Nabataeans first – as Josephus himself says. He stopped at Dion, having marched through Judaean territory on the Golan plateau and past, or through, the territories of several small Greek cities, some independent, some in the Judaean kingdom. Beyond Dion he faced Philadelphia-Gerasa, a joint state probably ruled by a hereditary tyrant of the family of Zenon Kotylas, whose enmity towards Judaea was a fixed political fact of the region; beyond that state was the Nabataean kingdom.[17]

Pompey would need to negotiate passage through Philadelphia-Gerasa, which would explain the stop at Dion, the last city before the northern Gerasene border. His forces also needed supplies, another matter for negotiation with both Philadelphia and Judaea. And by this time he presumably knew something of the country of the Nabataeans. The army had been marching through very difficult country since Damascus, and the march would only get worse south of Philadelphia – dry, hilly and stony country, which eventually dried into desert. Information about the length of the proposed march, and the fighting methods of the Nabataeans, had no doubt also been gathered by this time; so an expedition to suppress or control Nabataea came to seem more and more difficult the further south he went.

The other geographical point is that, when he followed Aristoboulos, Pompey went into Skythopolis' territory, but camped at Koreai, just north of the Auja River. Skythopolis was a Macedonian city which had maintained its full independence until about ten years before, and even then had only accepted Judaean suzerainty because it was surrounded by Judaean territory after the conquest and destruction of Pella, across the Jordan by Aristoboulos' father King Alexander Iannai. Skythopolis was still effectively autonomous within the Judaean kingdom, and no doubt it welcomed Pompey's arrival as a sign of a possible improvement in its political situation.

Aristoboulos, in the Alexandreion fortress, was only a short distance south of the Auja, perhaps six or seven kilometres from Koreai. He came out of the fortress and negotiated with Hyrkanos. Thus Pompey once again had put himself in the position of an arbitrator, but whatever inclination he had shown earlier towards Aristoboulos had evidently disappeared.[18] It would seem that at Dion Pompey finally realized the difficulty he faced in attacking Nabataea and was interested in finding a face-saving reason for his change of course. The purpose of Aristoboulos in leaving the army at Dion was not to 'rebel', for he only went as far as the Alexandreion, and had no forces to speak of there. The best explanation for the move is that he intended to organize supplies for the Roman forces and Alexandreion was a useful place at which to collect them. The Roman army was just across the river and was still expected to march on south.

Pompey's attitude to Aristoboulos had been friendly until then, as Josephus says, but he had made no decision about the Judaean kingship. By camping at Koreai, outside directly ruled Judaean territory, he was in fact respecting Aristoboulos' sovereignty (just as by camping at Dion, he had respected the autonomy of Philadelphia-Gerasa). But by deflecting his forces from the invasion of Nabataea, Pompey now had to make a decision about Judaea.

Just as it is likely that he learned about Nabataea only as he approached it, so it is probable that Pompey knew little about Judaea before he reached Damascus. Scaurus no doubt had told him what he knew, and the meeting with the rival kings and the third delegation at that city was also part of his education. Another aspect came to his notice on his march to Dion and then to Koreai. He passed Pella, a Greek city which had been destroyed by Alexander Iannai. He had also passed near Gadara, also destroyed – his freedman secretary Demetrios came from there.[19] He passed by, or through, the city of Skythopolis, whose people had long been threatened by Jewish forces, and had no wish to continue under Judaean suzerainty. They, and no doubt Demetrios, could also point to other destroyed cities: Philoteria on the shore of the Sea of Galilee; Samaria, a foundation of Alexander the Great which had been destroyed by Alexander Iannai's father; Gaza, and others. Pompey's contacts with the ruler or rulers of Philadelphia-Gerasa will have shown him the enmity felt towards Judaea there. In addition other enquiries will have told him that the Judaean kingdom, besides being politically unstable, controlled many Greek cities like Skythopolis who resented that control.

The meetings between Hyrkanos and Aristoboulos, under Pompey's supervision, were wholly unsuccessful, and Pompey now had to decide who should be king. He also had to make decisions about the future of the kingdom as a whole. He kept both decisions secret for a time, for he was now faced, for the first time in Syria, with a state capable of putting up a serious resistance to his demands. He persuaded Aristoboulos to give way in stages, so that the Roman decisions could be implemented peacefully. Aristoboulos was also under pressure from his own people, who clearly had a lively appreciation of Roman power and ruthlessness.

The population of Judaea was divided, some supporting Hyrkanos, some Aristoboulos, and others (the third delegation at Damascus) hoping for the abolition of the monarchy; the Greek cities within the kingdom could not be relied on to support any Judaean ruler in a confrontation with the Romans. In effect, the pressure exerted by the mere presence of Pompey and his army had brought the Judaean kingdom to the point of collapse.

Aristoboulos clearly understood that only by doing as Pompey demanded would he be able to remain as king. He was persuaded to surrender the strongholds his people occupied – which seem to have included the Alexandreion – and then returned to Jerusalem.[20] Josephus says he then 'prepared for war', which may be so, but Aristoboulos and his immediate followers did not want to fight the Romans. Pompey moved his camp to Jericho, just below Jerusalem, and this persuaded Aristoboulos to give in, promising to admit a Roman force into Jerusalem and pay tribute.

Josephus interprets these actions by Aristoboulos as demonstrating a continuing intention to 'rebel', but the steady reduction in his power argues the opposite. It is best to assume that he had hopes of being recognized as king, and that by acceding to Pompey's salami tactics he would eventually succeed. Aristoboulos' separation from Pompey during much of this time may have allowed Hyrkanos and Antipater to increase their persuasiveness on the Roman, though it seems likely that Pompey was not very susceptible to such whisperings in his ear. It is best to assume that Pompey made his decision during the meetings at Koreai, but had to operate as he did in order to reduce the chance of fighting. So now, with Aristoboulos' agreement to let him into Jerusalem, and, keeping the king with him, Pompey sent A. Gabinius, another of his legates, to secure the city. But it was too late. Die-hards in the city seized control. Gabinius was shut out.

Pompey took his full army up to the city. He was admitted by a group opposed to Aristoboulos, but Aristoboulos' supporters seized control of the temple area, which was fortified, and bade defiance to the Romans. Helped by Hyrkanos, whose day had come, Pompey at first tried to negotiate terms of surrender, then set about a regular siege, with artillery bombardments and counter-fortifications, and the construction of a ramp to reach and overtop the walls.[21]

It was perhaps at some point during the siege that the Egyptian King Ptolemy XII contacted Pompey. He offered a crown worth, according to Josephus quoting Strabo, 4,000 pieces of gold, and clothing for the army, but also asked that Pompey assist him in suppressing 'sedition' in Egypt.[22] This Pompey could not do, for, apart from being busy enough in Palestine, he had no authority to enter Egypt – he was already stretching his *imperium* by being in Syria. Had he gone into Egypt, there would have been a political explosion in Rome. (It is also claimed that Ptolemy sent, or offered, a force of 8,000 horses, but this is a misreading of the source, where Pompey and the force are mentioned in the same sentence.[23]) This contact was the beginning of a new involvement of Egypt, Rome, and Judaea, which developed over the next generation.

Josephus describes the siege of Jerusalem in fairly general terms. He claims that the Jews were beaten only because they would not fight on the Sabbath or on fast days; however, the siege took over two months so it seems probable that fighting was continuous, even during the Sabbath. The decisive action was the destruction by the Roman siege machines of a tower, part of the temple fortification. (This may have been finally achieved on a fast day, but it had obviously taken some time in preparation.) Then followed, as is only to be expected after a hard siege, a massacre of the defendants – Josephus claims a death toll of 12,000, though this is a number scarcely to be believed, as with all Josephus' figures. He displays a good deal less concern for these deaths than for the safety of the 'holy objects', and more horror at the invasion of the holy of holies by non-priests than the killing of so many of his fellow Jews.[24]

During the siege, Hyrkanos had been established as the ruler of what would remain of Judaea once Pompey had finished. He had been particularly useful in holding down the rural areas of Judaea during the siege. In return Pompey confirmed him as high priest and took Aristoboulos off to Rome with him when he left.[25] With Jerusalem conquered and occupied, Pompey set about attempting to create a situation in which a new balance in southern Syria could be achieved. After several months in the area he had presumably gained a clear picture of the general position. Hyrkanos' work during the siege in controlling the potentially hostile countryside had earned him install-ation (or restoration) as high priest, but the treatment meted out in the past to the Greek cities surrounding Judaea had to be reversed. Hyrkanos' territory was drastically reduced to highland Judaea, highland Galilee, and the trans-Jordanian Peraia; the first two areas were separated by the territories of inde-pendent Greek cities of the Vale of Jezreel. Other areas taken from the kingdom were most of the coastal plain, and the Greek cities east of the Sea of Galilee. Those cities which had been destroyed were ordered to be rebuilt, though only one, Gadara, was attended to immediately, as a favour to De-metrios. Josephus lists the freed cities, not altogether accurately (he was writing well over the century later), and, of course, it was not possible to re-store them all at once.[26]

The result was largely to de-urbanize the kingdom but to re-urbanize the surrounding lands. Jerusalem remained to Judaea, but had a Roman force stationed within its walls. Otherwise there were fewer towns of any size or military significance within the kingdom. And it was surrounded by cities, which, as Josephus pointedly states, 'Pompey set free and annexed to the province' of Syria. A line of independent cities occupied the coast: Gaza (which had been wrecked by Jewish conquest as far back as 96), Dor and Strato's Tower; the port of Joppa, held by Judaea for almost a century, was made independent. Ashkelon had always maintained its independence; this was confirmed, and it was joined by two more restored cities nearby: Azotos (Ashdod) and Iamneia. These are the cities Josephus mentions; there were probably others, and some can be added because of the activity of subsequent governors, such as Apollonia.

The inland cities, as noted above, divided Judaea from Galilee. Pompey himself ordered the rebuilding of Gadara, east of the Jordan (which took the name 'Pompeia' in commemoration), and Josephus lists several places which were 'restored to their inhabitants'.[27] The Judaean conquest of many of these places, some of them fairly small cities, had been fairly recent, so it was pos-sible to locate the refugees (such as Demetrios), and free those enslaved. The restored cities on the coast must have been inhabited by largely new populations, or perhaps by the heirs of those earlier driven out.

The recent conquest and/or destruction of many of the Greek cities indicates that they were vulnerable. They had earlier survived as cities of the Seleukid kingdom, and so under royal protection, but without it they had fallen, even to the poor siege technique of the Judaean army. The new Roman province and its governor thus now took the place of the Seleukid kings. That the cities still required protection was shown by the tough resistance of Jerusalem to the Roman attack, and by the fact that Pompey was unable to reduce the Judaean state any further: even shorn of all its Greek cities, it remained the largest state in the southern part of Syria – indeed it was the largest political unit in Syria, except for the Roman province itself. The cities on the coast were protected by their geographical position, being easily accessible to Roman sea power, but those inland required further measures.

Pompey formed them into a specific group, the Decapolis. It included cities still in ruins, like Pella, cities never conquered by the Jews, like Skythopolis, cities which had been conquered but retained, like Dion, and cities which had greater pretensions, like Damascus. Most of its members began a new era in 63, which implies Pompey's work. In addition Gerasa and Philadelphia were included, which makes it clear that the joint cities under their dictator had also succumbed to Pompey's pressure. The precise purpose of this league of cities is not altogether clear. If it was for defence it would clearly clash with the authority of the provincial governor. Membership tended to vary over time, so it was hardly stable. No league institutions are known, though they may have existed. It all looks rather like a political bluff. Putting the cities together like this produced a quasi-political grouping which was of a similar size to its monarchic neighbours, Judaea, Nabataea, and Ituraea; perhaps it was essentially an enlargement of the Philadelphia-Gerasa union.[28]

The final element in the region which had to be dealt with was the Nabataean kingdom. Pompey's dealings with it had so far been unsatisfactory. Scaurus had insisted that King Aretas take his army away from the siege of Jerusalem in 65, but since then there had apparently been no contact. Pompey's intentions in his march south from Damascus are obscure. Josephus at one point indicates that he was merely going to 'see how things were', but later he mentions that Pompey's force was 'prepared against the Nabataeans'. Pompey was then deflected, or deflected himself, into Judaea. There seems little point in marching with an army 'against' the Nabataeans without the intention of enforcing Roman authority over the king. So this was unfinished business.

Pompey returned north in 63, taking Aristoboulos and his sons and daughters with him, and leaving M. Aemilius Scaurus as his legate in Syria. The Roman governing arrangement was, of course, still provisional until ratified by the Senate. Pompey's journey north came soon after he received the news of the death of Mithradates. (Josephus, in keeping with his assumption that Pompey's prime interest was in dealing with Judaea, fails to mention this.) He went first to Kilikia and then to Asia Minor, so he probably attended to matters in North Syria while Scaurus operated in the south.[29] Scaurus was given the task of dealing with the Nabataeans.

Josephus is the only source for Scaurus' expedition, but he did not know much about it. He claims that Scaurus 'ravaged the country round about Petra', but that was desert, so Josephus was actually saying what he thought should have happened in such an expedition (unless it reflects Scaurus' own, propagandistic, account). More convincing is his statement that Scaurus' forces ran short of supplies, which were made good by grain and other things sent from Judaea, organized by Antipater, Hyrkanos' minister, who was married to Kypros, an aristocratic Nabataean woman.

The supplies were sufficient to keep Scaurus and the army going, but the distance and the conditions defeated him. He claimed on coins which he issued in Rome later that King Aretas succumbed to his armed pressure (the king is depicted kneeling in submission), but he had in fact negotiated Scaurus' retirement, with Antipater as the intermediary. Aretas agreed to pay 300 talents for Scaurus to go away, and Antipater, clearly anxious for his two friends to stop fighting each other, guaranteed the payment. (This may well have been in effect a Judaean pledge.) Aretas died (or was overthrown) soon after. It may well be that he was under even greater pressure to resist than Scaurus was to attack.[30]

The net effect, however, at least in Roman eyes, was that the Nabataean kingdom had entered the Roman system as a client state, on the same level as Judaea and Emesa and the Ituraeans. Scaurus' work completed Pompey's. Both had, in effect, simply accepted what was found, making a few indispensable adjustments. Over a century later the encyclopedist-admiral Pliny the Elder produced a version of a list of political units in Syria based in part on an official list dating from the time of Augustus.[31] It is, as Pliny gives it, rather confused, but the essential point here is that he noted a number of places with ethnic names, which were, so far as can be seen, not actually cities, but were anything from villages to monarchies, all autonomous within the province. And, as if weary of the number of strange names he has encountered, he ends by noting there were also 'seventeen tetrarchies with barbarian names' which he could not be bothered to list individually.

This is the legacy of Pompey's work. The disintegration of Syria in the first half of the last century BC had been halted by his expedition, but by recognizing and accepting the continued existence of most of those political units he encountered, Pompey had in effect frozen the situation as he found it in 64/63 BC. Only in the south, where the large kingdoms of Judaea and the Nabataeans had resisted him, had he employed violence, and even then both of these kingdoms survived – though he had contributed to the land's disintegration by his reduction of Judaea. Over the next 170 years the dozens of tetrarchies and kingdoms and cities and villages which Pompey had left autonomous were gradually annexed to the Syrian province. Pompey had thus left a great deal of work for his successors to do.

Chapter 2

Gabinius

The untidy situation in southern Syria left by Pompey and Scaurus was unstable and dangerous both to Syrians and to the Romans. The client states of Judaea and Nabataea and Ituraea were still stronger than many of the cities which had been 'freed' by Pompey, only to be incorporated at once into the Roman province. Pompey's order that they be restored did not make them instantly strong and populous. Further, Pompey found that political conflict in Rome blocked the ratification of his measures, though governors were sent out to take charge of the new province. In Syria the lack of ratification did not mean a great deal, but among the more politically aware – the kings and their ministers – the uncertainty sapped Roman authority.

The Jews in Judaea were perhaps in a state of shock as a result of the events between 67 and 63. They had seen their kingdom reach its greatest size in 74 and then collapse into civil war only seven years later, suffer invasion, the capture and sack of the Jerusalem temple, and then stripped of all its conquests. Yet it was still a substantial state. And the Nabataeans had been attacked for no reason that they could see, and mulcted of a large treasure. Both of these states, therefore, had been defeated and humiliated, but had been left relatively strong. It was a dangerous and uncomfortable mixture.

The governors of the province had to deal with the inevitable reaction. Pompey's return to Rome removed the driving force behind the evisceration, while the non-ratification of his deeds produced an accurate perception of the general Roman indifference to Syria. The size of the armed forces the governors could deploy to deal with any problem is rarely clear. Pompey had collected a miscellaneous force on his march south from Damascus, including Roman legions and the 'auxiliaries from Damascus and the rest of Syria'. These were the forces he used in attacking Jerusalem, and he had been assisted by some of the inhabitants. Yet the siege had lasted well over two months; no wonder he ordered the destruction of the city's walls. When he left Syria he allocated two legions as a garrison for the province, and probably he left two more in Kilikia.[1] But two legions is not a very large force for a province 600 km long still littered with potentially hostile kings and bordered by potentially hostile kingdoms. The governors could call on the same auxiliaries Pompey had used, men from the Greco-Macedonian and Phoenician cities, each of which maintained an armed militia. The client kings also had armies, kept fairly small in later years, but in those early years of varying sizes.

All these were available to assist the legions – but they might also be the basis for a rebellion.

Two legions would scarcely suffice in the face of a serious attack from outside, or if a rebellion by a large client state occurred. And both of these dangers threatened. Hostility between Rome and Parthia was developing, and there was certainly danger in the south, though the first Roman governors did not have much trouble. Scaurus had his confrontation with the Nabataeans, and his two successors had to fight, or deter, invasions by 'Arabs', who may have been raiders into the Decapolis area from the badlands of the borderlands between Judaea and Nabataea, taking advantage of the confusion which resulted from the dismantlement of the Judaean 'empire'. None of this had any effect on the general political balance, and invasions from the desert were hardly new in this area, nor were they all that serious.[2]

The next governor, who took office in 57, A. Gabinius, consul in 58, was more aggressive. He was ambitious to gain the wealth and renown by now vital to success in Roman politics. He was sponsored by Pompey and was given the power to recruit an army in Italy to take with him to Syria. It is not attested that he did so (though his consular colleague, with the same powers, did), but his ambition was to attack Parthia, which he could scarcely do with only two legions and some auxiliaries. So it may be supposed that he brought out two more legions.[3]

A minor insurrection had begun already in Judaea. It was led by Aristoboulos II's son Alexander, who had escaped from Rome some time earlier. He had made only slow progress for a time, but by the time Gabinius arrived he had gathered enough strength to threaten Jerusalem.[4] Presumably his progress had been slowed by opposition from Hyrkanos' forces, but he eventually captured the city. He attempted to rebuild the city wall, but was stopped by a force of Romans which were there. These men have been suggested to have been civilians – businessmen and others – but it is, in the circumstances, much more likely that they were the soldiers who had been left in the city by Pompey.[5] That they had not intervened earlier is a clear indication that Alexander's war was with Hyrkanos, not Rome, also that the Romans were not charged with defending Hyrkanos, only with enforcing the peace terms. But their intervention was the first stage in what became an escalating conflict between Rome and Alexander.

Alexander was thus rebuffed but, perhaps because he was opposed by the Romans in the city and hence could portray Hyrkanos as a Roman puppet, he was able to gather more support. Josephus puts his force at 10,000 hoplites and 1,500 horses, which can be no more than a guess and an exaggeration, but he was able to seize the Alexandreion fort in the Jordan Valley, the fortress of Machaerus on the east bank of the Dead Sea, and the fort of Hyrkania south of Jerusalem.

This was the situation when Gabinius arrived. He sent Mark Antony, one of his tribunes, on ahead with a cavalry force to gather local troops. He armed some Romans – certainly these were civilians this time – and collected a Jewish force under Peitholaos and Malichos, along with Antipater's own guard. These forces defeated Alexander in a pitched battle near Jerusalem. Gabinius arrived soon after and laid siege to the Alexandreion, which was only large enough for a small garrison. Then he marched through Judaea, no doubt primarily to suppress other insurgents. He also, much more significantly, ordered the rebuilding of many of the cities which had been freed by Pompey.[6]

Josephus lists the cities he knew about: on the coast, Raphia, Gaza and Anthedon, which controlled the road to Egypt, and Ashdod, north of Ashkelon, making a solid group in the south west; in Idumaea, Marisa and Adora (unless Josephus mistook this for Dor on the coast); in the centre, Samaria (destroyed almost fifty years before), and Skythopolis, which may not have needed much work. He adds 'and not a few others', which would include Apollonia on the coast, Gadara, rebuilt by Pompey's orders, and Gabai near Carmel, re-established before Gabinius' arrival.[7]

Alexander, shut up in the Alexandreion, finally surrendered; his three fortresses were demolished. Hyrkanos was therefore reinstated, but Judaea was left without any fortified centres at all, while all around new fortifications were being erected. The ease with which the authority of Hyrkanos had been overthrown persuaded Gabinius – who had been one of Pompey's legates and had experience of conditions in Judaea – to split up the country into five regions, each with its own council, or *sanhedrin*.[8] This scheme did not last beyond Gabinius' own time as governor, but it was an interesting experiment. It is clear that the Romans had little confidence in the ability of Hyrkanos to rule the state, but he was their choice, and to transfer the position back to Aristoboulos and his family would entail a significant loss of face; nor was Aristoboulos likely to be a loyal Roman client after his treatment.

Alexander was given into the custody of his mother (who had not been taken to Rome with Aristoboulos). But then Aristoboulos himself escaped from Rome and arrived in Judaea. He quickly gathered a force, 8,000 men, according to Josephus, and seized the Alexandreion. Gabinius sent a detachment to evict him, and he had to dismiss many of his people because they were unarmed. The demolished Alexandreion was no use to him, so he retreated across the Jordan to the Machaerus fortress, which was also partly demolished. On the way his force was defeated by the Romans, and having reached Machaerus he held out for only two days.[9]

It cannot be said that either of these Jewish rebellions was much of a threat to the Roman position, but to Gabinius they were a time-wasting nuisance, and to the Jews they emphasized that the real enemy was no longer Hyrkanos but the Roman Republic. Gabinius' military reaction in both cases had been swift and successful, and his political actions, in ordering the rebuilding of the surrounding cities, was sensible. But what he really wanted to do was to invade Parthia, for which he had been given *imperium infinitum* on his appointment as proconsul.[10] Josephus reports that he had actually crossed the Euphrates with his army when he was deflected by a message from Pompey. He was therefore in the territory of Osrhoene, one of the Parthian client kingdoms. However, the message from Pompey clearly took precedence, even though, as it proved, the authority with which he gave orders to Gabinius was less than complete.

The message was brought to Gabinius by the exiled Egyptian King Ptolemy XII Auletes, who had persuaded the Senate, through Pompey's advocacy, that he deserved to be restored to his throne. This was the latest development in the increasingly entangled relations between the Roman Republic and the Ptolemaic kingdom. This went back two centuries and more, to 273, when Ptolemy II made contact with the city which had by then come to rule almost all Italy. In the 160s a dispute over the Egyptian kingship involved Rome, with the result that one of the disputants had made a will leaving part of the kingdom to the republic, a tactic used in other disputes of this sort later. This bequest had become active in 96, when Rome inherited Cyrenaica, but it was only twenty years later, in 74, that Rome collected, and formed the region into a regular province.[11] Possession of Cyrenaica brought Roman territory to the border of Egypt proper on the west; and now Pompey's promenade through Syria brought Roman power to Egypt's eastern border.

Ptolemy XII Neos Dionysos (the new Dionysos) referred to also as 'Auletes', 'the flute player' by the disrespectful Alexandrians, had been king since 80 BC. In fact it had been the Alexandrians – that is, the ruling group in the city – who had made him king in the first place, when the legitimate Ptolemaic line had died out on the death of King Ptolemy X Alexander. He had been at the court of King Mithradates VI of Pontos, Rome's great enemy, when called to take over the Egyptian throne, a fact which delayed for some time Rome's recognition of his kingship, since he was assumed to be allied with Mithradates. He had the handicap of being of illegitimate birth by Greek reckoning, so he was insecure from the start. The power of Rome could, however, bolster his internal position.[12]

After a fairly rocky reign, Ptolemy had been expelled by the Alexandrians in 58 because of his extravagant payments to Rome and Romans, using money which had been collected by more than usually fierce taxation. These payments – 'bribes', to most historians – had been needed because the issue of direct Roman intervention in Egypt, even annexation, had become an active one in Roman politics. Ptolemy's problem was that, if he was illegitimate, the will of his predecessor Ptolemy Alexander became operative, in which he had bequeathed the kingdom to Rome (though he had been exiled at the time) in exchange for finance to mount an attempt to reconquer Cyprus. He was killed in the attempt. The terms of the will – there was clearly a problem with it, since Ptolemy Alexander was not in possession of that which he was bequeathing – were never enacted. But it was an issue which hovered over Ptolemy Auletes all his reign.

His method of dealing with his legitimacy problems was to use his wealth to secure Roman recognition of his kingship by an enactment of the Senate. Since it was not in the Roman interest to grant this, Ptolemy was handing out money in large quantities to prominent Romans in attempts to buy the measure. These huge payments had made the issue all the more controversial, for they drew attention to the wealth of Egypt, but that was something no Roman politician was prepared to see fall into the hands of a rival. Any proposal to do anything about Egypt therefore encountered strong opposition. In 65 M. Licinius Crassus, as censor, proposed the annexation of the country by Rome, but was stopped by the veto of his colleague as censor, Q. Lutatius Catulus. Cicero had made a speech against the plan also and no doubt congratulated himself on his success.[13]

In 63, when Pompey was in Judaea, another attempt to reach directly into Egypt was being made at Rome, by means of a proposed new agrarian law. Cicero again pointed out the dangers to Rome, and the proposal was defeated.[14] One reason for the defeat of this measure was the heavy payments Ptolemy was now making to many Roman politicians, and Cicero's speeches lent a respectable gloss to the rejection. In the meantime Ptolemy had established contact with Pompey in Judaea, as noted in the previous chapter.

What Ptolemy wanted above all was confirmation of his rule by Rome, for this would negate the provisions of the will of Ptolemy Alexander. His attempts to persuade or bribe Roman politicians were enormously expensive, yet had little or no result except to block changes. The campaign, at first financed by the taxation of Egypt, was also causing unrest. Taxes were raised, spending inside Egypt was reduced, and opposition to the king spread as conditions worsened. Ptolemy made the situation worse by then borrowing heavily in Rome to finance his bribing of Romans; his main source was a banker, C. Rabirius Postumus.[15]

The coalescence of Roman politics which produced the First Triumvirate (C. Julius Caesar, consul in 59, Crassus, and Pompey) was Ptolemy's opportunity. An offer of 6,000 talents to Caesar and Pompey secured the law he needed, and Caesar passed an agrarian law which omitted all reference to

Egypt. Part of the triumvirs' arrangement was that Gabinius would become consul in 58, which had brought him to Syria next year. By that time Ptolemy had finally exhausted the patience of the Alexandrians. Rome had summarily annexed Cyprus, a Ptolemaic province for nearly three centuries. The island's king was Ptolemy's brother, and he had been made king by the Alexandrians at the same time as Ptolemy Auletes had been made king in Egypt. Auletes, in hock as he was to the Romans, made no protest. At that point, the Alexandrians – that is, the leading members of the court – compelled him to leave the country. He went, of course, to Rome.[16]

If the Alexandrians intended to reduce Roman influence and meddling, Ptolemy's exiling failed. His succession produced continuous confusion in Egypt, and this encouraged further Roman interventions. Two queens, Ptolemy's estranged wife (and sister) and his daughter, ruled for a time. His wife soon died. The daughter, Berenike IV, searched for a husband through whom the royal line could be continued. Rather more important was the requirement for an adult man to be king. Marriage to a legitimate princess was a recognized route to the kingship – hence the Ptolemaic practice of brother-sister marriage, which annexed the royal women safely. Berenike had in fact two half-sisters and two stepbrothers, but all were too young, and their mother may not have been Ptolemy XII's wife.

Candidates for Berenike's husband had to be of sufficient rank to be acceptable, and there were not many men who could be considered. Three Seleukid princes were apparently available. Two were the dismissed claimants for the Syrian kingship, but they were obviously too dangerous to be given any power, and Gabinius prevented them from leaving Syria; the third, Seleukos Kybiosaktes, did get through and married Berenike, but he was so personally offensive to her that she had him strangled a few days afterwards. A new candidate was Archelaos, who claimed to be a son of Mithradates the Great of Pontos. He was also in Gabinius' custody at the time, but he was either allowed to go to Egypt or he escaped, perhaps by Gabinius' contrivance; bribery was naturally assumed. He turned out to be more personally acceptable to Berenike (though he was not actually a son of Mithradates).[17] This marriage put yet another obstacle between Ptolemy XII and his lost throne.

In Rome, Ptolemy XII's request for help to recover his kingship took a long time, and much money, to proceed. It was of course much entangled with the increasingly complicated Roman political scene, and contributed a good deal to that continuing complication. Pompey was Ptolemy's host, and pushed his case, hoping to be given the command. He was foiled by opponents who claimed that the statue of Jupiter Latiaris had been struck by lightning and that the subsequent consultation of the Sibylline books gave the advice that Ptolemy's friendship with Rome was needed, but he should not be restored by force. Since he could not be restored peacefully this effectively blocked his return. He gave up and went to Ephesos.[18]

This was not the end of the matter, however, and it dragged on inconclusively throughout 56. For a time it seemed that L. Cornelius Lentulus Spinther, consul in 57 and then proconsul in Kilikia, would take on the task of restoration, based on some ambiguous decrees of the Senate, but eventually he pulled out. The Senate did in fact produce a decree which might be used, and in the end Pompey, consul with Crassus in 55, gave Ptolemy the letters addressed to Gabinius.[19]

Gabinius withdrew from his Parthian campaign and marched his forces south, taking Ptolemy with him. Gabinius could clearly have refused to do this, as Lentulus had in effect refused, by delaying or by arguing that he was already involved in a war, but he went ahead. This is partly to be accounted for by Pompey's authority, partly by Gabinius' own greed, and partly by the presence with Ptolemy of C. Rabirius Postumus, who had financed Ptolemy's bribes and journey, and wanted his money back. It may also be that the prospect of a Parthian war had come to seem much more difficult from the viewpoint of Syria than it had been in Rome, and maybe Gabinius was glad of an excuse to call off his invasion.

Gabinius' Egyptian campaign was relatively straightforward. He marched south, through Palestine, where he was provided with supplies and arms by Antipater, who had secured Hyrkanos' instructions to that effect. Antipater was also able to make contact with the Jewish soldiers who formed the guard at Pelusion, the fortress which guarded the access to Egypt from the east.[20] Ptolemy's presence was no doubt also a means of opening the way. The Roman army was accompanied by a naval force, presumably recruited from the Phoenician cities along the Syrian coast.[21]

The sources for Gabinius' campaign in Egypt are a mixed set. It is briefly alluded to by Strabo, without detail.[22] Dio's apparently straightforward account is brief, and is included in a description of these matters which is chronologically confused.[23] Plutarch gives more detail in his biography of Mark Antony, in particular crediting Antony with the capture of Pelusion.[24] These partial accounts do not connect with each other, but they can be organized into an account which is probably as close to the truth as we can devise.

Antony clearly did capture Pelusion, but he had a cavalry command, which was of little use against the fortress unless, as appears in this case, the attackers had the assistance of traitors within. So his capture of the fortress was facilitated by the betrayal by the Jewish garrison just as Gabinius' main force was assisted by supplies from Judaea. He also no doubt got supplies from other places in Syria and Palestine – arranging for supplies to be available on the march was an obvious preliminary.

The capture of Pelusion was the crucial first step. In invading Egypt it was necessary to march along the east bank of the Pelusiac distributary as far as Memphis, cross the river there, and then march along the west bank of the Damietta distributary to attack Alexandria. The Delta, with its intricate streams and marshes, had to be avoided, since an army would merely blunder about getting nowhere. Capturing Pelusion gave access to the river, but the next step would be to defeat a defending army and fleet, since the march was then in desert territory, and the river was needed to bring up supplies.

It is clear that Gabinius knew all this, no doubt informed by Ptolemy and whatever Egyptians accompanied the king. The government of Berenike IV and Archelaos was also fully aware of the military requirements of defence. The treason of the Jewish guard at Pelusion was therefore of crucial import- ance, for as soon as he had passed that fortress, Gabinius faced the Egyptian forces, both army and fleet. The Romans were quickly victorious, which opened the way to Memphis and the route to Alexandria, but they had to fight again as they approached Alexandria; in this battle King Archelaos was killed. The Alexandrians gave in, for the city did not have to be attacked. Gabinius was therefore able to restore Ptolemy to what he considered his rightful throne in Alexandria.

Plutarch claims that Ptolemy set about killing his opponents at Pelusion, but that Antony stopped him. At Alexandria, however, Ptolemy had free reign. Archelaos being dead in battle, Berenike was at once killed, as were many of her former supporters – which must have cut a swathe through the upper ranks of Alexandrian society.[25] Partly because of these killings, as well as having been expelled once and then restored by force, Ptolemy could not expect to be safe in the city. Gabinius was therefore constrained to leave some of his forces behind in Alexandria as a royal guard, a group who became called the Gabiniani, apparently under the command of a former soldier of Pompey called L. Septimius. How large the force was is not known, but Pompey later was given 500 of them in 48, and there were still plenty more still in Alexandria later that year when Caesar reached the city, so we may perhaps think in terms of at least a couple of thousand men. Some of them were Gallic or German cavalry, so probably Gabinius did not leave any spe- cifically Roman forces in Egypt, other than the officers. By the time Caesar arrived, in 48, they had partly assimilated to the Alexandrian population, though they had been used on several occasions to suppress unrest; the unrest came from native Egyptians; the soldiers integrated with the Greeks.[26]

On the other hand, C. Rabirius Postumus stayed on as Ptolemy's *dioiketes* (his financial minister) in order to squeeze taxes out of the Egyptians to repay his loans to the king.[27] It may be that one of the tasks of the Gabiniani was to protect Rabirius. He certainly needed protection. According to a fragmentary papyrus he replaced the existing officials, who had inherited their posts from their fathers and grandfathers, in a drive for greater efficiency.[28] But it was only the inefficiency of the officials – no doubt fat, lazy, and corrupt, and supposedly secure in their inherited posts – which made the taxation system halfway tolerable to the population. Rabirius lasted less than a year before ending in protective custody; he was deported, or allowed to escape, to Rome where he (and Gabinius) faced trial.

As a result of this Egyptian diversion, profitable as it may have been (Gabinius is said to have been paid a fee of 10,000 talents), Gabinius' prospects of a victorious looting of Parthia, and the conquest of extensive provinces, was ended. He had only the rest of 55 as governor of Syria – Ptolemy was in place as king once more by mid-April of that year – and his forces had been reduced both by casualties in the fighting, and by the detached Gabiniani. And his absence had been the opportunity for more trouble in Syria.

The superficiality of the Roman conquest of Syria is demonstrated by the situation which faced Gabinius on his return from Egypt. There were strong complaints from much of the province at his brutal taxation policy. 'Gabinius had harried Syria in many ways, even to the point of inflicting far more injury on the people than did the pirates', as Dio Cassius summarized the condition of the country, and he reports that during his absence the pirates – supposedly suppressed by Pompey, of course – had been active, so much so that the tax-collectors had been unable to operate.[29] And there was an armed uprising against Roman authority in Judaea. Aristoboulos' son Alexander had returned to the fray and had roused the Jews once more, no doubt pointing to the absence in Egypt of the Roman forces. And this time the rebellion was specifically against the Romans. Alexander's forces targeted any Romans they could find for killing. The threatened Romans gathered for refuge at Mount Gerizim (not, interestingly, in any of the cities, for these were perhaps not yet fully re-fortified). They were obviously numerous enough to be able to stand and fight.

Gabinius used Antipater to divide his Judaean enemies. A considerable number of Alexander's followers were thus induced to go home, no doubt assisted in their decision by the news of the return of the Roman army. Alexander retained a large force – 30,000, says Josephus, another unbelievable number – and retreated north away from Mount Gerizim. He stood to fight at Mount Tabor, near Samaria, and there his forces were defeated with heavy casualties by Gabinius in battle.[30]

Gabinius then turned to take on the Nabataeans. Josephus gives no reason for this, but he states that Gabinius defeated their forces in battle. This has been expanded by Bowersock into an attack on 'the city of the Nabataeans', which he assumes to have been Petra, though Josephus does not say so, which was in fact what Scaurus had attempted several years before. Josephus is not so specific in the case of Gabinius, specifying only the Nabataeans as Gabinius' target. Further, it may be that the centre of such administration as Nabataea possessed was now in the north, at Bostra, from where the king could observe the dangerous events in Palestine more closely than from Petra. It is also assumed that Gabinius' purpose was loot, but even Josephus, ever ready to impute mercenary motives to Roman commanders, does not say so. Bowersock claims also that it was 'the new glamour' of conquests in Arabia which attracted Gabinius. In fact there is no indication of a conquest, despite the supposed victory in battle.[31]

It does seem clear that the Nabataeans had a new king by the year 55 BC. Which king ruled between the death of Scaurus' enemy Aretas in 62 and this invasion is not clear. Possibly it was a man called Obodas, whose coin image suggests he was old. The new king, who probably faced Gabinius, appears to be Malichos (which is Nabataean for 'king', so this may be merely his title). Obviously Gabinius felt that an expedition was necessary to remind the Nabataeans that they were clients of Rome. It was the normal practice among Hellenistic states that treaties between kings expired on the death of one of them. Two Nabataean royal deaths, plus the constant preoccupation of Gabinius with Jewish, Parthian, and Egyptian wars, may well have eroded any Nabataean appreciation of their client status to nothing – indeed they may well not have appreciated this essentially Roman concept in the first place. Gabinius chose the obvious means to persuade the new king to recognize this. Gabinius' victory was no doubt sufficiently persuasive.

In another swift decision Gabinius reorganized the Judaean government. He had been assisted in the attack on Egypt by Hyrkanos and Antipater with food and arms and equipment, which was in fact their obligation as a client state. But they had a grievance in that Gabinius' earlier reorganization of Judaea into five districts, each under a council (*sanhedrin*) had significantly reduced the authority of the high priest. They could point out that it was the high priest and his minister who had produced the supplies, not the districts, and that the *sanhedrin*s had been wholly unable to withstand Alexander and his rebels.

So, as Josephus says, Gabinius 'settled the affairs at Jerusalem in accordance with the wishes of Antipater'.[32] This can only mean that Antipater's own power in Judaea was increased, and, since Hyrkanos was his superior, that the responsibilities and administrative range of the high priestly government had been restored. Probably the five districts were consolidated once more, and possibly Antipater was awarded an official position and title. The general aim, from the Roman point of view, was to maintain control of Judaea and prevent further uprisings. In this, Hyrkanos and Antipater will have been helped by the heavy casualties incurred by their Jewish opponents at Mount Tabor.

Gabinius' governorship ended in 55, and he returned to Rome, to be replaced by M. Licinius Crassus, who was also intent on invading Parthia. Gabinius was tried for various crimes, principally for his invasion of Egypt, though this was, of course, a sideways route for their opponents to get at Pompey and the triumvirate. (Rabirius was also tried, for the same reason.) Gabinius was fined 10,000 talents, the fee he supposedly extorted from Ptolemy. He was not tried for extortion in Syria, despite the apparent complaints which Dio Cassius records. The overall achievement of his time in Syria was little more than a slow process of consolidating the work of Pompey. For all his activity, he had scarcely improved the lot of either his Syrian subjects or the Romans, had left the former to be harried by pirates, and had failed to provide a stable government for the latter.

The Syrians generally were impoverished and antagonized. The Jews had been repeatedly defeated in their rebellions, and their casualties had been heavy enough to stun them into quiet for a time, but the Roman authority in Palestine had improved only because the surrounding Greek cities had been refortified. The Jews themselves were clearly still unreconciled to their defeats, and had now identified Romans as their enemies and oppressors. Gabinius' expedition into Egypt had similarly not improved matters there. The king needed a Roman bodyguard; the Egyptians, like the Syrians, had been impoverished and antagonized, and Rome was now deeply enmeshed in Egyptian internal affairs. Gabinius had therefore, in his hyperactivity, largely worsened the Roman position, by angering the Syrians, the Jews, the Nabataeans, and the Egyptians.

Chapter 3

The Emergence of Antipater and Kleopatra

The events of 63–55 brought Roman power into Palestine, but had also left the two major kingdoms there still in existence as clients. None of the Roman governors in those eight years had extended their control into the hearts of either kingdom. Judaea had been deprived of its conquests, but Gabinius' experimentation in adjusting its government had eventually been revised and the kingdom was back to self-government by the high priest and his minister. Nabataea had been almost unaffected by Scaurus' and Gabinius' invasions and extortions. Its king ruled, and the royal succession was obviously in local hands. Nabataea was still effectively independent.

The Judaean succession, however, which was the problem which had allowed Roman power to penetrate into the kingdom in the first place, was the subject of the disputes which had repeatedly escalated to war.[1] Each successive bout of this fighting brought Roman power deeper into the state, so that, by 55, Judaea could no longer be regarded as independent in any serious sense. Gabinius' repeated interventions in its internal affairs had shown that.

Gabinius' other interventions, however, had only had a marginal effect on Egypt, and even less so on Nabataea. The presence in Alexandria of the Roman guard for Ptolemy XII was not really very different from the normal Ptolemaic practice of hiring mercenaries. It is clear that the soldiers, mostly not Italian to start with, were happy enough to become assimilated with the non-Egyptian part of the population. Their presence did not make for an increase in Roman influence, though they were under the command of Roman officers. The strongest influence after Gabinius left in 55 was that of C. Rabirius Postumus, given his head in collecting taxes until he had to be removed to save his life. What happened to the debt he was trying to collect is not known. Roman influence in Egypt was thus greater by the end of 54 than ten years before, but was less than might be expected after Gabinius' successful campaign.

If Roman authority was so clearly limited in the south-eastern corner of the Mediterranean, it was nevertheless not going to go away. The general political situation in the area remained unsettled, and difficulties and problems would inevitably arise. With each disturbance, each crisis, Roman involvement would increase, as had been the case already in Judaea. On all sides there was considerable reluctance for this to happen: on the Roman side an unwillingness to take on the responsibility for ruling what was evidently a difficult area, or to allow any individual Roman to get his hands on Egyptian wealth; and on the side of the locals a dislike at the prospect of any outside rule, and especially Roman. Egypt's wealth had already contributed a disruptive influence to Roman political life, and the restoration of Ptolemy XII continued to be a matter of contention there, with the trials of Rabirius and Gabinius. If Egyptian wealth became available again, it could obviously set off yet another prolonged political crisis in the city. On the Egyptian side everyone involved, from the king to the poorest taxpayer, had burnt his fingers in the Roman crisis; a repetition was not to be contemplated. While Ptolemy XII lived, therefore, Roman-Egyptian relations lost much of their heat.

In view of this it is hardly surprising that, after Gabinius' retirement from both Egypt and his governorship of Syria during 55, it was a quarter of a century before Roman control was fastened on Egypt, and seven decades before the same was finally done to Judaea, while Nabataea remained under the rule of its own kings for another sixty years after the incorporation of Judaea. The major Syrian client kingdoms similarly continued for another century or so, though all of them, with Judaea, Egypt, and Nabataea, had first to survive the Roman civil wars, and some of them vanished in that time.

In the south-eastern Mediterranean, however, two formidable rulers emerged in Judaea and Egypt in the years following Gabinius' governorship. Their abilities, in their different ways, contributed much to the delay in the Roman takeover: they were Antipater in Judaea and Kleopatra VII in Egypt. Curiously, in dynastic terms they were respectively the first and the last of their lines.

Antipater's wishes had guided Gabinius in the restructuring of the government of Judaea during 55. This put Antipater in the position of a major power in Judaea, under the nominal authority of Hyrkanos. The latter was perhaps not quite the nonentity he is often portrayed, but there is no doubt that he was dominated by Antipater.

Antipater was the son of Antipas (or perhaps Antipater), who came probably from Marisa in Idumaea, of a family which had been, like all those who survived in Idumaea, forcibly converted to Judaism in the early years of the Jewish rebellion against Seleukid rule, a century before Pompey's arrival. Antipas had been governor of Idumaea in the reign of Alexander Iannai, and it seems that Antipater succeeded him in that position; they thus combined a loyalty to the Judaean monarchy with local knowledge and influence.[2]

Antipater's scope for action in Idumaea was certainly reduced by Pompey's conquest, for a good part of Idumaea was separated off from Judaea when the city of Marisa (and perhaps Adora) was made free and put into the Roman province. He was married to an aristocratic Nabataean lady, Kypros, and had, of course, made himself useful as an intermediary between Scaurus and the Nabataean king in 62.[3] By acting as a guarantor of the Nabataean tribute of 300 talents, he was shown to be extremely rich.[4] He had assisted Gabinius in invading Egypt – technically on the instructions of Hyrkanos, but by naming Antipater even when he had no official position, Josephus shows that he was a major influence – and again made himself useful facing Alexander's insurrection, when he persuaded many of the rebels to go home.[5]

So when Gabinius, after this latest victory, reorganized Judaea 'in accordance with' Antipater's wishes, it is reasonable to assume that Antipater now took a formal position as the effective ruler of Judaea. Hyrkanos had been relegated by Gabinius' earlier measures to the care of the temple and his high priestly duties only, but now it seems that Antipater was given full political responsibility. By 48 he was being referred to as *epimeletes*, one of those vague but useful terms which imply a general managerial authority, and he may have acquired it at any time between 55 and 48.[6] It is generally assumed to be a Roman appointment, but it is more likely to be a general recognition of his position, perhaps formalized by an official appointment by Hyrkanos; no Roman need be involved.

Antipater was certainly a much more effective and energetic political operator than Hyrkanos, but his Idumaean origin half-damned him in the eyes of many Jews. His marriage to a Nabataean lady meant that his children were seen as half-Jews and subjected to the same social prejudice. But the connection was obviously useful to him, and to Judaea; while he was in power it helped to defuse any problems between the Nabataeans and Judaea. Antipater also deposited part of his wealth at Petra, presumably because he was fully conscious of the antipathy towards him among many of the Jews.[7]

The insurrection which had greeted Gabinius on his return from Egypt had been defeated by the joint efforts of Antipater's diplomacy and the Roman military, but it continued in a minor way under the leadership of Peitholaos. He had been one of Hyrkanos' commanders against Alexander's first rebellion, but had since changed sides.[8] It had only minor significance, but Roman actions in the years after Gabinius' victory helped fan its flames. The next governor, M. Licinius Crassus, stripped the temple of its gold and its accumulated money to help finance the war he embarked on against Parthia.[9] (He probably did the same in other Syrian temples, but the only specific case we know of is at Jerusalem.) When he was defeated and killed by the Parthians at the battle of Carrhae in 53, his quaestor, C. Cassius Longinus, faced a Parthian invasion and a revived Jewish rebellion, which had been stimulated by the Roman defeat. He marched south and captured the town of Taricheai in Galilee, and, in a deliberate act of terror, seized the inhabitants (30,000 people – another exaggerated figure by Josephus) and sold them into slavery. Antipater persuaded him to attend to Peitholaos, who was caught and killed, at which the rising faded away.[10] Cassius returned to the north and succeeded in beating back the Parthians.

It should have been clear to the Romans by now that only vigilant control in Palestine would prevent constant trouble, just as it should have been obvious to the Jews that Rome regarded them as subjects, and that their independence was an illusion – and that insurrections against Roman rule were futile. Cassius held Syria until 51, when a new governor was sent out by the Senate.

In Egypt, meanwhile, Ptolemy XII purged his opponents, and then made his arrangements for the succession. He had murdered his only legitimate child, Berenike IV, so his four illegitimate children were now designated to be his successors, though they were all still children. He had thus contrived a repetition of the problem he had struggled against all through his own reign, of securing the succession to children who were not technically eligible.

By his will Ptolemy XII appointed his elder daughter Kleopatra (aged about 18 when her father died) and his eldest son Ptolemy as the joint queen and king. They were intended to marry, in the tradition of the family, when Ptolemy was old enough. He also made the Roman people the executors of the will, and a copy was sent to Rome (where in fact Pompey kept it at his home).[11] Ptolemy died early in 51; almost at once Kleopatra deprived her brother ('Ptolemy XIII') of any power. He was, after all, several years younger than she was, perhaps only 10 years old, and she was the only one of the siblings old enough to exercise any real power. No marriage seems to have taken place. She ruled alone, husbandless, for the next year and a half.[12]

The last years of Ptolemy XII's reign and the early years of the reigns of his children, say 53 to 48, were a difficult time in Egypt. There was near famine, with hunger riots in Alexandria, and at the same time heavy taxation. The peasantry reacted by striking, which make the food problem worse, and just at this time there was the prospect of the removal of the Gabiniani.[13] This did not please the Egyptian government, which was not fully seated in control. This difficult economic and military situation was the background to the gradual unseating of Kleopatra from power in those years.

The suggestion of the removal of the Gabiniani came from Syria, where the Roman war with Parthia thus had its repercussions in Egypt just as in Palestine. The successor of Cassius as governor in Syria, M. Calpurnius Bibulus, was eventually successful in deflecting Parthian attacks, largely by cunning, by setting the Parthian commanders against each other.[14] Before this success, however, when he still expected to have to fight an invasion and so, probably in late 51, he sent two of his sons to Alexandria, to ask for the return to his command of the Gabiniani. It is said that the soldiers, on learning

of this possible fate, mutinied and killed the two Romans. Kleopatra demanded that the murderers be surrendered; the soldiers, now secure in the
knowledge that they would not be used as cannon fodder against the Parthian
bowmen, meekly complied. The guilty men were sent to Bibulus for punishment; he returned them, saying punishment was in the power of the Senate,
not him, and they thereupon vanish from the record.[15] The reaction of the
soldiers in this episode suggests that already by 51 they had shed any residual
Roman loyalty and had become Egyptianized. The reaction of the queen is
indicative of a desire to avoid conflict with any powerful Roman politicians.

More important than the exclusion of the child Ptolemy XIII from power
was the fact that those around him, his tutor, his 'nurse', and so on, were also
excluded. They now intrigued and operated within the court to return their
protégé to power, and so themselves also. They could argue that it was un-
constitutional (if such a formal term can be applied to an absolute monarchy)
that a woman should rule alone, though it was not unprecedented in Egypt.
By late 50 they had succeeded in returning Ptolemy to his throne, and his name
now appears before Kleopatra's in the decrees issued by the government. By the
middle of 49 a new dating formula indicates the Kleopatra had been pushed
out altogether.[16] She went to the south of Egypt, to the area around Thebes,
which is an interesting move.[17] This was the region which had in the past been
the most 'nationalistic' area of the country, where an independent state had been
maintained for twenty years a century and more ago, and was liable to rebel. It
is possible that Kleopatra's parentage was half-Egyptian. We do not know who
her mother was, but it could be that she was a daughter of one of the powerful
native priestly families, perhaps from Thebes.[18] This is a probably unsolvable
question, though it is relevant that Kleopatra is reputed to be the only Ptolemaic ruler who spoke the Egyptian language, presumably learned as a child.[19]
The south was, even when not in rebellion, always semi-independent by virtue
of its distance from the seat of government in Alexandria; Kleopatra's move
may have been a search for political support in an attempt to return there.

The men around Ptolemy XIII took up official positions which gave them
control of the government system. The most important of them was the eunuch Potheinos, Ptolemy's 'nurse', who became *dioiketes*, in charge of state
finances (the position which Rabirius Postumus had held for a time).
Theodotos of Chios was Ptolemy's tutor, and the third man was Achillas,
guardian of the king; these then were the actual rulers operating in Ptolemy's
name.[20] They clearly owed their access to power by their access to and control
of the king, which gave them the authority to ease Kleopatra out of power.
She learned the lesson.

Kleopatra was clearly seen as a threat by her brother's entourage, and so
she was in danger herself. She left Egypt, or fled or escaped or was driven

out, and went to Syria, taking her younger sister Arsinoe with her. The city of Ashkelon minted silver coins in her name in 49 and she may have lived there, but it had minted coins for her father and her grandfather on various occasions, so too much cannot be made of this coincidence. On the other hand, the city minted more coins in her name next year, and successive annual issues had never happened before. It has been suggested that these coins financed the recruitment of the troops she commanded a little later; there is neither proof nor evidence for this. More likely the city was invoking Ptolemaic protection against Judaea, and had done so successfully. Pompey had also left the city alone.[21]

By the time Kleopatra was in Syria the Romans – or some Romans – had again intervened in Egyptian affairs. Roman politics had at last collapsed into open civil war during 49, when Julius Caesar, threatened with prosecution by a Senate dominated by his enemies, invaded Italy from his province of Cisalpina by 'crossing the Rubicon'. He swiftly conquered Italy, and his senatorial enemies retreated to the Balkans. There they constituted themselves as the real Senate and appointed Pompey as their military commander. He gathered troops from the whole of the east, and called in help from his clients as well, who included both the Judaean and Egyptian rulers. Hyrkanos and Antipater in Judaea are not recorded as having assisted Pompey in any way, but the Egyptian government was more generous, or compliant.

Pompey sent his son Gnaeus to Alexandria to negotiate assistance. The government there at this time (late in 49) was for the moment still headed by both Ptolemy XIII and Kleopatra, though the real decisions were being made by Ptolemy's men, who had now installed themselves in the major administrative positions. The younger Pompey was provided with 500 men from the Gabiniani (without any argument from them this time, apparently), and, more usefully, with fifty warships from the Ptolemaic fleet, which was used to some effect in the naval fighting around Dyrrhachium.[22] It was not long after this that Kleopatra was pushed from power.

In the autumn of 49 the Senate, meeting at Thessalonika in Greece, recognized Ptolemy XIII as sole Egyptian king, and so his government also – thus setting aside the precise terms of his father's will, but accepting the new situation which had come to be in Alexandria.[23] Not long after this Kleopatra reached Syria; the Roman recognition of Ptolemy had obviously increased her danger, even in the south of the country. In Syria she recruited an armed force with which she intended to return to Egypt to claim her throne. (Yet again, we have a repetition of past events, for her father had aimed to do the same – but for the moment Kleopatra had no Gabinius and no Roman army to assist her.)

The Egyptian fleet, commanded by the younger Pompey, was taken to the Adriatic and used to try to blockade Caesar, whose army had landed at

Dyrrhachium, only to be besieged by Pompey's land forces. A blockade was very difficult to maintain using galleys, and various forces got across from Italy with men and supplies for Caesar's forces. The Egyptian fleet acquitted itself well, but Pompey was compelled to retreat eastwards into Thessaly, and there his army was defeated in battle at Pharsalus.

As the news of the result of the battle spread through the East everyone had to reassess his or her own situation. For the Judaeans the crisis had to some extent cleared the dynastic air. In Rome Caesar had contacted Aristoboulos, the former king, and in Palestine Alexander had re-emerged, yet again. Josephus has a story that Caesar gave Aristoboulos two legions and sent him to Syria where he was poisoned by the governor Q. Caecilius Metellus Pius Scipio Nasica. Meanwhile Alexander went north to Antioch and was there arrested and executed by Scipio for having killed Romans in his earlier rebellions.[24]

This latter case seems reasonable enough, though why Alexander went to Antioch, which was in the hands of his enemies, is not clear. His opponents in Judaea – Hyrkanos and Antipater – were pro-Pompey, as was the governor, but perhaps he hoped to enlist himself on Pompey's side and so gain credibility for a later return to Judaea. This would suggest that he thought Judaea's rulers were wobbling in their support, and the fact that no contribution was made to Pompey's forces from Judaea suggests that Alexander was right. But it was not reasonable for Pompey to expect a contribution, given the instability of the land, and this was no doubt fully appreciated.

Hyrkanos and Antipater, and thus the Jewish state, were clients both of the Romans and of Pompey, so that they inevitably had to line up on Pompey's and the Senate's side, in much the same way as did the Egyptian government. Given that Caesar was Pompey's enemy, and Aristoboulos and Alexander were enemies of Pompey's Judaean clients, it is no surprise that these two pretenders should emerge on Caesar's side. But the story that Caesar gave Aristoboulos two legions and sent him to Syria to stir up trouble for the governor there, Scipio, is clearly a nonsense. Apart from not having two legions to spare, Caesar had no ships to move them, being blockaded first at Brundisium and later at Dyrrhachium (in part by the Egyptian fleet). On the other hand, it is clear that Caesar had Aristoboulos released from confinement, and perhaps it was planned for him to go to Syria, but he was swiftly poisoned and killed by Pompey's partisans, probably before he left Rome.

Alexander's journey to Antioch suggests that a family rendezvous may have been planned. The deaths of the two men produced a curious display of royal solidarity from Ptolemy son of Mennaeus, the ruler of the Ituraeans. He now gave refuge to Aristoboulos' other children, a son and two daughters who had been living at Ashkelon (the only city in Palestine never taken by the Judaean kings). The involvement of Ashkelon in Ptolemaic affairs made the city vulnerable, for if it was aligned with Kleopatra, it was also thereby aligned against Pompey's enemies. The move of the Judaean royal exiles may have been a matter of self-protection, though Josephus ignores the Ptolemaic involvement of the city.

Their arrival at the Ituraean court caused a domestic upset in Ptolemy's family when both he and his son wished to marry one of the princesses. The son Philippion married her first, but old Ptolemy won the contest in the end, and Philippion was then killed: she was then married to the older man.[25] In a wider political sense the family was now clearly safer than in Ashkelon, and, from the point of view of Hyrkanos and the Romans, they were under firmer control and perhaps less likely to stimulate more trouble in Judaea. An attempt to reconcile the two branches of the Hasmonaean family came when Hyrkanos' daughter Alexandra had married Alexander.[26] This must have taken place while Alexander was confined to Ashkelon, by 54 or 53, but as a reconciliation attempt it was only marginally effective.

Pompey escaped from the Pharsalus battlefield with a small force and some ships. He could assume that all parts of the Roman Empire were now hostile, and the eastern regions had been denuded of Roman troops to join his army at Pharsalus – Scipio the governor of Syria, for example, had taken his two legions to Greece and commanded them in the battle.[27] The many client kingdoms and cities were now, like Hyrkanos, busy switching sides. Pompey still had control of a major fleet, though the Egyptian ships returned to Egypt, but he needed a place to revive and recruit his land forces. He sailed first to Attaleia in Pamphylia, then to Paphos in Cyprus. He had four possible destinations in mind: Syria, where he had many clients, both kings and cities, or Parthia, which he had already contacted before Pharsalus, though probably only to assure himself of Parthian neutrality during the Roman civil war. Caesar knew of the mission to Parthia but says nothing of any request for help. King Juba of Numidia was another possible refuge. Some of his supporters, with ships and soldiers under command of the M. Porcius Cato, had already gone to him. Egypt, whose government he could claim owed its position to his advocacy with the Senate, was still another possibility.[28]

At Paphos these options were discussed and narrowed. Syria, partly disarmed, was now generally hostile. At Antioch the citizens and the Romans there had seized control of the acropolis, and had sent word to any refugees from Pharsalus not to go there – probably Pompey also received one of these messages.[29] The lack of support from Judaea he already knew about. The idea of taking refuge in Parthia sparked strong protests among his companions; after all, Romans and Parthians had been fighting each other in Syria not much more than a year ago, and might be considered to be at war still.

Nobody seems to have trusted Juba, though this would probably have been the best place for him to go. So, by elimination, Pompey sailed from Paphos, avoiding all the Syrian ports, to Egypt.

He went to Pelusion, the fortress defending Egypt from an attack from Syria, because that was where the government of Ptolemy XIII was concentrated, defending themselves from an attack by Kleopatra and her forces.[30] Neither Pompey now, nor Caesar later, seem to have had any conception of the difficulty their arrival in Egypt would cause for the Egyptian government. Both men arrogantly assumed that simply because they were Roman commanders their wishes took precedence over any local issues. But the Egyptian government naturally had its own priorities, and these were not Roman. Above all, the Egyptians were extremely sensitive to any threats to the independence of their country, and assumed that any Roman commander who turned up had designs on that independence.

Pompey's arrival was thus highly unwelcome for any number of reasons. First, there was already a civil war between the forces of brother and sister. Kleopatra had evidently recruited a large enough force to compel a full Egyptian army to stand on the defensive at Pelusion. This was always the best way of defending against an attack from the east, since it put the attacker in the desert. The arrival of a Roman general who had just been defeated in a civil war into the midst of their army was likely to result in his assuming command over it, if he could. His intention to continue the Roman war would inevitably bring Caesar to Egypt, with his own forces, which would result in fighting and requisitions and destruction – and would, most difficult of all, force the men controlling Ptolemy to choose sides. As an instance of likely trouble, Pompey's messengers who took his letter to the king asking for hospitality and protection tried to recruit some of Ptolemy's soldiers, and the Gabiniani, even as they stood waiting for a reply to Pompey's request.[31] This was obviously tactless, but typically Roman.

Ptolemy's senior advisers, Potheinos, Theodotos, and Achillas, discussed the request, as Pompey and his party waited on their ship. Their conclusion was that it was too dangerous to let him land, even more dangerous to refuse him hospitality, and absolutely necessary to gain some credit with Caesar. But Pompey had money, 2,000 men, and a fleet with him, and he was clearly capable of forcing a landing. The Egyptians decided to tempt him ashore with the promise of discussions and then kill him, while using their ships to impose a blockade to prevent Pompey's own ships from getting away. Achillas took a small group of men in a small vessel out to Pompey's ship. They included the tribune L. Septimius and a centurion called Salvius, both former comrades to Pompey in his pirate campaign, who were serving with the Gabiniani. The presence of these men helped persuade a reluctant Pompey to land, though he could see the king's forces lining the shore and the Egyptian ships moving to blockade him, to go ashore. He perhaps expected to be made a prisoner, but he certainly expected to be able to discuss matters, and began checking over his notes on what he would say when he met the government. As he reached the shore, first Septimius, then Salvius and Achillas, stabbed him. He covered his head with his toga, and died.[32]

Chapter 4

Caesar

The anxious calculations of the Egyptian rulers had led them into a grievous mistake. Possibly the lack of reaction by Bibulus to the killing of his two sons had beguiled them into thinking that killing prominent Romans was not going to incur punishment, at least during a civil war. Once again we find mutual incomprehension. When Caesar was presented with Pompey's severed head by Theodotos of Chios as proof of his death, he burst into tears – not a reaction any Ptolemy or any Ptolemaic official would have, or understand.[1] (They had also murdered L. Cornelius Lentulus Crus, who had landed in Egypt soon after Pompey's killing; he had been consul the year before, and was another of Caesar's Roman enemies, but Caesar showed much less remorse in his case; but then Lentulus Crus was not, as Pompey had been, his son-in-law, and long-time colleague.[2])

The killing of Pompey was, therefore, a great political error. Caesar arrived two days after the murder, and was annoyed. Had the Egyptians simply imprisoned Pompey and handed him over to Caesar when he arrived, they might have persuaded him to leave. More likely, though, Caesar would have landed anyway; murdering Pompey just gave him a better excuse. And when he went ashore into Alexandria he did so surrounded by the lictors of a Roman consul with *imperium*, and moved immediately into the royal palace. The precise symbolism of the lictors and the implication of *imperium* may have eluded the Alexandrians, but the arrogance of his arrival and his appropriation of the palace were unmistakable messages which they could not miss.

It was then Caesar's turn to misunderstand the situation. Given the killing of Pompey, it was reasonable for him to assume that the Egyptian rulers were acting in support of him and his cause, whereas their aim was to get him to go away and let them rule Egypt in independence. So when he landed and brought 4,000 Roman troops with him, and marched through Alexandria as if he had authority as consul in the royal city of the Ptolemies, and automatically took up quarters in the royal palace, the Egyptians inevitably concluded that he was seizing power, and perhaps even annexing the country. Opposition developed at once, manifesting itself as hostility to his soldiers.[3]

It soon became clear that Caesar had another motive for landing in the city. He had never received the full amount of the fee promised by Ptolemy Auletes in arranging, ten years before, for the king's recognition by the Senate. He had probably also arranged for the cash supposedly still owed to

Rabirius Postumus to be assigned to him, and now demanded its payment. The sum he stipulated he required, on account, so to speak, was 10,000,000 *denarii*.[4] With Caesar in occupation of the palace, Potheinos the *dioiketes* had no choice but to make an effort to pay, but he did so in such a way – using temple treasures and royal plates, and then serving meals on wooden platters – as to put Caesar in a bad light with the Alexandrians.[5]

The Alexandrians were thus quite right to be suspicious of Caesar's presence, and this suspicion quickly developed into hostility. He played the tourist, visiting such sights as the tomb of Alexander the Great. The hostility which greeted him as he stepped ashore had persuaded him to order up reinforcements from Asia Minor. This may or may not have been known in Egypt, but it was clear to all that the man who was still engaged in a civil war was not staying in a foreign kingdom merely to see the sights.

It is unlikely that Caesar or any of his party had any direct up-to-date information about the conditions in Egypt when he arrived; he had, after all, been preoccupied and rather busy with more immediate matters for the past few years. When fully informed, however, he sought to extend his influence and Roman power into the heart of the Egyptian government by aiming to settle the dynastic dispute. This would permit him, as Pompey had, to act as patron of the claimant to whom he judged the throne. He stated he was acting on the authority he had as consul in 59, when he sponsored the recognition of Ptolemy Auletes, and on his current position as consul again; he had also been reappointed dictator, but it is not clear that he knew this yet. This was all, of course, extremely flimsy reasoning, and neither party in Egypt would recognize or accept such authority. But he had troops, and in recognition of the realities of the situation, he ordered up more. In order to magnify his power, as a first step he ordered the disputants to dismiss their armies, which should have made the Roman force the only power around.[6]

Neither did, of course. Ptolemy XIII arrived in Alexandria in person to make his case, but he was backed by his troops and his ministers;[7] Kleopatra had to get to Caesar secretly, being carried in hidden in a coverlet.[8] Probably she seduced Caesar that night – he was always susceptible to women of charm and beauty, and besides that, she was a queen; how could he resist? There is no doubt that she was thereby able to influence him to her support. At the same time, she was politically the weaker of the disputants, and so, if he placed her in power, she would be much more reliant upon Roman support, and so easier to control. There was politics as well as personal regard in his Egyptian policy. Caesar's manoeuvres were thus mainly aimed at promoting Kleopatra to power once more, but the exact mix of the various authorities was yet to be decided. He must have had doubts about her ability to rule alone, for her first attempt had hardly been successful.

With Kleopatra in the palace, Ptolemy XIII was infuriated, appreciating at once that his own position was under threat. He rushed into the crowd, tore off his diadem, and shouted that he had been betrayed (not an accurate assessment, of course). He was captured by Roman troops, and Caesar staved off the threatened riot by bringing both candidates out, and announcing that he had decided to re-establish the original provision of the will of Ptolemy XII, which he read out loud, to place Ptolemy XIII and Kleopatra as joint monarchs. This was perhaps not quite what Kleopatra had really wanted, but then neither was it acceptable to Ptolemy. It did quieten the crowd, perhaps by the sheer surprise of Caesar's action. As part of the settlement, and to get them out of the way, the youngest siblings, Ptolemy (later 'XIV') and Arsinoe were to be made joint rulers of Cyprus, which was thus returned to Ptolemaic rule after ten years as a Roman possession.[9]

One of the curiosities of these events was that, since Kleopatra's arrival, all parties were living in the royal palace. On Ptolemy's side it was Potheinos who controlled events (as much as anyone did). He had helped rouse opinion against Caesar by handing over the temple and royal treasures, claiming there were no other resources – which may actually have been true. Ptolemy's histrionic claim of betrayal may have been set up by Potheinos. And he was organizing the opposition to Caesar from, so to speak, the next room.

Potheinos now called up the full Ptolemaic army under Achillas from Pelusion, leaving a small force to hold the fortress.[10] Kleopatra's attacking force had probably retired to Syria once more. It would not be able to subsist in the desert, and she had to make some gesture of disarmament in the face of Caesar's demands. The approach of the Ptolemaic army caught Caesar by surprise. It is said to have been 20,000 strong, and included the Gabiniani, now loyal to Ptolemy. This figure is Caesar's estimate, and he is not above exaggerating the size of his enemy's forces – he had done this repeatedly in his Gallic wars. On the other hand, he was certainly outnumbered. He sent out two men, prominent Ptolemaic courtiers, to negotiate, but Achillas ordered them arrested and killed, though one of them escaped, wounded. Caesar had Ptolemy, and the king could be a hostage of a sort, but Achillas was able to occupy the greater part of the city.[11]

Caesar's force was able to hold on in the solid buildings of the palace quarter and repelled a variety of relatively small attacks, deploying his forces by cohorts. Much destruction was done, including the Museon library. Achillas controlled all the city except for the small part Caesar held, which he had fortified. Now Achillas made a serious attempt to gain control of the harbour, where over seventy Ptolemaic warships, quadriremes, and quinqueremes, including those recently used by Pompey in the Adriatic, were berthed, though it is unlikely they were manned. Caesar's naval force was much smaller, so the

Ptolemaic fleet could blockade the palace (which was close to the harbour) and so block the arrival of supplies or reinforcements. Caesar replied by having all the enemy ships burned. The fighting then centred on a contest for control of the Pharos lighthouse, whose commanding position controlled the harbour entrance. Caesar could reach the island with his own ships, and gained control of part of the island after some fighting, but he did not have the strength to defeat the Alexandrians and so had to wait for reinforcements to reach him.

The Egyptian forces which Caesar faced were partly the regular Ptolemaic army, including the Gabiniani, but also, he says, mercenaries from Syria and Kilikia. He calls them brigands and pirates, which they may well have been, for these were always the alternative professions for unemployed soldiers. Also runaway slaves had joined the army, which gave them a home, and where their fellow soldiers protected them against their former owners' attempts to recover them. Caesar's description is redolent of aristocratic Roman contempt for the non-Roman lower orders, but he cannot evade describing the success of these forces against his own legionaries.

With the Ptolemaic army besieging the palace district, it was relatively easy for Caesar's hostages and prisoners to communicate with them. Arsinoe escaped from the palace, along with her tutor, the eunuch Ganymedes, and joined Achillas' forces, possibly in order to inspire them, possibly in an attempt to seize the throne. But then she, or rather Ganymedes (Arsinoe was only ten) fell into a dispute. It is likely that her escape had been engineered by others, and Caesar indirectly points to Potheinos, who was discovered sending messages to Achillas. In this scenario Potheinos will have become jealous of Achillas and apprehensive that his command of the army gave him too much power. Another possible culprit would be Caesar himself. It was surprisingly easy for Arsinoe to leave the palace (Caesar does not say she escaped), and she and Ganymedes almost at once quarrelled with Achillas over the command. Possibly Potheinos and Ganymedes were allied, but it is more likely that, linked as they were to different royal claimants, they were rivals. This was presumably clear to Caesar. The quarrel between Achillas and Ganymedes – and Arsinoe – is the main ground for suggesting Caesar's involvement, for when his enemies quarrelled he was obviously the beneficiary. Potheinos, in the palace with Ptolemy, was executed for sending messages in an attempt to control Achillas. Then Ganymedes drove Achillas from control of the army and had him killed. As a direct result of Arsinoe leaving the palace, two of Caesar's main enemies had been eliminated.[12]

By this time we are dependent very largely on a new source. Caesar's own account in the *Civil War* ends with the execution of Potheinos. The narrative is taken up by a different author, possibly A. Hirtius (who had completed

Caesar's account of his Gallic wars) in the *Alexandrian War*. The tone is, of course, different, and perhaps less artfully propagandistic than in Caesar's account. Hirtius may have been present in Alexandria; if not, he had access to first-hand accounts, no doubt Caesar himself being one. Certainly some of the descriptions of the fighting are clearly based on eyewitness accounts.

Ganymedes had Arsinoe proclaimed as queen, clearly in direct opposition to Kleopatra's claims, and as a new partner for Ptolemy XIII. He also infused new energy into the fighting. Having a royal sibling in hand he could disregard the threats Caesar made against his hostages. He poisoned the water supply with seawater; Caesar had his soldiers dig new wells. The Alexandrians organized the manufacture of arms, and recruited more troops, including slaves.[13]

They gathered up all the ships they could collect into a small fleet, about the same size as that which Caesar controlled. The two fleets fought a battle off the island of Pharos. The author of the *Alexandrian War* claims the Egyptians 'fled', but Caesar was sufficiently concerned that he decided he must gain control of the whole of the island, where until then he only held the lighthouse area.[14] He sent landing forces which succeeded in conquering the island, which was a built-up suburb of the city, but an attempt to gain control of the Heptastadion, the causeway connecting the island to the mainland, failed with considerable losses. Caesar himself had to swim for his life when the ship he was on was captured and sunk. He maintained control over the island end of the causeway, but by controlling its landward end, the Egyptians could still get raiding forces into the harbour.[15]

As a gesture, and as a possible means of dividing his opponents Caesar released Ptolemy when the Alexandrians requested this. He presents this as a peace gesture, though his troops thought he had gone soft, and in fact Ptolemy's release only stimulated more fighting, since the king himself energized his followers even more than Ganymedes. Another naval battle was required in order to keep open the Roman supply lines.[16] It cannot be said that Caesar ever came to understand the Egyptian situation, but then it was a situation which was repeatedly changing. Every action he took indicates that he was aiming to establish Roman influence over whatever Egyptian regime emerged from the confusion. And this was his aim only in part because of the personal relations between them, for any settlement had to include Kleopatra as queen.

By now the reinforcements Caesar had sent for were approaching. Some ships with the Thirty-seventh legion had waited for some time off Canopus, held there by foul winds, and where they were menaced by Ptolemy's fleet; Caesar sent out his own fleet as protection.[17] In addition, Mithradates of Pergamon (who, despite his city of origin, was a descendent of the Gauls of Asia Minor) had gathered troops in Asia Minor and marched through Syria, collecting more soldiers on the way, paced along the coast by a fleet. He was given 3,000 troops by Hyrkanos of Judaea, commanded by Antipater in person, who is given the credit by Josephus for persuading other clients to contribute. From north and central Syria two contributors are named: Iamblichos, probably a member of the Emesan royal family, and Ptolemy son of Soemos 'who lived in Mount Lebanon', possibly the lord of the principality of Arqa. (It seems unlikely they needed Antipater's persuasion to contribute.) Mithradates also collected troops from 'almost all the cities', and it is difficult to see what influence Antipater could have here, though he had used his Nabataean connections to persuade King Malichos that it would be a good idea to help out, and a Nabataean cavalry force was sent to assist (though Josephus actually refers to the donor as 'the chiefs of the Arabs'). These cities and princes contributed because they were Roman clients, and because it was now good politics to support Caesar, not because of Antipater's supposed persuasiveness.[18] This had all been a splendid opportunity for the Syrians of all types, in cities and kingdoms, to jump on Caesar's bandwagon.

By the time he reached Pelusion, Mithradates of Pergamon had a substantial force, including the Syrian contingents. There was also another legion marching through Syria some way behind, though it did not reach Egypt in time to join the fight. It may also be that the force which Kleopatra had recruited earlier joined in as he approached Pelusion. The fortress was held by Ptolemy's troops, but it was captured by escalation, with the Jewish forces in the lead according to Josephus, though the author of the *Alexandrian War* describes a series of attacks which wore down the defenders; the two are not, of course, mutually exclusive, but one must always be wary of Josephus' tendency to boost Jewish prowess. Further, Dio Cassius adds that Mithradates got his ships into the Nile by hauling them overland and so could attack from the river side simultaneously with the landward attack.[19]

From Pelusion, Mithradates' army marched along the banks of the Pelusiac distributary of the Nile to Memphis, and then north along the Damietta branch towards Alexandria, the same route used by all invaders, including Gabinius. The march must have taken some time. The distance from Pelusion to Memphis and then on to Alexandria is at least 350 km, which will have taken Mithradates' forces at least a fortnight to cover, and probably a good deal more. The Egyptians certainly had time to organize a defensive deployment which fought two battles, the first against Mithradates' fortified camp, in a fight Dio thought was an Egyptian victory.[20] A Ptolemaic force commanded by Dioskorides was met and defeated, but these may be the same battles as described in the *Alexandrian War*. As with the Pelusion fight several sources all seem to have got hold of just part of the story. The very fact that this army was on the march will have relieved the pressure on Caesar in Alexandria; the

Ptolemaic army met by Mithradates mainly came from the forces facing Caesar.

How committed the ordinary Egyptians were to this fight against the Romans is never clear. On the way Antipater persuaded various Jewish groups living in the country to join the Caesarians, a fact pointedly noted by Josephus, but we gain no information about Egyptian responses. It does seem unlikely that the over-taxed peasantry would have supported the greedy government in Alexandria. Caesar and the author of the *Alexandrian War* both claim that the Ptolemaic army was filled out by ex-slaves and such riff-raff, and imply that the fighting was done mainly by and for Alexandrians. There is in fact little sign that anyone else in Egypt took part, and the *Alexandrian War* author notes that Mithradates' march was nowhere contested, while Josephus says that the Jews in Egypt were supportive of it.[21] On the other hand, the Egyptian priestly and landowning classes were surely fully aware at what was happening in Alexandria. Kleopatra is said to have gained some popularity early in her reign by attending various ritual celebrations.[22] Ptolemy XIII had not had time to do this, and it was in any case a fairly superficial popularity. On the whole it seems reasonable to assume that a majority of the Egyptian population, Egyptian and Greek, living outside Alexandria (and Pelusion) were indifferent to the result of the fighting, so probably there was neutrality at worst from the Egyptians, and perhaps even some support for the Romans.

Ptolemy moved his main army from Alexandria along the river, using ships, and took up a strong and naturally defensive position to block the invaders' further advance, by which time they were fairly close to Alexandria. Sufficient men were left in Alexandria to contain Caesar's troops. But Caesar had control of the harbour and of his ships, and by this time he had received the Thirty-seventh Legion and the supplies on the relief fleet. It is probable that he could have taken control of the city by assault in the absence of much of Ptolemy's army, but this would still leave the main enemy force intact. If Dio Cassius is correct in his estimate of the result of the battle by the river, he might also find that Mithradates' army had been destroyed while he fought in the city. The main target therefore had to be the Ptolemaic main army and not the city, and his first priority was to unite his forces. As Mithradates squared up to the Egyptians near Mareotis, Caesar moved his forces out of the city by sea along the coast, landed them, and marched to join his two armies together.[23]

It is an impressive decision. After concentrating on the fighting for the city for several months it must have been tempting to let the troops loose. It would hardly have been surprising if he had by then become fixated on the desire to defeat the enemies in front of him. Caesar's grasp of the whole picture is admirable, especially when his information about Mithradates' forces and their position must have been only partial. And, of course, he was right.

This was a notable march, for the king's army had been transported by river, and so were rested. They will have moved faster than Caesar's forces by land, yet Caesar's force was able to meet and defeat the Egyptian army in the field, though admittedly only in a skirmish. No doubt the Egyptians were defensively-minded from the start, and having secured a defensible position had no wish to march out and engage Caesar in the open country. It cannot have helped that they knew they were about to fight the conqueror of Gaul and Pompey. Caesar's forces constructed a camp – so both armies held fortified positions – and he no doubt brought up Mithradates' army; Antipater and his Jewish forces were certainly present. A small river with high banks was between them, and Egyptian cavalry and light infantry went out to secure the crossing places. But the river was not really defensible. Some of Caesar's German cavalry swam across where the banks were low, and then the legionaries used tree trunks laid across the river and surfaced with earth to make bridges. The Egyptians withdrew to their fortified camp.

This camp was formidable, and Caesar refused to attack it until his men were rested and fed. It was close to the Nile, where the king's ships formed an outflanking guard. On the landward side of the fort a wall had been built to connect it with a fortified village. It was clearly a formidable position, and no doubt another reason for Caesar's caution was that he would want to examine the enemy's position before making his attack. He located three points of apparent weakness. One was the village, for once that was taken access to the main fort could be had on more than one side. It also looked as though there was an unguarded area near the Nile, and another place where the approach was not blocked by any obvious impediment.

Caesar committed most of his force to the attack on the village. Its fortifications were less robust than the main fort's, and the Roman forces were able to concentrate at one point, whereas Ptolemy's forces had to be on guard everywhere. The village was stormed, and the fugitives were pursued towards the main fort. However, if the aim really was, as the *Alexandrian War* author certainly claims, that the Romans were to rush the fort alongside the fugitives, it failed.

Presumably after some reorganization and redeployment (though the only source for all this, the *Alexandrian War*, does not say so) the two apparently vulnerable points of the main fort were then attacked. The force which aimed to attack along the bank of the river was bombarded by missiles by men in the ships and by others in the fort, and the other, unencumbered, approach route was defended by the best of the Egyptian troops. Neither attack came anywhere near succeeding.

The fighting at these places, however, had attracted reinforcements from the interior of the fort. This had denuded one particular spot of troops, a high area which appeared to be well protected by its natural defences. Caesar spotted this and sent 'some cohorts', whom he had clearly kept in reserve, to attack this point. This was decisive, for the defendants suddenly realized that they were now under attack from a third point, and one which had become effectively unguarded. The defence faltered and the Roman troops broke in at all three points of attack. The Egyptian army was thus comprehensively defeated. King Ptolemy died in trying to cross the river to escape. Caesar at the head of his victorious (and now much larger) army, moved on Alexandria, which surrendered to him.[24]

Historians of Rome commonly criticize Caesar for wasting time in Egypt while the rest of the empire slipped from his grasp.[25] During the nine months or so he spent in Egypt the Pompeian/Senatorial cause revived in many areas, Africa and Spain notably, with the result that the work accomplished at Pharsalus and before had to be done again – though he could not be everywhere at once, and these revivals would no doubt have happened anyway. But Caesar, once in Egypt, had become trapped in a situation where he could not allow himself to be beaten (which would give his enemies even more encouragement), and he also believed he needed access to Egypt's wealth, and above all he had to be sure that the country remained in friendly hands. Even with an unfriendly and reluctant government, Pompey had secured a small land force and a fleet of fifty ships from Egypt. Caesar's experience in Alexandria dictated that the only friend he had in Egypt was Kleopatra. Every other person in authority was hostile so he needed to stay long enough to ensure that Kleopatra was firmly placed in control. As a result of the fighting, most of his Egyptian opponents were in fact now dead.

He spent some more time in the country after the victory, enjoying Kleopatra's company (she was pregnant by this time), but also, and perhaps more important in his eyes, he put in position government structures to support her rule and to ensure that Rome's authority was accepted. (The story of his enjoying a romantic voyage up the Nile with Kleopatra is not true.) Kleopatra's other brother was made king along with her (Ptolemy XIV); Arsinoe, whose anti-Kleopatra sentiments had been made clear during the fighting, was banished to Ephesos, and she was later exhibited in Caesar's triumph as a symbol of his victory in Egypt. After the events of the recent past it is not surprising that Kleopatra was deeply unpopular in her kingdom, so when at last he left Egypt Caesar left her a guard of three legions. These were somewhat understrength units, but they were the troops who had won the war, and were unlikely to be soon attacked.[26]

Kleopatra's unpopularity was thus an excellent excuse to increase the Roman military presence in Egypt, and she and her country had now become a client state of the Roman Empire. What had become of the Gabiniani, who had fought against him, is not known; probably the survivors faded into the

Alexandrian population. Most of the men of the legions left in Egypt had been originally on Pompey's side at Pharsalus, so it was useful to be able to leave them well away from Rome: also their pay and maintenance lay with the Egyptians, which helped relieve Rome's finances somewhat. The queen had to rely on these men for some time, though she energetically set about recruiting her own forces, both army and fleet, and soon was able to assert a good deal of independence, helped by yet another bout of Roman civil warfare. This policy will have helped reconcile at least some of her Egyptian enemies to her rule. And if she was overthrown or assassinated, Caesar had to hand yet another member of the family, Arsinoe, whom he could use. For the rest Caesar was probably uninterested in how Kleopatra ruled, only that she remained in power and in control.

The first problem Caesar dealt with after the Egyptian settlement was the defiance of King Pharnakes of Pontos. Leaving the three legions in Egypt, to which a fourth was later added, he took the rest of his forces on a march to Asia, through Syria. The several Syrian contingents were either allowed to make their own ways home, or were dropped off on the way, and on the journey Caesar could express his thanks to those who had contributed forces to help him in Egypt. Of these we know he had troops from Judaea, Nabataea, Arqa (probably), and Emesa, while Ashkelon had been hospitable to Kleopatra, and many of the Syrian cities had also contributed to the army Mithradates of Pergamon had recruited on his way through, since by then it seemed prudent to do so. Caesar distributed rewards to these temporary friends. Only in the case of Judaea are they known in any detail, but others can be deduced.

It is possible that Caesar rewarded the Emesan kings. Iamblichos was the son of Samsigeramos I, who was still alive, but he seems to have entrusted Iamblichos with the more active work. They were probably rewarded by the return of the small city of Arethusa to their rule. Pompey had taken it from them in 64, when the city adopted a new dating era, but a comment in Strabo that it 'belonged to Samsigeramos and Iamblichos', might suggest its return, and only Caesar was in a position to do this. This is by no means certain, but we must expect that those who, like Hyrkanos of Judaea, gave Caesar substantial help, would expect rewards. Some of the Syrian cities, in particular Antioch and Laodikeia show signs of being grateful to Caesar, which implies that he had rewarded them with privileges, but little detail can be discerned.[27]

Hyrkanos and Antipater had been particularly active in the relief expedition, perhaps more so than anyone else in Syria – but then they controlled the largest Syrian state, and were neighbours of Egypt, so more would be expected of them. Antipater's connections with Malichos I of the Nabataeans had brought in a contingent of Nabataean cavalry, and Hyrkanos had contributed

3,000 of his own troops. Antipater himself had led the assault on the walls of Pelusion and had been particularly prominent in the fight outside Alexandria – or so Josephus says, though no one else reports this. Caesar prudently gave the kingdom substantial rewards. Hyrkanos was made *ethnarchos*, meaning chief or ruler of a people, which the Jews sensibly simply translated as 'king'. His kingdom recovered the city-port of Joppa, one of its long-standing targets, together with an area to the north-west called the 'Great Plain', an agriculturally rich area inland of Mount Carmel. This was the beginning of the territorial revival of Judaea. For the moment any other wishes were ignored or refused, though the message was clear: active loyalty would be rewarded. At least Caesar did not meddle any further with the internal affairs of the kingdom, other than giving Hyrkanos his new title.

Antipater was also possibly rewarded by being recognized in his dominant governing position in Judaea, and was given Roman citizenship. The Judaean state tribute was fixed at a reasonable amount, with the concession that this was not to be levied in sabbatical years. At the same time Antipater's request to be allowed to refortify Jerusalem was refused. But Caesar also refused the request by Antigonos, the surviving son of Aristoboulos II and brother of the troublesome Alexander, to replace Hyrkanos as ruler in Judaea. Antigonos returned to his refuge in Chalkis with Ptolemy son of Mennaeus; Caesar will have taken due note that, as in Egypt, he may have favoured one faction, but a rival was available if needed.[28] He cannot have been unhappy that Hyrkanos was thus under permanent threat.

The result of the crisis in Alexandria had been to establish the power of the two new rulers in Egypt and Judaea more firmly. These would in their different ways dominate the region for the next two decades, Kleopatra as queen of Egypt, and Antipater and his family as the governors of Judaea under the ethnarch, and as it turned out, he was also the founder of a new dynasty (which in fact outlasted that of which Caesar was the founder). In Egypt the war had eliminated most of Kleopatra's competitors and most of her prominent opponents and had left her in sole effective power, but all too obviously under Roman protection. In Judaea, Hyrkanos may have received a sort of promotion in formal terms, but it was clearly Antipater who had established himself as Rome's favourite, as his Roman citizenship demonstrated. Both of these rulers were thus in place because Rome had favoured them. This is most obvious in the case of Kleopatra, whose position as queen was entirely due to Caesar's support, and his soldiers' protection; for Antipater his rise had been assisted by the repeated Roman interventions in Judaean affairs, which he had exploited personally with great success. These two now dominated their respective kingdoms, but in effect only as Roman clients.

Chapter 5

Herod

After Caesar's gifts and commendations Antipater had become even more important than before. His Roman citizenship – a status almost unique in the Near East except for immigrant Romans – marked him out, and together with his position as an *epimeletes* in Judaea established him firmly as Hyrkanos' dominant minister. It also made him a prime target for those in Judaea who disliked the whole governmental set-up.

Caesar's promotion of both Hyrkanos (to ethnarch) and Antipater (to Roman citizen) led directly to the emergence of Antipater's elder sons as active political figures. He and his Nabataean wife Kypros had four sons and a daughter, who were also, of course, now Roman citizens. The eldest son Phasael was made governor of Jerusalem, which put him at the centre of power; the second son, Herod, was made governor of Galilee. In fact, Galilee was the more difficult proposition, for there was a revolt in progress at the time of Herod's appointment. The rebels, led or commanded by a man called Hezekiah, were actually referred to as 'bandits' by the Judaean government, but denigrating enemies, particularly internal political enemies, is standard practice for governments, then as now.[1] Hezekiah's purpose was no doubt anti-Antipater, anti-Hyrkanos and anti-Roman.

Herod set about suppressing Hezekiah and his rebels, who operated on 'the borders of Syria' which would seem to mean the border country between Galilee and the Syrian province, either inland of Ptolemais-Ake or towards Samaria and Skythopolis. Basing themselves inside Judaean territory, they were largely immune from retaliation if they raided into the Roman province, yet plenty of Jews would be quite happy to see them continue unpunished. Herod's action was therefore praised by the Syrians, and commended by the new governor of Syria, Sex. Julius Caesar (the great Caesar's cousin).[2] Such praise, from such a quarter, rasped the nerves of those who already disliked the family, whose rise was resisted by those they displaced or whose ambitions were thereby thwarted.

Herod's success had in fact given his enemies an opening. He was charged with having killed Hezekiah and his followers illegally, since it was claimed that Jewish law prohibited any Jew being killed unless they had been condemned by the Jerusalem Sanhedrin first. Of course, Herod was not the real target for this attack, but the whole family. Hyrkanos, no doubt already apprehensive at Antipater's new powers, and whose attitude towards Antipater was never anything but ambiguous, was persuaded that Herod should be tried. As Herod was travelling to Jerusalem for the hearing, a message reached Hyrkanos from the governor Sex. Caesar, enjoining aquittal. This Hyrkanos arranged, throwing the blame onto the governor. Josephus' various accounts of the trial are confused, but the essential points are that Hyrkanos willingly submitted to instructions from the governor, and that out of it all Herod became a staunch Roman ally.[3]

Sex. Caesar made his confidence in Herod clear by appointing him as subgovernor in Koele Syria. Presumably his accusation and trial had involved Herod's removal from the governorship of Galilee, and he had gone out of Judaea to Damascus, but the new appointment was in the same region. At this time the term Koele Syria seems to have meant the Decapolis cities, the group of Greek cities straddling the Jordan but mainly on the eastern side. (Indeed it may have been along the borders of this area and Galilee that Hezekiah had mounted his raids.) From his new position Herod gathered some forces and began to march in Jerusalem, supposedly intent on attacking Hyrkanos in revenge for his humiliation at the threat of a trial. Antipater and Phasael calmed him down, and possibly Sex. Caesar also intervened (though the distances involved and the short timing would make it difficult for him to do so).[4]

Antipater and his family were clearly wedded to the Roman alliance, for they owed their recent rise to Roman patronage, but by 46, only a year after Julius Caesar's visit to Palestine, the question of which Romans they should support returned. Not long after Herod's appointment to Koele Syria, Sex. Caesar faced a rebellion. Q. Caecilius Bassus, a Pompeian, intrigued with others to subvert Sextus' control of the soldiers. At first victorious, Sextus was later murdered by some of the soldiers Bassus had subverted.[5]

This rebellion was timed to coincide with Julius Caesar's invasion of Africa, and was helped along by forged letters (or perhaps just rumours) of Caesar's death. Caesar sent out a new governor, C. Antistius Vetus, who succeeded in collecting enough forces to blockade Bassus in the city of Apamea, but was unable to capture the city. Both men appealed for help to local potentates. Bassus persuaded an Arab chief, Alchaudonius, and a Parthian force to join in; Vetus brought in help from Judaea. Antipater sent two of his sons with part of the Judaean forces to assist him. Bassus recruited soldiers and ex-slaves and others locally in Syria to form a new legion – so presumably up to 4,000 men.[6] This competitive reinforcement merely continued the stalemate at Apamea, where the siege continued all through 45 and into 44.

A new governor, L. Staius Murcus, was sent out, with three more legions, arriving early in 44, and the Bithynian governor, Q. Marcius Crispus, came to help with another three.[7] This should surely have been enough to deal with Bassus, but then came the news of Caesar's assassination in Rome in March. A further layer of complexity now supervened. Caesar had appointed C. Cassius Longinus as Syrian governor for 43, but Mark Antony now appointed P. Cornelius Dolabella instead. Cassius ignored this change, reached Syria first, and was able to take over Murcus' and Crispus' armies, and, being now anti-Caesarean (he was one of the assassins), persuaded Bassus' army to join him as well. Suddenly he had an army of seven or eight legions, and this increased again when he met, defeated, and recruited Dolabella's single legion, and to twelve or thirteen when he persuaded the commander of the legions left in Egypt by Julius Caesar to join him. These troops had originally been some of Pompey's soldiers at Pharsalus; Cassius in his new anti-Caesarean role was perhaps congenial.[8]

Antipater and his sons were now clearly in real danger. They extracted their forces from the confrontation at Apamea before Cassius arrived, for when he came south to collect the Egyptian garrisons they were back in Judaea. He knew of the earlier preferences of the Judaeans, however, and imposed a massive tribute of 700 talents on the kingdom. Herod rapidly produced his quota of 100 talents from Galilee, and succeeded in gaining Cassius' confidence. The others were slower, and Cassius seized the people of the four towns of Gophna, Emmaus, Lydda, and Thamna, and sold them as slaves to make up the difference. Further seizures were stopped when Hyrkanos produced 100 talents and had them delivered to Cassius by Antipater.[9]

The speed and slickness of the family's switch is impressive. But it was done, as Josephus says, 'at the expense of others', both the taxpayers and the citizens whom Cassius had enslaved. And further Roman demands would come. This all stoked the opposition in Judaea, already substantial after Herod's activities in Galilee. The family was fully identified as Caesar's and now Cassius' men; now they were identified as likely to suck up any Roman in power. And the population of Judaea would pay.

This was a tailor-made situation for an opponent to gather support. One such opponent was Malichos. He was presumably a governor of the same sort as Herod and Phasael, for he had some responsibility for raising the money to pay off Cassius. He had failed or refused to pay up, and was then protected from Cassius' vengeance when Hyrkanos' 100 talents were paid over. One of Malichos' motivations was his animosity towards Antipater, and Antipater's role in saving him from Cassius cannot have reconciled them. Josephus' account of their feud is scarcely clear. It is evident that they plotted against each other, though it is Malichos' plots against Antipater which are mentioned. Already, early in 44, Murcus had offered to kill Malichos after one episode, but Antipater refused. At one point Antipater had to go across the Jordan, presumably into the Peraia, to escape. He collected 'an army of Arabs as well as natives' – the latter presumably Jews – and faced down Malichos. Such a reaction shows how serious and dangerous the feud was, for the two men came very close to instigating a civil war. Malichos backed down, denying on oath that he was plotting.[10]

In early 43 Antipater died. Josephus says that Malichos persuaded Hyrkanos' butler to kill him by poison. There must be much doubt about this, for deaths by poison were impossible in the ancient world to distinguish from other internal illnesses, or even from heart attacks or strokes. Josephus states the poisoning as a fact, but that is not evidence that poisoning took place. All one can say is that Antipater died. He was, after all, about 60 years old; death could have come from natural causes at any time.

Malichos 'restored order' in Jerusalem, which implies that there were disturbances as a result of Antipater's death. Herod and Phasael, evidently outside Jerusalem at the time (even though Phasael was the city's governor) immediately accused Malichos of the murder, since Antipater had been in the company of both Malichos and Hyrkanos when he died. It looks as though these two were taking the opportunity created by Antipater's sudden death to carry through a coup against Antipater's family. By doing so, of course, they inevitably brought suspicion on themselves, and Herod and Phasael immediately exploited this.

Herod was all for marching on Jerusalem, but Phasael dissuaded him and saw to their father's burial.[11] They reported Antipater's death to Cassius, accusing Malichos. Cassius was facing a major problem in the re-emergence of the Caesarean party in Italy, headed by Mark Antony and Octavian, Caesar's heir, and he had no wish for trouble in Judaea. He already knew of Malichos as a nationalistic Jew and a strong ant-Roman. In effect he told Herod to do as he wished, for he understood that Antipater's family was the best bulwark of Roman authority in the kingdom.

Herod, with Cassius' clear backing, brought a force to Jerusalem. Malichos and Hyrkanos tried to prevent him entering, but failed. Then Cassius' defeat of Dolabella provided a reason for all these men to gather with Cassius at Tyre to congratulate him. There Herod, in complicity with Cassius, and assisted by Roman soldiers provided by Cassius, had Malichos killed. Hyrkanos was shocked into speechlessness for a time, but then recovered. On being told Cassius had authorized the killing he was adept enough to praise him and damn Malichos.[12] Antipater was not the only man who could switch sides in an instant.

Herod successfully cast the blame for Malichos' death onto the governor, whose soldiers, after all, had wielded the daggers, just as Hyrkanos had been able to cast the blame for Herod's acquittal onto Sextus Caesar. A man who bade fair to replace Antipater as Hyrkanos' chief adviser had therefore been removed, and that position could now be taken up by Phasael and Herod. But Malichos' murder angered his family and his supporters just as that of Antipater had angered his sons. Malichos' brother controlled a large part to Judaea, presumably as governor. His territory included the fortress of Masada, which suggests his province was in the south; the commander of Malichos' forces in the Jerusalem area, Helix, immediately moved against Phasael. Malichos had no doubt had strong suspicions that he would be attacked at Tyre, or perhaps he had made plans to extend his earlier Jerusalem coup to gain control of the whole kingdom.

Herod fell ill, and Phasael conducted the campaign against Helix, who commanded a substantial armed force and was assisted by the citizens of Jerusalem, and by Hyrkanos, whose condemnation of Malichos at Tyre had clearly been opportunistic and insincere. Phasael eventually besieged Helix in a tower, presumably after defeating his army, but he was allowed to leave under a truce; by this time Herod had recovered and attacked Malichos' brother, capturing all his forts. He also was released after capture, under a truce.

The result of the deaths of Antipater and Malichos, therefore, had been an open civil war, which the two principals had avoided while alive. Their military mobilizations, like that by Antipater across the Jordan, had been in the nature of posturing and bluff, but once they were removed their sons and associates quickly resorted to violence.[13] The bluffs and posturings of the elders would probably have led to fighting anyway; Herod's entry into Jerusalem despite the prohibition of Malichos and Hyrkanos came very close. The fighting in Judaea took some time, probably several months. In theory the Romans should have intervened, but Cassius was preoccupied with the threat to him from the west. And if Jews in Judaea were fighting each other they were no threat to him; he could let them get on with it. Then Cassius marched off to the west to face the coalition of Octavian and Mark Antony, and Phasael and Herod suddenly found themselves facing a new threat. Antigonos the son of Aristoboulos II, the pretender to the Judaean throne, had organized an alliance with his brother-in-law Ptolemy son of Mennaeus of the Ituraeans and the tyrant of Tyre, a man called Marion, who had been put in place by Cassius, probably to dominate the region while he was away. Cassius left just one legion in Syria under the command of his nephew (whose name is not known). Antigonos, Ptolemy, and Marion enlisted a Roman commander called Fabius, who was based in Damascus, and this probably means that Cassius' nephew was involved as well. Their aim was to remove the trio ruling in Judaea, Herod, Phasael, and Hyrkanos.

This attack was just what was needed to stop the disputes within Judaea. Herod had been sorting out problems in the Samaria region, which had presumably been the scene of the fighting between Phasael and Helix. When the attack by Antigonos' coalition came he was the one in a position to combat it. No doubt Phasael was left in Jerusalem in order to maintain control, and deal with any manifestations of support for Antigonos. The territory of Tyre, under Marion's control, stretched inland for a considerable distance, as far as the headwaters of the Jordan, and so his land bordered on Galilee for some distance. His forces invaded Galilee, capturing 'three strongholds' (which are not named). Herod is said to have evicted the Tyrian troops, sending them off with gifts, but it is evident later that Marion held on some of his conquests, so he was apparently bought off.

Antigonos had also invaded Galilee, presumably out of Ituraea, and so somewhat to the east of Marion's attack. Herod defeated him in a battle, but we do not know where. Evidently Herod gauged the situation well. The lack of coordination between the invading forces meant that they could be dealt with separately. The more dangerous to the two was, of course, Antigonos; all Marion wanted was territory, and he was allowed him to keep some. Antigonos, on the other hand, wanted the whole country, and the deaths of Herod, Phasael and Hyrkanos. So Marion was bought off, and Herod then concentrated the whole of his forces to fight Antigonos' more dangerous invasion.

Antigonos' attack had also reconciled Herod and Phasael with Hyrkanos, since all three were threatened by the invasion. When Herod returned to Jerusalem he was greeted by 'Hyrkanos and the people', who 'wreathed his head with crowns'.[14]

This all took place between Cassius' departure from Syria and the defeat of his and Brutus' army at Philippi in October 42. When the news arrived, just as after Pompey's defeat, everyone in the Near East had to make adjustments to their relationships with Rome and Romans. This turned out to mean conciliating Mark Antony, who was assigned the task of dealing with the eastern provinces, while Octavian attended to Italy and the west. It was therefore to Antony that representations, backbiting, bribes, and entreaties had to be addressed. He stayed at first in Athens, then at Ephesos. Hyrkanos' representatives met him at the latter city with a golden crown, but it was only when he reached Bithynia on a tour through Asia Minor that Herod reached him in person; another delegation of Jews was also there, accusing Phasael and Herod of ruling in Hyrkanos' place; presumably they wanted all three removed.

The initial encounter of Hyrkanos' representatives with Antony at Ephesos presumably revealed that Antony above all required money. The presentation of a crown to the victor was normal diplomatic practice, not tribute. When Herod met Antony after he had left Ephesos and had started on his tour, he arrived with a substantial contribution, probably after being warned by Hyrkanos. It was also the case, of course, that the fighting in Judaea had pitted Hyrkanos and Herod against Cassius' supporters, so both men could claim to be allied to Mark Antony. When the anti-royalist delegation complained, they therefore received short shrift. The timing of all this makes it clear that Herod's journey was a result of Hyrkanos' report when he returned from Ephesos. Antony had had a difficult time in Ephesos trying to persuade the local cities to produce money they did not have. Herod's gesture was therefore all the more pleasant, acceptable and timely.

Hyrkanos had a number of complaints which he wanted Antony to redress. He wanted the return of those Jews whom Cassius had kidnapped in place of the tribute he had demanded, and the return of the territory which was still occupied by Marion of Tyre. (Since Marion had been a creature of Cassius, his days were clearly numbered.) It all helped that both Herod and Hyrkanos had met Antony earlier, as far back as at the time of Pompey's conquest. Furthermore he and Herod could offer money, stability, and to a record of constant loyalty to Rome (if not to individual Roman warlords) over the past few years.

Their diplomatic campaign was successful. Marion, soon to be deposed, was ordered to return his Galilean conquests.[15] Hyrkanos was confirmed as ethnarch, and in Judaea his alliance with the brothers was enhanced by the betrothal of Herod to Hyrkanos' daughter Mariamme. Antony was met by another hostile delegation at Antioch, 100 men this time, complaining again about Herod. Hyrkanos himself was present, and stood up for Herod, as did M. Valerius Messala Corvinus. Antony signalled his clear favour by appointing Phasael and Herod as tetrarchs, subordinate to Hyrkanos as ethnarch. Yet another delegation met Antony at Tyre. This time, being closer to Palestine, the complaining group numbered 1,000 men. Hyrkanos and Herod tried to get them to go home, after Antony had decided that they were bent on revolution – which was probably true. They were also defying him, after his clear decisions at Antioch. Despite the warnings given by Herod and Hyrkanos the men refused to budge, whereupon they were attacked by Roman soldiers and dispersed, several of them being killed.[16]

All this showed that opposition to the Idumaean family was still strong among the Jews, and that since Herod, Phasael, and Hyrkanos were firmly and publicly wedded to the Roman alliance, Antony was all the more wedded to Hyrkanos and Herod. But it could not be claimed that their position was in any way secure. The increasing numbers of opponents encountered by Antony – a delegation, 100 men, 1,000 – on his journey made that quite clear.

Antony's stay in Syria occupied the latter part of 41, during which he conducted an unsuccessful raid on Palmyra, and he spent the winter of 41–40 in Egypt. A crisis developed in his relations with Octavian, and he was preoccupied with western affairs for the rest of 40. While he was in Egypt the Parthians invaded Syria. It was well known that Antony intended to invade Parthia, in part as revenge for Crassus' death and in part because Caesar had intended to do so. The Parthians were also persuaded by Labienus, a former commander of Caesar's who had been sent to solicit Parthian aid in the time before Philippi. The defeat of Cassius and Brutus cut the ground from under his mission, but by now the Parthians had watched the Roman civil wars long enough to wish to take advantage. They had, after all, been gratuitously attacked more than once – and the Palmyra raid might have been interpreted by them as another. The previous fighting had not ended in a definitive peace agreement – how could it, when the responsible Roman authorities changing so often? – so they could legitimately invade Syria in continuation on that war. Antony had carried out a raid on the oasis of Palmyra while in Syria in 41, and this no doubt alerted the Parthians to his ambitions.

Labienus' presence was decisive in the early stages of the Parthian attack, and he quickly persuaded the Syrian garrison to join him, and went on to do the same in Asia Minor. Antony's army in the east thereby evaporated just when he needed its strength most in order to face Octavian. The Parthians themselves concentrated on conquering Syria, and their army came south, meeting no effective resistance except at Tyre.[17]

The Parthian forces were commanded by their king's son, Pakoros, and by a satrap, Barzaphranes. Tyre resisted (having just been liberated from its tyrant by Antony), but the new ruler of the Ituraeans, Lysanias, joined them. Ptolemy son of Mennaeus, his father, had just died after a reign of nearly half a century. Lysanias may well have been persuaded by Antigonos, the Hasmonaean pretender, who saw yet another opportunity to displace his rival Hyrkanos. The Nabataean King Malichos also seems to have favoured the Parthians, though he did little actually to assist them.

With Antigonos as a Parthian ally, Hyrkanos, Phasael, and Herod had no choice but to oppose the invaders. When Antigonos arrived in the Plain of Esdraelon he reached the area devastated by Cassius, and fought over by Phasael and Malichos, and the population rose in his favour. An initial fight in the plain was a victory for Antigonos, and he and his people laid siege to Jerusalem. Phasael and Herod intervened with some success, and defeated the untrained and poorly armed army Antigonos had gathered.[18]

Antigonos asked for Parthian help. A general, Pakoros the cup-bearer, intervened and persuaded Phasael and Hyrkanos to see Barzaphranes with a view to negotiations. Herod was suspicious, but this was his nature, so they discounted his doubts and went to the meeting. This time Herod's warning was accurate and both were arrested. Pakoros with a bodyguard stayed with Herod, ostensibly as hostages, actually to seize him also if necessary. Herod's suspicions were again justified, and while the Parthians debated on methods, he organized his and his supporters' escape. Taking his family, Hyrkanos' family, his servants and his soldiers, he left the city and went south, having to fight much of the way against local enemies. (This was the area where he had fought Malichos' brother.) He put his family into the Masada fortress with a guard of 800 men and supplies, and sent the rest of his people into Idumaea, where no doubt many of them had originally come from. He went himself into Nabataea.[19]

This, despite the well-organized flight, amounted to a comprehensive defeat for Herod and his family. The Parthians occupied Jerusalem and looted it, then went south and seized Marisa in Idumaea, which they may have assumed to have been Herod's destination, since it was the family's original home. Antigonos thus arrived on the Parthians' spear points, though with a large amount of popular support, and was installed as king – not a mere ethnarch – and high priest. The action of the Parthians in plundering Jerusalem cannot have endeared them, or their protégé, to the citizens. Antigonos secured his position by mutilating Hyrkanos, which was supposed to make him ineligible to be high priest. Phasael committed suicide when it was clear he was to be executed. Hyrkanos was sent away, and received a warm welcome amongst the Jews of Babylonia, despite his mutilation.[20]

For a time in 40 the Roman Empire's eastern boundary had been pushed westwards to the Aegean Sea. Antony sent an army from Italy to Asia Minor under P. Ventidius Bassus, probably the best general Rome produced, apart from Julius Caesar. In a series of battles and marches he drove the Parthians out of Asia, then out of Kilikia, captured Labienus (who was later executed), and in 38 defeated and killed Pakoros the king's son, who was making a new invasion. By 38 he had cleared the Parthians from Syria and was besieging Samosata, the headquarters of the Kommagenian king, yet another local king who had joined the Parthians.[21]

Herod, without family and forces, tried to recover the treasure his father had deposited at Petra, but King Malichos refused to give it up. Herod's purpose was to use the money to ransom Phasael, but he was deflected by a message from Malichos, who reported that the Parthians had forbidden the meeting between them. It seems likely that Phasael was already dead, so Malichos could refuse, but that he cast the blame on the Parthians indicates his submission to their authority – or his fear of them. Herod did not, could not, insist, but turned away for Egypt.

Kleopatra suggested that he be given command of an expedition, probably one she was preparing to assist Antony (she must have feared a Parthian attack on Egypt), but Herod would not accept. He sailed to Rhodes, acquired a ship – a warship – and sailed on to Italy. However, there is more to this than the mere journey. Herod's first destination had been Pamphylia whence he could reach Ventidius, who was preparing to drive out Labienus. Perhaps Herod thought Antony was there, or more likely he may have intended to gain points with Rome by joining Ventidius in the fighting. His arrival at Rhodes, therefore, was accidental. He was driven there by a storm, and once there he stayed for some time. It was now winter and sailors were always reluctant to go to sea at that season. But Herod did not merely take ship from there. He had one built and hired a crew for it, and further it was a trireme, at that – a warship. He clearly had plenty of money, and he used more of it to help finance the restoration of the city of Rhodes, which had suffered in the Roman wars.

In this journey, and in his partly enforced stay in Rhodes, he had clearly had time to consider what he wanted from Antony, and what he could offer. The last was obvious – loyalty to Rome, of which he had given plenty of evidence already. What he wanted in return was subject to negotiation. It seems clear from the swift passage he made in and out of Italy when he finally got there, that the negotiations had resulted in at least an outline agreement before he left Rhodes, and that the delay there was not merely to have a ship built for him, but to investigate the reaction he could expect in Italy. Someone in his party made more than one journey between Rome and Rhodes in that winter.[22]

He landed at Brundisium and reached Rome in December. He was introduced to Octavian by Anthony, then taken to the Senate, where it was proposed that he be named king of the Jews (a measure formally proposed by Messala Corvinus, again). With an endorsement from Antony, and with Octavian also present, the Senate agreed unanimously. After sacrificing to Jupiter and a banquet of celebration, he was off the next day back to Brundisium and his ship. The whole process in Rome had taken just one day. The royal title – he was already tetrarch – was required because his opponent was himself a king, and this would give Herod the necessary prestige.[23]

When he returned to Palestine, early in 39, Herod found that Ventidius had beaten the Parthians (though they returned for another attempt next year) with the result that they had evacuated Syria. Antigonos, however, was still firmly in control of Judaea, though his forces were unable to capture Masada. Herod landed at Ptolemais-Ake in 39 and set about recruiting his own forces. Later in the year Ventidius came to Palestine, presumably to clear up any Parthian problems. While there he in effect recognized Antigonos' authority, by extracting a large tribute from him (the words 'extortion' and 'bribe' are usually used). When he returned north he left 'a certain number of soldiers' in the region, under a legate called the Pupedius Silo.

Silo was no doubt puzzled as to what he was supposed to do, and his force was not large. He was a legate of Ventidius, who was in turn Antony's legate, whereas Herod had authority direct from Antony, and recently, so Silo tended to bide his time. If he fought Herod on behalf of Antigonos, as Ventidius seems to have intended, he might fall foul of Antony, yet if he joined Herod this would leave him possibly disobeying Ventidius. Added to which it is clear that he did not have a large enough force to make much difference, though his presence marked continuing Roman interest. He would no doubt recognize whoever won the fight between Herod and Antigonos, as would both Antony and Ventidius (it was still possible to disown Herod) so Silo was able to slide aside and let them fight it out.[24]

Herod was therefore on his own. If he failed, or died, Antigonos would probably be accepted by the Romans, so long as he had the sense to be subservient enough to the latest Roman warlord. He had made a good start with Ventidius, and he would be able to do so with Antony if necessary. Therefore if Herod wanted the kingdom to go with his royal title he would need to win it for himself. But he needed also to keep the various Romans on his side.

He began by recruiting a small army of mercenaries, both 'foreigners' and Jews, at Ptolemais. While doing this an envoy from Antony, Q. Dellius, arrived and persuaded Ventidius, and therefore Silo, to look favourably on Herod's enterprise, which will have boosted Herod's confidence, but neither was able to provide much immediate help so Herod was thus still essentially on his own. He began with Galilee, which he had governed for some years, and where he had supporters. He recruited his forces to the point where he felt strong enough to try to relieve the siege of his family at Masada. To do this he had to march south along the coastal plain and then east through Idumaea. Near Joppa he met Silo, who was being attacked by a force from Jerusalem, no doubt one result of Dellius' instructions to favour Herod. Herod saved the Roman force, and then took Joppa, which gave him a defensible place within Judaea. More supporters joined as he passed through Idumaea, and when he rescued his family at Masada he acquired also the 800 troops he had left there a year earlier.[25]

Antigonos harassed Herod's march where possible, but it seems that he did not have forces large or professional enough to defeat Herod's growing army. Herod and Silo now joined together and set siege to Jerusalem. Herod hoped that his presence, his support from Rome, and the memory of the behaviour of the Parthians might persuade the citizens to let him into the city. He had no wish for a long siege. The rivals harangued each other. Antigonos decried Herod's half-Idumaean ancestry (though the family had been Jews for three generations), his new royal title, and non-priestly status, which he contrasted with his own royal ancestry.

The allies did not have sufficient forces to mount a direct attack on the city, nor were supplies easy to obtain. Silo made it clear that he could not remain long in front of the city if it did not surrender. He may well not have been happy to be involved in the siege in the first place. The local area had evidently been stripped of resources to stock Jerusalem, and the Roman soldiers were not willing to stay long under such conditions – it was hardly their fight, and the city's fortifications were formidable. They withdrew into a camp nearby. Antigonos did not attack the Roman forces, but did not hesitate to attack Herod's. Herod set about gathering provisions, making a logistics base at Jericho where he gathered 'grain, wine, cattle, and other things'. To get the supplies from Jericho to Jerusalem involved a steep climb up the near cliff which is the edge of the Rift Valley, and it proved comparatively easy for Antigonos' forces to intercept the convoys. Then the arrival of winter compelled the Roman troops to take up winter quarters, and they and Herod's forces were distributed through Idumaea, Samaria, and Galilee.[26]

Herod spent the winter extending his control of Galilee, captured Sepphoris (with substantial supplies) and clearing out a group of 'brigands', in fact supporters of Antigonos, from caves on the east. It appears that Antigonos maintained some diplomatic contact with Silo, whose quarters were at Lydda. According to Josephus, Silo established them there by agreement with Antigonos, but when the Romans ran short of provisions they had to turn again to Herod.[27]

In the spring of 38 a new Parthian invasion was expected in Syria, and Ventidius recalled Silo's force to assist in the defence of North Syria. A gesture was made to Herod by suggesting that Silo should help Herod first, but Herod could see that defeating a new Parthian attack was the first priority. Silo went off to the north, where Ventidius in a masterly campaign triumphed by the middle of the year – though the campaign took some time. Meanwhile Herod crushed the last resistance in Galilee, not without difficulty.[28]

After his victory Ventidius sent two legions to help him. These Roman troops, however, were only recently recruited, probably in Syria or Asia Minor, and were commanded by Machairas, a Greek or Asian; 'legion' seems to be only an indication of their numbers, not their prowess. Machairas was contacted by Antigonos (as Silo had been), but rebuffed the approach. He went up to Jerusalem, probably hoping to conclude the war by himself, but was repelled. He took his anger out on the local population, infuriating Herod. These legions were clearly not enough, either numerically or martially, given Antigonos' powerful local support and his strong position within the well-fortified city – ironically the walls had been rebuilt by Antipater. Herod, now knowing that Antony had arrived in Syria, went off to see him. This would be a sensible diplomatic move anyway, for it is clear that the situation in the north was changing, and Roman support largely depended on personal contacts being maintained. Antony had dismissed Ventidius and had taken over command at the siege of Samosata. The country was very disturbed after the Parthian invasion, which had been widely welcomed. Herod had to fight his way through from Antioch to Samosata, and then had to be escorted into the Roman camp by a Roman detachment.

There was clearly much for Antony to do it in the north. However, the Kommagenian war soon came to an end in a compromise – King Antiochos kept his kingdom on payment of a tribute. Now Antony could now devote more resources to Palestine, the only area of his half of the empire where fighting was still going on. Herod returned south with two more Roman legions. The result of the fighting in Kommagene, in fact, was a warning to him that even fighting on behalf of the Parthians would not necessarily mean that a king would be removed. Antigonos might survive even yet. Once again it was clear that Herod had to win his kingdom for himself.[29]

Herod had left his brother Joseph in command in Palestine, but Joseph divided his forces and was defeated and killed by Antigonos' army; his army was dispersed and the virtually untrained Roman troops under Machairas were part of this humiliating defeat. Antigonos followed this victory by instigating a rebellion against Herod and his family in Galilee. Machairas, having lost a considerable part of his forces, together with his ally, camped in Idumaea at a place called Gittha, so it seems he was making an attempt to hold on to part of Herod's conquests, possibly on the advice of Herod's surviving brother Pheroras. Antigonos did not by any means recover all the lands he had lost.

Herod returned south with one legion (the other following on), and went immediately into Galilee. The arrival of the second legion was then sufficient to force the surrender of the last of Antigonos' ephemeral conquests. Herod moved to Jericho, where his army was attacked by a large Antigonid force; the Romans saw them off, though Herod himself was wounded. Fighting concentrated on Herod's attempt to open up the route to the Judaean plateau from the north, from the direction of Samaria. A bloodthirsty battle in the village of Isana finally opened up the route.[30]

A new siege of Jerusalem followed. Roman expertise in siege work was employed, and the new governor of Syria, Q. Sosius, came south to direct it, with both more legions and Syrian auxiliaries. The siege followed much the same pattern as that by Pompey nearly three decades earlier. The besiegers concentrated on attacking the north wall of the city, once they had established a camp and blocked egress with a triple line of entrenchments. The first wall was taken after 'forty days', and the second after 'fifteen days' – neither figure looks more than a guess. The final fighting was in the Upper City, where Antigonos held a castle and the temple. After much killing, Antigonos surrendered.

Herod, whose city Jerusalem now was, persuaded Sosius with some difficulty to stop the wholesale looting which had begun, pointing out that he was now king in the city, but he did not want to be king in a wilderness – though this may well have been the condition of the surrounding countryside after it had been fought over for the past three years. He also protected the temple from looting and from prying Gentile eyes, but this cost him a considerable donation to each soldier. The siege lasted as long as that of Pompey. Antigonos was carried off to Antony, who had him executed.[31]

This final result, of course, showed that, despite all his efforts, Herod had been unable to conquer his kingdom by his own and his supporters' efforts. Massive Roman support was needed – Sosius had deployed at least six legions in the siege, maybe more. If Antony and Antigonos could have negotiated sensibly the Romans could have secured their loyal king in Judaea without all that effort. But Antigonos was, as he kept saying, the descendant of a royal house, and he would not be able to adapt himself to subordination to Rome.

Chapter 6

Kleopatra

In June 47, a couple of months after Caesar left Egypt, Kleopatra gave birth to a son whom she named Caesarion.[1] By then Caesar was far off, dealing with problems in Syria, Pontos, Italy, and so on, though the name given to the child proclaimed his paternity. Only Kleopatra had any power in Egypt's government; her husband-brother Ptolemy XIV had no influence, partly because he was too young, but mainly, one suspects, due to Kleopatra's dominance. She was supported in Alexandria for the next four years by the Roman forces left by Caesar. These had constituted three legions at first, under the command of Rufinus, the son of a freedman of Caesar, but by 44/43 they had increased to four legions.[2]

The presence of the Roman troops was necessary because the main opposition to Kleopatra had come from the Alexandrians. A garrison of three or four legions, 12,000–16,000 men, was clearly sufficient to dissuade any further manifestations of opposition, for there seems to have been no further trouble in the city after Caesar left. Outside the city, in the *chora* – the rest of Egypt – conflict had been minimal. The army of Mithradates of Pergamon faced opposition only at Pelusion, garrisoned by Ptolemaic royal troops, and near Alexandria, where he was opposed by the royal army brought out from the city. In his march from one to the other there was no fighting. So the *chora* could be effectively ignored as a source of opposition and the Roman troops kept in Alexandria.

The government had to be reconstituted after the fighting. The heads of the administrative departments, Potheinos and his colleagues, had all been killed or driven out. Any who had survived the fighting owed their positions to Kleopatra's enemies and so were liable to dismissal or execution. A clean sweep allowed Kleopatra to appoint her own men, who were clearly largely reliable, though, this being a totalitarian monarchy, the system was so organized that they spied on each other; a balance was thus created.[3]

The lack of hostility in the *chora* meant that it was not necessary to carry through a wholesale purge there. So far as can be seen the local administration was largely unaffected, and there are cases of officials holding their offices all the way through from the reign of Ptolemy Auletes before his exile and into the reign of Kleopatra.

A particularly noteworthy example is Kallimachos, of a family well entrenched in the Theban region in the south. He himself was *strategos* and *epistrategos* and 'general of the Red and Indian Seas' between 74 and 39. In the 40s he was responsible for relieving a two-year famine, and was honoured with an inscription which called him *soter* – 'saviour' – a title generally applied to, and reserved for, kings.[4] He was known to and clearly trusted by Kleopatra, for she took refuge in his area in 49. Kallimachos had clearly taken the place of the king in the local minds in the Thebaid. He is perhaps a fairly extreme example, but others seem to have been similarly well entrenched in local affairs, so much so that they could generally ignore events in Alexandria.

It seems that Egypt, both the city and the country, settled down to relative peace quickly. The return of Kleopatra to power was of course what her father had intended, accompanied by her brother – though it was supposed to be a different brother. This had clearly been Caesar's intention, despite any personal regard he had for the queen. The Roman garrison cowed the city. The bureaucracy, as bureaucracies always do, was relieved to be able to function once more. By the middle of 46, only a little over a year after Caesar left, Kleopatra was confident enough of the condition of her kingdom to be able to accept Caesar's invitation to join him in Rome, though she took Ptolemy XIV with her.

This 'invitation' may or may not have been actually a directive. One source, Suetonius, says that Caesar 'summoned' the queen to Rome, but he wrote in the early second century AD, and was clearly envisaging Caesar as an emperor of the imperious type he knew, like Trajan or Hadrian.[5] It is quite likely that Kleopatra could have refused, or at least prevaricated, had she wished, or had the situation in Egypt been difficult – though in that case, Caesar would probably not have issued the invitation in the first place.

She stayed in the city for almost two years, accompanied by her royal brother, and possibly by her son, though this is not certain – if Caesar acknowledged him it was only in private, and only after his death was this revealed, by Antony, who had a particular political purpose in the statement, which therefore cannot be accepted without corroboration. P. Cornelius Dolabella did so as well and also had a particular motive apart from the truth.[6] To leave Ptolemy in Egypt would obviously risk her overthrow, if not by him, then by men acting in his name – it had happened before. The reason for her presence in Rome is not altogether clear. It has been theorized that Caesar's aim was to set up a Roman monarchy, which had to be hereditary, and Caesarion was the only child he had fathered, so she and the child were required. He was certainly in a political cul-de-sac, since he could not abdicate (as Sulla had) while surrounded by enemies, and this would undoubtedly set off a new civil war. One escape would be a Parthian war; a Roman monarchy seems rather unlikely. Perhaps he brought Kleopatra to Rome to ensure a distinct Roman control over Egypt, which would be easier in her absence. We do not know.

When Caesar was murdered she returned to Egypt. Life was now clearly much more dangerous. She soon had her brother murdered, so compromising her own position.[7] She promoted her son as pharaoh and publicized this in temples and on inscribed stelai.[8] He was three in 44, and so had survived long enough to escape the likelihood of an infant death. The next two years, 43 and 42, were times of famine in Egypt, with low or non-existent Nile floods. The royal granaries in Alexandria were opened to distribute food, but no doubt many died there and in the *chora*.[9] It was probably in this time that Kallimachos was so successful in feeding the people of the Thebaid.

The renewed Roman civil wars threatened to involve Egypt directly when C. Cassius Longinus in Syria appeared ready to march on Egypt because Kleopatra favoured his opponents. He was diverted by the threat from the west. Kleopatra had in fact started her four legions on the march north through Syria to help Dolabella, who was besieged at Laodikeia. She had contacted Dolabella (or he had contacted her) and in return for the offer of support he had provided a sort of recognition of Caesarion as Caesar's son. He had been consul in 44, the year before, with Antony, so he may well have known the truth – or he may have been prepared to say anything to get the use of the four legions. He sent an ex-praetor, A. Allienus, to take command of them, but Cassius marched south and intercepted them unexpectedly in Palestine. With only four under-strength legions against eight or nine, Allienus had the good sense to surrender at once.[10] His troops enlisted with Cassius; the Egyptian fleet stationed in Cyprus and the governor of the island, Serapion, also joined him.[11] These defections indicate the limited authority of the queen, not merely over the Roman forces supposed to protect her, but over at least one of her officials – no doubt others were uneasy or even treasonous, especially when they could detect that she was vulnerable. The main fleet, based in Alexandria, was started on a voyage westward, commanded by the queen in person, to assist Antony and Octavian, but she became ill and it ran into a storm and had to turn back (or so she claimed later).[12] By the time she and the ships had recovered the battle of Philippi had been fought and Cassius was dead.

If Kleopatra was able to dispense with a large Roman bodyguard – she had despatched the whole of the Roman army in Egypt – and to mount an overseas expedition, it follows that her kingdom was now well armed. The royal army which Ptolemy XIII had commanded in battle in 47 had been defeated, but by no means destroyed, and the survivors could either go home or re-enlist in Kleopatra's army. It had consisted of the Gabiniani, who may have been reclaimed by the Romans, but who in any case are not heard of after the battle with Caesar in Alexandria. There were also the cleruchs, Greeks descended from settlers whose lands were held on condition of military service.

Then there were the mercenaries, recruited usually among the wilder populations of Asia Minor. The cleruchs were still there and still liable to serve, though they may not have been very efficient, and were surely unwilling to serve abroad in pursuit of a quarrel between Roman warlords. But mercenaries were always available, and were willing to serve in most armies so long as they were paid.

Further, if she had a fleet, the queen had a supply of sailors, and each ship was manned by marines. The ships were quadriremes and quinqueremes, though later she had several larger vessels. According to Caesar he had caused seventy or so such ships to be burned in Alexandria harbour during his Alexandrian War, but it is clear that others had survived elsewhere, and in 43 there was one Ptolemaic fleet in Cyprus and a larger one in Alexandria. The size of these fleets at the time is not known, but several tens of ships may be presumed. These had been built in the period between 47 and 43, long enough for the purpose; no doubt there had been substantial stocks of wood in the Alexandrian dockyards. Conjuring up a substantial fleet was something which was repeatedly done by the major powers of the Mediterranean at the time. Her kingdom was well armed.

The result of the Roman civil war for Kleopatra, therefore, was her reclamation of effective independence. She had built up her own army (or so we may presume), she had built a new fleet and she had rid herself of Caesar's protective but expensive Roman army. This last was the decisive change, for under their protection she was hardly independent. Further, her new fleet was the largest in the eastern Mediterranean, and with Cyprus under her control (despite Serapion's treason) she could dominate the whole sea as far as Greece.

The elimination of the anti-Caesarians at and after Philippi was a process in which she had no obvious part (other than inadvertently supplying them with ships and soldiers). She now had to deal with a new group of Roman authorities. This, as it turned out, was Mark Antony, whom she may have met years ago when he was in Egypt with Gabinius. She had first to excuse her lack of participation in the war, which she was easily able to do, having dazzled him in the meeting at Tarsos.[13] She had deliberately delayed the meeting – and had then contrived one in which she was the centre of attention – until well after the other client kings had met Antony in Ephesos. Now clearly independent, she was claiming to be treated as an equal by the Roman warlord, and had to ensure that the new Roman rulers kept out of Egypt. This she was able to do by inviting Antony personally to Alexandria as her guest. He brought only a personal guard with him, and spent the winter there.

She had presented herself to him in the guise of Aphrodite at Tarsos, and he had responded by playing the part of Dionysos. The two revelled in each other's company, and entranced Alexandria with festivities and play-acting.

She was pregnant again when he left in the spring.[14] She was able to use him to remove her enemies: her sister Arsinoe, whom Antony ordered killed even though she was under the protection of the goddess at Ephesos; Serapion the traitorous former governor of Cyprus, whom the Tyrians, freed by Antony of their tyrant Marion, surrendered for execution; a pseudo-Ptolemy XIII at Arados was also delivered up by the Aradians. Her vengeance soon extended to persecuting the priest of Artemis who had sheltered Arsinoe, but Antony heeded pleas by the Ephesians and released him; but it was a nasty display of vindictiveness by a woman who was playing at being Aphrodite.[15]

Kleopatra was free of family competitors, but was entangled all the more with a Roman warlord. She used the same methods, charm and sex and luxury, as had worked for a time with Caesar. She bore twins in 40, children of Antony; and yet Antony clearly regarded her and Egypt as just another Roman client kingdom, and generally ignored her for the next three years. He was just as generous to Herod as to Kleopatra, though in both cases he allowed them plenty of leeway, Herod to conquer his kingdom if he could, Kleopatra to rule hers as she wished. This, after all, was the point of a client: to remove the burden of administration from Rome, and to provide support – material, human, and financial – when required. Antony would take no heed of any Egyptian pretensions to full independence; it had taken only one visit to reveal the limits of that independence. Antony had not needed to bring his army with him.

This was Egypt's role in the next ten years. It is a mistake to concentrate on the romantic relationship between Kleopatra and Antony, just as to pay much heed to the previous romantic relationship between the queen and Caesar is politically misleading, though in that case the fact that they were fighting a war at the same time thrust her pretensions to the forefront. The essential relationship between Kleopatra and both her Roman lovers was always political. Kleopatra's prime purpose was to maintain her independence and freedom of action. This was a vain hope, but for Antony it was worth indulging her fantasy. He was willing, as Caesar had been, to give her presents of bits of territory which the Ptolemies had controlled in the past, but these were never seen as permanent additions to the continuing Ptolemaic kingdom. As early as 40, he had added Kilikia to Cyprus (Caesar's gift) as a Ptolemaic province, but this was a region important only for its timber resources and as a source of mercenary soldiers.[16] The timber was useful for shipbuilding to increase Kleopatra's fleet, but this was a fleet which was at Antony's disposal if he needed it; the mercenaries increased her military resources and hence her internal security, which relieved Anthony of any duty to repeat Caesar's protective garrison of Roman troops, and provided a reserve of soldiers for his use in an emergency. Egypt was a semi-detached part of the Roman Empire, her resources being utilized for that empire's benefit.

Kleopatra therefore is best seen as a vigorous and greedy client of Antony, whose independence was much circumscribed even when she thought it increased. She was given various other items of territory in parts of the Near East, but these lands were only provided when the transfer could be justified within Antony's overall rule.

Antony left Alexandria and Kleopatra in spring 40 and spent the next three years disputing with Octavian while his legates, and eventually he himself, fought the Parthians and their supporters and their supporters in Syria. It was only in 37 that the fighting in Syria died down with the submission of Antiochos I of Commagene and the capture of Jerusalem by Herod and Q. Sosius. Then Antony set about organizing, or reorganizing, the whole region.

Kleopatra attended his court, at Antioch, during this process, for she and her kingdom were bound to be affected by any changes.[17] Antony was busy adjusting boundaries, provinces, and kingdoms throughout his territory, and Kleopatra was one of those who benefited. Herod was confirmed as king of the Jews; Lysanias the ruler of Ituraea was executed; kings in Asia Minor were rewarded or punished similarly. This was reward and retribution: Herod had fought the Parthians, while Lysanias had welcomed them. Since Antony planned an invasion of Parthia, clearing house in this way was clearly essential. But the reason these client kingdoms existed continued to be valid, so Ituraea was not annexed to the Syrian province, but was presented to Kleopatra. Their personal relationship inevitably revived (even though Antony was married to Octavian's sister), and another son was born to them next year.

The ancient sources are confused, contradictory, and summary about the lands presented to Kleopatra. Dio says she received 'extensive portions of Phoenicia and Palestine, part of Crete and Cyrene and Cyprus as well'. Plutarch lists them as 'Phoenicia, Koele Syria, Cyprus, Cyrene, and a large part of Kilikia', and adds the Jericho balsam groves and 'all that part of Arabia Nabataea which slopes towards the outer sea'. Josephus points to the Jericho balsam groves, and 'all the towns to the south of the Eleutheros River to Egypt, Tyre and Sidon excepted'.[18] It is evident that Josephus was not really interested in anything outside Palestine, and that Plutarch and Dio were exaggerating Antony's gifts to substantiate their claims that he was besotted by her and would do whatever she asked. This has been all too readily accepted by too many modern historians, who produce maps which imply that she now ruled virtually all Syria, Cyrenaica, Syria, and Kilikia.

This is clearly wrong, in detail and in total. Cyprus, for example, listed by Dio as Antony's gift, was actually Caesar's a decade earlier; Kilikia, listed by Dio Cassius and Plutarch, had been handed over by Antony much earlier, and in 37 he allocated other parts of it to other kings. Josephus and Dio say that 'parts' of Phoenicia were handed over, but Plutarch implies all of it. Lysanias' kingdom in Ituraea was certainly one area, and was probably the only part of Syria which Kleopatra came to rule directly. For the rest, two small parts will be considered later, but it will be well to attempt to account for the exaggerations first.

The alliance of Rome and Egypt, of Antony and Kleopatra, was celebrated in the usual Roman and Hellenistic way, by the publication of sets of coins. These depicted the head of Antony on the obverse and that of Kleopatra on the reverse, and were produced at several cities in Syria: Antioch, where the conference probably took place, the Phoenician cities of Arados, Tripolis, Orthosia, and Balanaea, Damascus, and the Palestinian cities of Ptolemais-Ake, Dor (probably), and Ashkelon.[19] All these were cities in the Roman province, and responsibility for their coin designs and production lay ultimately with Antony. Such coins did not mean that Kleopatra had any authority in the cities which produced them. Ashkelon, for example, as noted earlier, had issued coins honouring Kleopatra before, as well as her father and her grandfather. The only coins she may have been responsible for were those from Chalkis, the main urban centre of her new territories in Ituraea.

Here we can now therefore eliminate the idea that she was given control over Phoenicia. This area included Tripolis and Orthosia, but their coin issues are no different – except for the cities' names – than other cities' coins at this time. Had Kleopatra ruled them her coins would have been in her name, not Antony's. Those produced at Chalkis, certainly her territory, usually were in her name alone. The conclusion must be that the written sources, all of them a century and more later than the events they discuss, and all of them with no interest in accuracy in this matter, are wrong.

The precise significance of the appearance of the two portraits on the coins is not all that clear. First, it is obvious that Kleopatra was not regarded as an equal with Antony, since her portrait is always on the reverse (except in the case of Dor, where their portraits are together on the obverse, but even here Antony is depicted in front). They cannot mean that the two were joint rulers of these cities, any more than they can be taken to mean that Kleopatra had acquired more territory than Ituraea. The maximum meaning is only that Kleopatra's kingdom was supporting Antony and the Roman Empire in its forthcoming struggle with Parthia. After all it was in order to arrange matters – politically and militarily – that the conference was held and its measures implemented.

In considering the relationship between Antony and Kleopatra it is necessary to recall that the sources we have to use are almost entirely Roman and were almost entirely produced after their eventual defeat. The anti-Kleopatra propaganda put out by Octavian in the years before the final conflict has contaminated the sources irretrievably. Also the age-old romantic view of Kleopatra, and her affairs with Antony as a great love affair, fogs the mind most effectively. And then there is the modern romantic view of Kleopatra, seen as a feminist icon – a role she would have found incomprehensible – manifested in the curious construction of her as 'Cleopatra the Great'.[20] This all blocks understanding what she was about, and what Antony's intentions and ambitions were.

For we have to remember that Kleopatra was originally driven from power by her own government, then returned to power in a civil war when the Roman soldiers beat down her own people, and that she was then used as a resource for Roman military campaigns, both of foreign conquest and in civil warfare. Her independence, no matter how complete she may have wished it, was always limited, and increasingly so in her last years. There is little in all this to justify her being regarded as 'great'.

The joint coins issued in Syria are not repeated in the coinage of Egypt, for which Kleopatra was ultimately responsible. There she is depicted as queen in the regular Ptolemaic succession. In the Egyptian temple inscriptions, Antony is scarcely mentioned, though Caesarion is.[21] In other words, Kleopatra's policy in Egypt was to detach herself as much as possible from Rome – that is, she insisted on claiming that her kingdom was independent.

Antony, on the other hand, was an ambitious Roman warlord, in the tradition of Marius, Sulla, Crassus, Pompey, and Caesar – and Octavian. The destruction of the Roman political system which these men had accomplished was complete by the 30s, when, for example, the Second Triumvirate (of Antony, Octavian, and M. Aemilius Lepidus) was renewed without any reference to the Senate or people. There is no sign that any of these men was a true republican Roman, only that they hungered for more, and sole, power.

Antony's way of progressing towards this goal was to conduct a major conquest of eastern lands. In this he required the support and the resources of his client kings, including Kleopatra. The independence of Egypt did not signify in his plans, or even perhaps in his thoughts. Of this Kleopatra could not but be aware, but she had no choice but to be involved and supportive, though the divergence in political aims between them was a source of tension. Just as Caesar had quartered a Roman army on Alexandria, from whose resources that army was to be fed and paid and clothed, to the relief of the Roman treasury, so Antony allocated certain lands to Kleopatra from which her government could support his adventures. The Ituraean kingdom was given her not in order to feed her vanity – though it may well have done that as well – but to relieve the Roman forces in the east of the need to control a difficult mountainous region (which was why Pompey originally left it as a client kingdom); Kilikia was hers because its timber resources were needed to help build up the Ptolemaic fleet, and that fleet was at Antony's disposal when he required it.

Some of the transfers to Kleopatra were as much for financial reasons as the allocation of Kilikia had been for its timber. Ituraea and Kilikia were the only items on the list of transfers, or gifts, of any geographical size. (Cyprus had been Kleopatra's since Caesar's transfer in 47.) The balsam groves in the area of Jericho, within Herod's kingdom, became hers for financial reasons. It was also helpful that this transfer put Herod's nose out of joint, and demonstrated just who was in charge. Herod's accomplished sycophancy was accompanied by the arrogance of a successful warrior, but Antony knew full well that it was Roman arms which had been the real instrument of conquest in Palestine. The balsam groves were therefore taken from him and given to Kleopatra as a gesture to both; the ultimate purpose of the transfer to Kleopatra was financial, for she leased the groves back to Herod in return for an annual fee of two hundred talents.[22] No doubt Herod still made a profit for himself. A similar mixture, financial and political, no doubt lay behind the transfer of part of the Nabataean kingdom on the Red Sea coast to Kleopatra. This was an area where the Nabataeans had developed ports for the Red Sea–Indian Ocean trade, which competed with Egypt's. Kleopatra's acquisition, which may have been leased back to the Nabataeans like Herod's balsam groves, would restrict Nabataean profits, and enhance the profits of Egyptian merchants, who could be taxed directly.[23] She was given some estates in Crete (an old Ptolemaic area of activity) and Cyrene. This last gives away the secret: the status of all these places was fundamentally unchanged. The grant in Cyrenaica continued to be administered by the same Roman officials as had done so earlier.[24] The purpose of the gifts was therefore merely to transfer some financial resources into Kleopatra's hands – and that money was used to develop naval and military resources which were to be used in Antony's campaigns.

Antony's campaign into Parthia in 36 was a failure, and the retreat was a disaster. Having begun with an army possibly numbering up to 100,000 men, he lost about 35,000 killed in battle or dead of disease or exposure, and Artavasdes of Armenia deserted with his army of 13,000 men at a crucial moment.[25] These figures are all probably exaggerations, but Antony's army was certainly very badly damaged. He sent messages to Syria when his forces came close, and went on ahead to arrange relief. Kleopatra came with her ships, with clothing for the ragged soldiers and some money, but she is said not to have provided as much as Antony wanted. He supplemented what she provided from his own resources, and gave her the credit, perhaps to lay the blame on her for any shortcomings. Almost lost in this curious exchange is a little note that more money and resources used came from the 'allies', that is, the other client kingdoms, and the cities in Antony's half of the empire.[26]

Meanwhile Octavian had finally succeeded, after a long struggle, in eliminating Sextus Pompey, who had controlled Sicily and the nearby seas for some years. He had been greatly assisted by 120 ships 'lent' to him by Antony, who was supposed to get 20,000 soldiers in exchange. These had never arrived, and the ships were not returned either. Yet Pompey was actually finally caught and executed by Antony's men in trying to rouse the east. All Antony gained was a memorial in the Forum at Rome.[27] Octavian had gone on to eliminate the third triumvir, Lepidus, who had been based in North Africa, and had taken over his army. The military balance thereby had abruptly tilted during 36 towards the west, as Octavian's strength grew just as Antony's was wasted. The reduction from four to two warlords also made it all the more likely that a decisive conflict would arrive soon.

Kleopatra's strength thus became all the more important to Antony, and her failure to produce the expected money in Syria in 36 may be a sign that she now understood this change and was prepared to exploit her increased relative power. By paying out from his original resources – that is, from the treasury he had extracted from cities and clients earlier – Antony's dependence on Egypt's wealth increased.

Antony prepared for a new campaign next year, but was able to put it off, perhaps with relief. He had more success in 34, when he captured Artavasdes.[28] Then he went to Alexandria where he staged a triumph in which he once more played Dionysos to Kleopatra's Aphrodite.[29] By this time he was being portrayed by Octavian as ensnared into helplessness by Kleopatra's seductive wiles. This was all the easier since he had sent his Roman wife, Octavia, back to Italy the year before without even meeting her, and had accepted that Kleopatra's twins were his children, and fathered another boy on her.[30] He made Alexandria his headquarters for the next three years. The triumph in Alexandria was followed by a new eastern dispensation, in which Kleopatra's children were given honorary titles and theoretical kingdoms. Caesarion was to be 'King of Kings', Alexander Helios (the elder twin) was to be king of Armenia, Media, and the East, his sister Kleopatra Selene was to be the queen of Cyrene and Libya, and the latest child, Ptolemy Philadelphos, was to have Syria and Kilikia.[31]

None of this had any direct effect on the ground, and Alexander Helios' kingdom remained to be conquered. All the client kings and Roman provincial governors and autonomous cities remained in place, just as the Romans administering Cyrene first for Antony and then for Kleopatra did not move. The whole scheme has an air of unreality about it, particularly as it followed a resounding defeat for Antony's invasion of Parthia and the loss of tens of thousands of his soldiers. But for kings and governors it was scarcely encouraging to have such a world division hanging over them, possibly to be implemented at some time at the whim of the Roman warlord. It was, of course, a gift to Octavian in his anti-Antony campaign. Further, during 34

Antony and Kleopatra went through a ceremony of marriage. This was scarcely legal in Roman terms, especially since he was already married under Roman law. So here was another propaganda gift to Octavian; it is difficult to avoid concluding that Antony's absence from Rome had detached him from Italian political realities.

What it all amounted to was that Antony had ended in the same political cul-de-sac as Caesar. The only way out he could see was by establishing himself as an hereditary monarch. His present position as a Roman official was non-hereditary – and in 33 even that fell away as the triumvirate expired – but if he could hold on long enough he could perhaps revive the old Hellenistic kingdoms for his children, with himself and Kleopatra as universal monarchs, and with the overlord position being inherited by Caesarion. It was in fact not far from what Octavian himself eventually achieved.

Chapter 7

Octavian

From 40 BC onwards, King Herod and Queen Kleopatra were neighbours, and Malichos I was the contemporary Nabataean king on Herod's other flank. These three were all uncomfortable in their roles as Roman clients. Herod exploited the situation to his own benefit, but to almost everyone else's cost; Kleopatra made a bid through Antony for the whole Roman Empire, or at least the eastern part of it, and failed disastrously; Malichos kept as clear of involvement as possible, with only limited success. Relations with Antony the Roman warlord were most important for all these rulers, but they also had relations with each other of the sort which we might expect from touchy, ambitious, and suspicious monarchs.

Kleopatra and Malichos ruled their kingdoms with little trouble. Kleopatra had no opposition to speak of at home, though she knew that certain important Alexandrians detested her, not surprisingly after the way she had come to power.[1] No trouble is known for Malichos, but that is because virtually nothing is known of Nabataean internal affairs. Herod, on the other hand, because of his origin, his nature, and the history of his kingdom, faced constant trouble at home. Josephus' detailed account of these years concentrates on murderous goings-on within the royal family, but Herod also feared and faced uprisings by other internal enemies. The unstable situation in Judaea is emphasized by the continued presence in and about Jerusalem of a legion of Roman soldiers[2] – something no longer necessary in Egypt. This was either left there by Sosius or sent in by Antony. The commander did not involve himself in the royal family's disputes, presumably on Antony's instructions; the legion was there to safeguard Roman interests, which included Herod's kingship, but not necessarily his family.

Herod's problem was one of legitimacy. He had won his kingdom in part by his own military efforts, but these were only successful because he had had the full support of Rome, including a large army which conquered Jerusalem for him – and which now remained on guard to protect his position. But there were still several members of the Hasmonaean royal family alive and present, and these were regarded by many, and regarded themselves, as the legitimate rulers of Judaea. Herod had married into the family, to Mariamme, the daughter of that Alexander who had repeatedly attempted to secure the throne in defiance of constant Roman victories. She was also the niece of Antigonos, Herod's enemy in his war of conquest. Mariamme had a younger brother, Aristoboulos III, who might soon be old enough to challenge Herod, while her uncle Hyrkanos II, the mutilated high priest, returned from Babylonia, released by the Parthians to make trouble for Herod and Antony. These were all part of Herod's court, and constantly sniped at him and argued for the promotion of Hasmonaeans.

Even before Hyrkanos returned, Herod's kingdom was damaged by its overlord. The conference at Antioch in 37 produced no concrete results for Judaea, certainly nothing to compare with the gains Kleopatra made. She gained control of parts of Phoenicia, the Ituraean kingdom on Herod's northern boundary, was presented with the Jericho balsam groves, which Herod had to lease back.[3] No doubt all these last were designed to bolster Kleopatra's revenues, for Antony's ultimate benefit, but the balsam groves grant was a clear warning that Herod's position depended on Antony's goodwill, and that Herod's kingdom was really Antony's to dispose of.

In the same way Antony allocated the Nabataean Red Sea coast to Kleopatra.[4] This allowed Egyptian officials to tax the goods passing through the Nabataean ports. It was also a defensive measure, for Nabataeans had used these ports in the past to launch raids from them on Egyptian ships and territory. It seems also that Malichos was billed with an annual tribute of 200 talents, to be delivered to Herod, who was made to guarantee that payment.[5]

This little tangle was clearly devised by Antony as a means of setting these three rulers against each other. A combination of the three, especially if he was away fighting in Parthia or Armenia or Greece, could well sabotage his military efforts. Between them these three powers could field a considerable force, both at sea and by land and all three could call on a substantial anti-Roman sentiment among their own people – more so among the Jews than the others, but in no kingdom was the emotion absent. If they rose against him, northern Syria would be an easy target – Kleopatra's territories stretched as far north as Tripolis. By sowing enmity amongst them Antony obviously hoped to prevent such an outcome. The continued presence of a Roman legion in Judaea was a further element of insurance. It was there not just to protect Herod, but to dissuade him from any hostile actions. It is evident that Antony did not trust any of these three monarchs, any more than he trusted his partner in power, Octavian.

Herod reacted to the problems he faced within the royal family by progressively killing off those he deemed a threat. The position of high priest was crucial, since for the past century every high priest had been a Hasmonaean, and the post had been hereditary. Herod himself was not eligible, not being of a priestly family. Perhaps on the advice of the returned Hyrkanos II he appointed Hananel, a Babylonian of a priestly line, but he only lasted a year.[6] Pressure from his Hasmonaean wife and relatives persuaded him to replace

Hananel with his brother-in-law Aristoboulos, only seventeen at the time, but then the boy looked as though he was becoming popular, and he was drowned in a swimming pool, supposedly on Herod's instructions.[7] Hananel was reappointed. The net result was to break the hereditary succession of high priests, and the office became appointive.

Alexandra, Hyrkanos' daughter and Aristoboulos' mother, complained about Herod through Kleopatra's contacts with Antony. He summoned Herod to a meeting at Laodikeia in Syria to investigate his conduct. Antony was probably not in the least interested in the internal economy of the Herodian family, but he was concerned that the kingdom should be stable under Herod's rule, and at the same time, such a summons clearly showed Herod who was boss. Herod clearly convinced him, if he needed convincing, of his loyalty, but next year (34 BC) he was stripped of more territory, some of which was given to Kleopatra.[8] Josephus has a fantastic story whereby Kleopatra visited Herod, tried to seduce him, then tried to have him assassinated, while Herod at the same time, tried to have her assassinated. It is probably all invented, but her gains at his expense were real. One of the prizes she gained at the time was apparently the city of Gaza, Nabataea's main exporting outlet. Possibly she also acquired Joppa, and the coastal cities of Palestine on the same terms as those in northern Phoenicia, that is, the cities retained their autonomy, but paid their tribute to Kleopatra.

Herod solved the problem of the high priest by first reappointing Hananel, then after 30 BC he appointed a succession of men, each of whom served for a few years. This created a new Jewish aristocracy, but none of the men achieved sufficient prestige to be able to challenge his own position. It was not customary to dismiss high priests, but there were precedents.[9] Herod also eventually solved the problem of his disloyal relatives by progressively killing them off, a habit he later extended to his own descendents. After the death of Aristoboulos III the only male Hasmonaean left was Hyrkanos II, whose mutilation barred him from the high priesthood, but whose royal descent was clearly a threat. After the meeting at Laodikeia, however, Herod was clearly safe; Antony had endorsed his kingship, and was unlikely to renege on that for some time at least. Herod's difficulties were clearly well known, and he was therefore all the more dependent on Antony's support, a situation which suited Antony perfectly well.

By 33 Antony was heading for a new confrontation with Octavian. Their triumviral agreement expired late in 33, and Antony and Kleopatra spent the winter of 33/32 at Ephesos making preparations, then moved on to Greece. The likelihood of a war between the two Romans was clear to every observer in the Mediterranean area. Quite possibly it had been clear earlier, for Octavian had been intriguing and manoeuvring for eastern support well before the expiry of the agreement.

So it was time for the client kings and the cities to make their choices yet again. Kleopatra had little choice since, apart from her personal attachment to Antony, she had been demonized by Octavian's propaganda, and neither she nor Octavian could abandon their chosen positions, even if they felt inclined to.[10] For Octavian, the queen was far too convenient an enemy to be discarded. At the same time her wealth and power also pushed Antony into enmity to Octavian, and, even had he wished, he now found it impossible to reach agreement with him.

Antony's previous dealings with the three clients, however, now came back to hamper him in developing his full strength. Herod and Malichos developed considerable fear of, and antipathy towards, Kleopatra, perhaps all the stronger in that they could not display such policies towards Antony himself, who they clearly knew was the real author of their difficulties – even if the historians blame Kleopatra's influence. As a result it proved impossible for Antony to induce all three to work together in his support.

Relations between Herod and Malichos deteriorated when Malichos ceased delivering the tribute which Herod was guaranteeing. Since this was money which should go on to Antony, Malichos' failure to deliver affected him as well. He and Kleopatra both urged Herod on to attack Nabataea in pursuit of what was owing. At the same time Antony accepted Malichos' offer of troops for the coming campaign. Herod had also proposed and prepared a contingent, but Antony refused it.[11] The Roman legion had presumably by now been removed from Judaea, so one reason for refusing is that Herod needed all his forces at home. And indeed, at this very time Herod had to put down a rising centred on a Hasmonaean princess he had imprisoned in the castle at Hyrkania.[12] Herod was encouraged or directed to use his forces against Malichos.

So, during 32, two of Antony's client kings went to war with each other, while Antony himself moved his forces westwards into Greece to challenge Octavian's control of Italy in the west. Kleopatra, having reinforced Antony's fleet with her own, and provided extra rowers for his ships, sent some of her army to assist Malichos in defending himself against Herod's attack.

This needs explaining. Herod proved willing enough to attack Malichos, though it is unlikely he realized he would be up against Ptolemaic forces as well. Antony's refusal of the soldiers he offered was perhaps not unexpected if the legion had been withdrawn. Herod would need a powerful force of his own in Judaea to keep control of his own kingdom. It was also clear to all that so long as the tense situation between the three rulers continued, so would Herod's internal problems, since it was only by external pressure that he could be removed; internal and external tensions thus reinforced each other.

Malichos had been compelled to submit to Antony, though there is no evidence that this pleased him. He was the only one of the three rulers who had acquired his throne without Roman help or interference, and this gave him a more stable internal position. His resentment at the treatment meted out to him by Antony was therefore likely to be particularly acute. The delivery of tribute to Herod was both debilitating and humiliating, so it is scarcely surprising that he ceased to do so when it became clear that Antony would be preoccupied with western affairs. (If the grant of Nabataean territory to Kleopatra, and the organization of the payment, had been arranged in 34, it may be that Malichos had only made one payment.)

Kleopatra had encouraged Antony to push Herod into the war with Malichos, and she sent a general and soldiers to help Malichos. The easiest explanation is that she wanted to cut both kings down to size, in the hope that a prolonged war would weaken both. Assuming Herod was beaten, which her support for Malichos suggested she expected, this would help Malichos to make Nabataea her client rather than Antony's. Herod's defeat might also lead to the break-up of his kingdom, and Kleopatra might be able to grab some of the cities. Behind it all, of course, was the assumption that Antony would beat Octavian in the coming war. She could then go to rule in Italy, leaving her independent and enlarged kingdom unsupervised by Romans and surrounded by territories he handed over to her and client kings she thought she could control.

None of this worked out as intended by anyone. Herod mustered his army. He began with raids, perhaps intending to discover the location of Malichos' forces, or to distract him. Presumably in the knowledge that Malichos had dispatched part of his army to join Antony, Herod then marched across the Jordan into the northern part of Nabataea. The two armies met near the city of Dion – so both had invaded Decapolis territory.[13] The early raids had actually alerted Malichos to what was happening, and his army was prepared. He had moved forward, for the two battles which followed were both fought in the lands of the Greek cities of the Decapolis. The battle near Dion was a victory for Herod, but this was against only part of Malichos' forces. Herod then advanced against a muster of Nabataean troops at Kanata.[14] We get a glimpse of Herod's army here. Part was clearly barely trained and undisciplined, and Herod could not control it. The men charged without formation or preparation at the enemy they could see. Herod's intention had been to establish a camp, and he was able to control the more professional section of his army. The undisciplined charge was blocked by a disciplined Ptolemaic force commanded by a general called Athenion. This encouraged the Nabataeans, probably also barely disciplined, to attack. The attacking Judaean force was routed. Herod arrived with the troops he had kept under control, but he could not retrieve the situation.[15]

Herod, no doubt after rebuilding his main force, continued the war by more raids into Nabataea, but the war was interrupted by a great earthquake in spring 31, and this was followed by Nabataean counter-raids.[16] Herod made peace overtures, but his envoys were killed. He mounted a new attack, probably in autumn 31, since soon after the fighting the news arrived of the battle of Actium. The new offensive was once again through the territory of the Decapolis, this time further south in the region of Philadelphia. A 'stubborn battle' resulted in defeat for the Nabataeans. Malichos now also sent peace envoys but, having had his own envoys killed earlier, Herod was determined on revenge and pursued the full humiliation of his enemy. A second battle was a second Jewish victory. The Nabataeans gave in and submitted. The peace terms are only implied by Josephus, not stated, though Herod's victory was clear. The terms were, of course, irrelevant once the result of Actium was known.[17]

The campaign against Octavian in 32–30 was the great test of the governing system which Antony had put in place in the east. He could call up troops from the Roman provinces in Greece, Asia Minor, and Syria, which boosted his regular forces to 75,000 infantry, but he also needed the forces which were maintained by the client kings. This produced a further 25,000 infantry and an unknown number of cavalry, so that the clients contributed perhaps a third of his manpower. The cultivation of Kleopatra now paid its full dividend. She provided a fleet of up to 200 ships and a war chest said to amount to 20,000 talents.[18] This first figure is credible, and amounted to almost half of the fleet; the second figure is probably exaggerated, but even half of it was enough to fund the campaign. The care with which the wealth of Egypt, and of the territories she taxed, had been accumulated over the previous ten years is evident.

On the other hand, Antony's evident dependence on Egypt for ships and resources, and on Kleopatra personally, was a distinct source of weakness, since she was unpopular with many of his Roman supporters, a fact which Octavian had been exploiting for some time. Her presence at Antony's strategic conference at Ephesos early in 32 was disruptive. He was joined there by the consuls in office and by several hundred senators, who claimed to be the official Senate, but these men were not pleased to see that there was a considerable basis in fact for Octavian's anti-Kleopatra charges. Antony tried ordering her to go home, but she did not move, and the contribution she made to the forces rendered her continued presence necessary – if she left, she would take her money and half the fleet with her. Octavian capitalized on this and on his earlier propaganda, by having his own rump Senate declare that she was an enemy of the state.[19] When fighting came he could claim to be fighting Egypt, not Antony's Romans.

These tensions among the most prominent men aggravated the increasingly awkward situation Antony's army was in at Actium. Desertions had begun even earlier, notably after Antony sent Octavia a letter of divorce, probably at Kleopatra's insistence.[20] This was something which particularly affected and annoyed prominent Romans, some of whom left to join Octavian. Notable among those who left were L. Munatius Plancus and M. Titius, who are said to have told Octavian that Antony's will was lodged with the Vestal Virgins in Rome. Octavian seized the document, illegally, and published a version of it, in which Antony was said to have left all to Kleopatra. It is highly unlikely that Antony would either leave his will in Rome (he knew Octavian's ruthlessness) or that he left his property to a non-Roman, which was against Roman law. The whole thing was transparently an Octavianic invention, but it was effective propaganda.[21]

More serious, when it became clear, by the middle of 31, that the army was trapped in Actium, the client kings began to leave, some taking their forces with them, others denying supplies to the army. The ruler of Sparta, Eutykles, was impressed by the naval successes in the Peloponnese of M. Vipsanius Agrippa, Octavian's commander, and switched sides – his father had been killed by Antony, so he had a personal motive as well.[22] King Deiotaros of Paphlagonia, whose very kingdom had been created by Antony, deserted when M. Titius, who had been Antony's general against Sextus Pompey in Asia Minor but had changed sides, defeated Antony's cavalry.[23] Detachments of Octavian's forces penetrated into Macedon and eastern Greece, and this may have persuaded King Rhoemetalkes of Thrace to desert.[24]

There were also casualties among the kings in the fighting. The exiled Mauritanian King, Bogud, died when Agrippa captured Methone in the Peloponnese.[25] Iamblichos of Emesa was detected attempting to desert, and was executed, in part as a lesson to others not to do the same.[26] The kingship went to his brother Alexander who, surprisingly in the circumstances, remained loyal. The king of parts of Kilikia, Tarkondimotos, died when an attempted naval breakout was blocked.[27] Amyntas of Galatia, another who owed his kingdom and kingship to Antony, deserted with his 2,000 cavalrymen not long after.[28] In effect, by the time the decisive sea battle took place in September, virtually all of Antony's client kings who were present had left or had been killed. Those contingents not commanded by their kings were left high and dry, and no doubt were watched carefully.

The one exception to this catalogue of desertion and death was Kleopatra. She could not leave, though if she had done so there may have been no battle. But Octavian's war had been declared on her personally, and one of the objects of his aggression was clearly to gain control of Egypt and its wealth. It is precisely Kleopatra's huge contribution to Antony's war effort which showed just how dangerous she and her kingdom were. In the event the sea battle concluded with her fleet, carrying her treasure, escaping from the fighting.

This is the basis for the later interpretation that she deserted Antony – though the manoeuvre had probably been intended from the first.

So the three client rulers in the south-eastern corner of the Mediterranean all survived without changing sides, in contrast to many of the kings of parts of Asia Minor and the Balkans. Kleopatra returned to Egypt, Malichos survived his conflict with Herod, and Herod had been spared the embarrassment of fighting on Antony's side by the manufactured war with Nabataea. Kleopatra could expect no mercy from the victor, though she had a powerful state in which she could have made a last stand. The others might be able to survive if they made the right moves, but this took care and thought. The kings who deserted Antony before the battle all survived. The most unfortunate were the kings of Emesa: Iamblichos had been executed by Antony for trying to desert; his brother and successor Alexander was executed by Octavian for not deserting.[29] It was clear that extreme care was needed.

The defeat of Antony's fleet left Octavian master of the seas; similarly the negotiated surrender of Antony's army in Greece left the way open for Octavian to campaign towards Egypt. The enormous increase in his armed forces also made it absolutely vital for Octavian to acquire Kleopatra's treasure and her tax-rich kingdom, since he would need to pay off the soldiers soon; here also was a way to his stony heart, by offering him money. Herod was fully alert to this aspect of affairs. Antony's forces outside Greece also fell away into Octavian's hands. The four legions in Cyrenaica were taken to Octavian's side by the governor and commander L. Pinarius Scarpus, a decision which even Antony's persuasiveness in person could not reverse.[30] But Octavian had to attend to many things before he could reach Egypt, so Kleopatra reigned on for almost another year after Actium.

During that time Octavian steadily picked off any surviving allies Antony still had. Pinarius in Cyrenaica was the first, various kings in Asia Minor went next, and the governor of Syria, Q. Didius, deftly shifted sides as well. He was menaced by a gang of escaped gladiators who were marching towards Egypt to offer their services to Antony. Didius probably had few troops and the gladiators were a formidable and brutal enemy. They had already fought their way through Amyntas' kingdom in Galatia and against the sons of Tarkondimotos, thereby proving especially useful to others besides Didius in demonstrating their loyalty to Octavian. Didius was helped by the resourceful Herod, fresh from fighting Malichos. Herod speedily detected a ploy by which he could align himself with Octavian – no doubt the same calculation had occurred to Didius. Between them Didius and Herod caged and dispersed the gladiators, who were gradually picked off and killed later.[31]

Herod now went to meet Octavian at Rhodes. He had two military achievements to his credit, the defeat of Malichos, some of whose forces had been with Antony in Greece, and who had been allied with Kleopatra, and the gladiators. There was also the memory of being sponsored as king by Octavian as well as Antony in Rome ten years before. A certain manipulation of the facts would allow him to assert loyalty to Octavian just as he had been loyal to Antony.[32] But he also took the precaution of ordering the killing of Hyrkanos II before he left Judaea, so that there remained no credible Hasmonaean alternative to himself as king.[33] Hyrkanos had planned to escape to Malichos, where he would certainly have been able to make trouble for Herod; this is a clear sign that the dispute between Judaea and Nabataea was unfinished. But by executing the old man, and by reaching Octavian first, Herod would block any moves by Malichos. Octavian, whatever his original intentions, had the sense to grin and bear it. Herod was confirmed as king.

There were also good military reasons for Herod's confirmation. Egypt was still a formidable military target, even for a victorious Roman army. The country's defences were strong, and it could defy large armies by holding just a few fortresses. It had a considerable army, and with Antony as commander it had a formidable general, and Kleopatra still had a major fleet. Octavian had no wish to have a turbulent or hostile Judaea in his rear while attempting to break into Egypt. Herod had already shown that he had the skills and ruthlessness needed to hold Judaea down. He probably had no need to fear a Roman deposition in favour of a Hasmonaean restoration, since the Hasmonaeans, as every Roman who had ever come into contact with Judaea could attest, were wedded to the concept of Judaea as a wholly independent state. Since this was also Kleopatra's basic aim for her country, there was always the possibility of a Ptolemaic-Hasmonaean alliance if Herod was removed. Octavian surely knew all this. Herod was quite safe, but Octavian will have enjoyed the sight of Herod grovelling before him.

What had become of Athenion and the Ptolemaic detachment in Nabataea which had beaten Herod at Kanata is not known; no doubt once Malichos had submitted – through Didius – and made peace with Herod, the troops had returned to Egypt, or maybe he was withdrawn when Kleopatra returned from Actium, intent on defending her kingdom. She and Antony made some preparations to resist the enemy assault. As soon as she arrived in Alexandria, Kleopatra carried through a purge of prominent Alexandrians who appear to have all too quickly voiced their discontent at her rule.[34] (It would therefore seem that the political quietness in Egypt in the previous decade had been due to her ferocity rather than to contentment at her rule.) She also gathered up as much treasure and she could find, even stripping some temples, no doubt on the pretext of financing the defence of the kingdom. Recruiting also went on, both in the country and among the kings she and Antony could reach. She prepared a bolt-hole on the Red Sea, having ships moved there and others

1. Caesar. Roman portraiture had settled into a pattern of emphasising the careworn features of busy men. Caesar was in his fifties when this was made.

2. The Colossi of Memnon. One of the two great statues of seated pharaohs which Strabo records visiting with Aelius Gallus in 25 BC.

3. Ptolemy Auletes is crowned by the goddesses of Lower Egypt (on the left) and Upper Egypt (right).

4. Kleopatra VII and Ptolemy XIV. The joint reign of brother and sister is commemorated at Dendera.

5. Qasr Ibrim. The southernmost point of Roman control at the time of Cornelius Gallus, but abandoned by Augustus in the treaty of 20 BC. The original construction dates from about 1000 BC, and it remained occupied by a garrison until AD 1810.

6. The Temple of Isis, Philae. The main religious site on the island, built in the Ptolemaic period and in use through to the Byzantine, when it was a centre of the local tribes from the south. Clearly an official Roman site, it also contained a temple to the Kushite god Mandulis.

7. King and Queen of Kush. The pylon of the Lion temple at Naqa not far from Meroe city, showing the basic Egyptian style of architecture and bas-relief carving. But the two main figures are King Natakamani and the Kandake Queen Aminatore.

8. The battle of Alexandria. During the battle, Caesar launched an attack using a variety of ships, light vessels, transports and warships to seize the strategic Pharos Island where the famous lighthouse stood. The attack ended in failure and many of Caesar's soldiers crowded aboard the ships to escape. Some ships therefore capsized including the one Caesar was on, forcing him to jump overboard and swim to safety. The Roman historian, Appian, records that Caesar left behind his purple cloak which was later captured by the Alexandrians as a battle trophy, an embarrassing fact that Caesar neglected to mention in his own account!

9. The battle of Actium. At the height of the battle, a Roman-Egyptian centurion informs Marc Antony that Cleopatra and her squadron of ships are leaving the action. The centurion wears a padded garment based on an interpretation of equipment shown on the near contemporary Arch of Orange in France. Antony himself carries a shield bearing images of the gods Helios and Selene, after whom he and Cleopatra had named their children. The shield is based on a sculpture of a shield in Tarragona Archaeological Museum. The Roman-Egyptian troops in the foreground wear a variety of late Hellenistic and Roman equipment and have inscribed their own shields with Cleopatra's name in Greek.

10. The battle of Beth Horon. Roman cavalry attempt to break out of the ambush in Beth Horon pass. The army of Cestius Gallus was ambushed on its withdrawal after its failed siege of Jerusalem. The cavalrymen wear standard cavalry equipment of the period, the leading trooper has a helmet which incorporates a cheek-piece found in Jerusalem. Although most of the Jews were lightly equipped, like the man armed only with a wooden club, the foreground warrior has managed to acquire some captured or looted equipment. Although Gallus and the bulk of his forces escaped, they had left behind all their baggage and siege train, including valuable artillery pieces and ammunition and the equivalent of a legion and an auxiliary cavalry *ala* in dead comrades.

11. The siege of Gamla. Although Gamla (Gamala) was in a difficult position on top of a hill, the Romans under Vespasian managed to breach the city walls. However, the Romans faced more difficulties once inside the city. At first in the narrow alleys they were pelted with missiles from the roof tops by the defenders. When they attempted to scale the rooves, according to Josephus, they collapsed under their weight, burying many Romans under the debris. The body of one such unfortunate legionary was found during the excavations at Gamla. The legionary equipment is based on these finds and those from Masada. The Jewish clothing is based on the slightly later finds from the Nahal Hever caves.

12. The tell at Samosata, the centre of the Commagenian kingdom, with the remains of one of the grandiose temples built by the later Commagenian kings. This place was one of the main sources of Commagenian strength since it was extremely difficult to capture.

13. Caesarea. King Herod developed the old town of Strato's Tower on the coast into a major city, which he named for Augustus. It eventually became the capital of the Roman province of Palaestina and a Roman colonia.

14. Herodion. Herod built a number of fortress palaces-cum-prisons out in the Judaean desert. Masada was one, and Machaerus, and the Herodion south east of Jerusalem was another.

15. The city of Sepphoris (now Zipori) has been extensively excavated. It was well built, and was clearly a wealthy town with an elaborate artificial water supply. It was also a town which determinedly kept out of all conflicts in Judaea, surrendering to whoever turned up, and thereby survived.

16. Masada. The plateau-top fortress in the Judaean desert was also a royal palace. The steep sides of the rock suggested invulnerability, and the actual fortifications are no more than a wall around the edge. This sufficed to protect Herod's family while Herod went to Rome.

17. The Captured Menorah. The conquest of the Jerusalem temple was completed when Titus seized – 'rescued' – the holy objects.

18. A coin of Vespasian celebrating his victory in Judaea. The reverse shows a triumphant Roman leaning on a palm tree, with a despondent (female) Judaea.

gathered. The idea was perhaps to continue the fight there, or to transfer some forces to the south and then across the desert to the Thebaid, or even to evacuate to Yemen or to India. But Didius pointed this out to Malichos, who first reclaimed his lost lands on the Red Sea coast, then launched an attack to destroy the Egyptian ships.[35] This must have been as satisfactory for him as Herod's submission was to Octavian.

This was scarcely a vital blow, however, and if Kleopatra wished to retreat to or along the Red Sea, no doubt other ships could be found. For the rest it was clear that she intended to fight for her kingdom. So, having made that clear, it was then time for negotiations. Predictably they came to nothing. Octavian did not need to offer any terms; and the only thing which would satisfy her would be the continued independence of Egypt, either under her or her son Caesarion. But it was exactly the continued Egyptian independence which had become impossible for Rome and Octavian to accept. First, Octavian needed to gain possession of the Ptolemaic treasure to help finance the demobilization of his grossly swollen army and fleet; second, Egypt had been the source of continuous trouble for Rome for the last forty years, and it was therefore time, in Roman eyes, that it be incorporated decisively into the empire. Its resources could then be used for Rome as a whole, rather than for a warlord. (Or rather, this last warlord could use Egypt's resources to maintain his rule, thereby, of course, benefiting the whole empire.)

This final campaign, against Egypt, was relatively easy, as it turned out, if only because the forces of Kleopatra and Antony lost heart. Three attacks were made, not necessarily intended to coincide – such coordination was beyond the ancient world. From the west C. Cornelius Gallus, in command of Pinarius' old army, advanced as far as Paraetonium, which he captured. Antony transported an infantry force in ships to confront the invaders, and since it was his old army he tried once again to persuade the soldiers to revert to their old allegiance, but Gallus got his trumpeters to drown his voice. An attack on the fort from the sea then failed with the loss of most of the ships.[36]

Octavian approached from the direction of Syria. He took the opportunity to sort out Syrian problems on the way, so his progress was probably slow. He was received and feasted by Herod when he got to Ptolemais. Herod handed over 800 talents to help fund the Egyptian campaign, money no doubt very welcome, since Octavian had already had to make donations and promises to his troops.[37] Presumably he had also acquired similar 'gifts' from others on his way south through Asia Minor and Syria.

From the Eleutheros River southwards Octavian had travelled through lands which had been under Kleopatra's rule for the past several years. The cities had retained their autonomy, but the tribute they paid had gone to Kleopatra – hence some of the '20,000' talents she had contributed to Antony's war chest.

Apparently no definitive changes were made during his journey, for Herod had to meet Octavian in Egypt later to finalize the changes along his borders in Palestine. However, it must have been clear that the Ptolemaic empire was being dismantled. In Ituraea, Zenodoros, the son of the dead Lysanias, had been managing the region on behalf of Kleopatra, and he continued in office, though no longer responsible to her.[38]

Octavian advanced south through Kleopatra's territories, therefore, being enigmatic about the future of both cities and kingdoms. His army advanced through Gaza and on to the Egyptian frontier fortress of Pelusion, which should have posed the same formidable difficulty it had for earlier invaders, but the fortress fell at once, producing rumours of treachery by its commander, Seleukos. These were surely correct, for the place should have been able to hold out for some time. (Antony had Seleukos' wife and children killed in revenge – these Roman warlords were deeply unpleasant people.[39]) Once Octavian's army was past Pelusion and inside Egypt the war was effectively over. Antony, like Ptolemy XIII facing Caesar, came out of Alexandria and drove back the Roman cavalry, but then was defeated in attacking the infantry; the Ptolemaic navy went out to dispute the arrival of Octavian's fleet (this was the third prong of the invasion), but the Egyptian sailors knew a certainty when they saw one, and surrendered without a fight. Antony's cavalry now deserted.[40]

This was effectively the end. Antony committed suicide, slowly, and Kleopatra, failing again to interest Octavian in any sort of terms, was also induced to kill herself, and without destroying the treasure.[41] The heirs of these two, Caesarion and Antony's son Antyllus, were killed, the former having made a break for the south, quite possibly aiming to continue the fight from there.[42] Afterwards Kleopatra was remembered and honoured in Alexandria and Egypt, rather late in the day.

Herod had to go to Egypt to learn what Octavian intended for Syria. No doubt others attended on the victor as well. Egypt was to be annexed, with Octavian as the next pharaoh. It followed that this obviously included Kleopatra's old Syrian lands, and the kingdom had to be regulated. Alexander of Emesa was reserved for Octavian's triumph and execution, but it seems that no decision was yet made about his kingdom – in effect for the next decade it was part of the Syrian province.[43] Malichos I died in the next year or so; rumour had it that Kleopatra was responsible, though it was probably old age, and she died first. Malichos had put himself right with Rome by burning Kleopatra's getaway ships in the Red Sea. Whatever political arrangements existed earlier were no doubt continued, and renewed with Malichos' successor, another Obodas.[44]

Herod's obsequiousness and ruthlessness earned his reward. Several cities which had been Kleopatra's were now given to him. Some of those in Judaea who did not like him would thereby undoubtedly be reconciled to his rule. The territories he acquired included Joppa, returned to his rule once again, and Gaza. Some serious military power needed to hold the gateway to Egypt in case of a rebellion or a Ptolemaic revival. North of Joppa the territories of Apollonia, Dor, and Strato's Tower became Herod's. Together with Ashdod and Iamneia, this gave Herod the whole Palestinian coast from Carmel to Gaza (except for the small territory of Ashkelon). This was in effect a reconstruction of the old kingdom of Alexander Iannai, which had been dismantled by Pompey, with the exception of the Decapolis. Samaria, if it was not Herod's before, became his now, so that the two main parts of his kingdom in Judaea and Galilee were now once again linked. Across the Jordan he was given two of the Decapolis cities, Hippos and Gadara, though the rest of the Decapolis remained separate.[45]

Regions outside Egypt which were Kleopatra's showed little trace of her brief rule, and scarcely any indication of Octavian's decisions. The former Ituraean principality was managed by Zenodoros for a time for Octavian, as he had for Kleopatra. The Phoenician coastal cities reverted to the province. Only one city was relieved enough at the change to begin a new era, the era of Actium; this was Botrys, scarcely the most important place in the region.[46]

Octavian had been careful to conduct the conquest of Egypt personally. He now made himself, by right of that conquest, Egypt's ruler, the new pharaoh, and dated his rule from the day he entered Alexandria, not the day of Kleopatra's death (which was ten or so days later).[47] By his reckoning therefore Kleopatra had not died a queen, but as a former ruler, and Caesarion had no claim. He took the Ptolemaic treasure and used it to pay off his surplus soldiers. So, right to the end, the Ptolemaic kingdom financed Rome's civil war.

Chapter 8

Holding Egypt: a New Roman Frontier

The Egypt which Octavian – soon to be 'Augustus' – seized from Kleopatra in 30 BC had been rigorously administered by Kleopatra's ancestors for three centuries, in succession to the similarly rigorous pharaonic administration, all with the object of gaining wealth and power for the rulers; and from 30 BC onwards it was to be rigorously administered for the benefit of Roman emperors and the citizens of the city of Rome. These were the Roman priorities, signalled from the beginning by Octavian's appropriation of Kleopatra's treasure, confiscations from those judged to have committed crimes, seizure of the public treasure in Alexandria, and a tax demand which provoked almost instant rebellions. The result was that Octavian was able to pay his soldiers a donative of 1,000 sesterces (with appropriate scaling up for officers), pay off many debts, and give presents to senators, knights, and temples.[1]

Technically Egypt was a province. 'I added Egypt to the empire of the Roman people' Augustus stated in his record of his deeds, the *Res Gestae*, which was carved on temple walls in many provinces.[2] But he, of all people, knew that Egypt could not be treated as a normal province. It had been so rich that even barely competent Ptolemaic kings had been able to play havoc with Roman politics by throwing money into the city; even a woman ruler, a clear anomaly to ancient politicians, had mounted a major challenge to the whole Roman Empire. So Egypt could not be treated as if it was Spain or Gaul or Syria. If it had been possible to sub-divide the country, it might have made several provinces, but its geography made this very difficult.

As a temporary measure, since it was expected that trouble would follow the Roman annexation, a large garrison under a competent general was left in the country: three legions, three cavalry *alae*, and nine infantry auxiliary cohorts, about 25,000 men.[3] It was not perhaps a really large garrison for such a populous country, with maybe four million people, but the great majority of these millions showed no interest in who ruled or governed them, other than the continued performance of religious rites and the payment of a large part of their produce in taxes – or perhaps their interest was more in trying to avoid as much payment as possible. But these three legions and the associated auxiliary regiments sufficed to put down risings by the more politically conscious elements in the population and at the same time to defend the country.

There were two risings, both quickly suppressed, and a more serious frontier problem. The risings were provoked by the heavy tax demand. Those who might have risen in support of a Ptolemaic return were thwarted by the absence of any Ptolemaic candidates. Kleopatra's surviving children were shipped off to Rome, where they were taken into the household of Octavia, Antony's divorced wife, though only the girl, Kleopatra Selene, is ever heard of again.[4] Otherwise there were no Ptolemaic claimants left. It may be pointed out that three times in the previous fifty years the Ptolemaic succession had gone to a son or daughter born to a marriage which in Greek terms was unrecognized. This had certainly worn thin the loyalty of the Greek population of Egypt to the Ptolemaic house. The Roman garrison was a guarantee that any peasant risings would be dealt with swiftly, and probably harshly, and this was clearly an acceptable replacement.

The legions were stationed at Nikopolis, close to Alexandria, a 'city' founded by Octavian in memory of his victory over Antony's army, at Babylon near Memphis, the old royal capital, and at Thebes in the south, the centre of native Egyptian sentiment.[5] The auxiliary regiments were scattered more widely, but particularly in the south and on the eastern frontier, where the possibly hostile client kingdoms of Nabataea and Judaea, and the desert tribes of Sinai, had to be watched. Of the forts in Egypt which were occupied by the Romans, six out of perhaps twenty were along the southern stretch of the Nile River from Luxor to the second cataract, and five more faced the eastern border.[6]

The early garrison was commanded by C. Cornelius Gallus, who had commanded the invasion from Cyrenaica in 30, and was now appointed as prefect of Egypt.[7] Originally from Forum Julii in Gaul, he had been a Caesarean, then a Pompeian, then had campaigned with Octavian. He was an *eques*, of a social rank below senator, unusual in a provincial governor, though several other *equites* were employed by Octavian as governors – 'prefect', in Egypt – in parts of the empire, though not in full-blown provinces. This may well have simply been a pragmatic matter of finding a competent man for a difficult post, but Gallus' post was especially noteworthy, for no other *eques* controlled so rich a province or so large an army.[8] Octavian later ruled that no senator could be allowed to visit Egypt without his express permission, which was generally refused. A senator outranked an *eques*, and could have made all sorts of trouble by interfering.

Octavian did not stay long in Egypt, and saw little of the country beyond the Delta and Alexandria – though he is depicted in an inscription in the south installing a new Buchis bull at Hermonthis near Thebes (the ceremony had previously been performed in person by Kleopatra twenty years before[9]) and Dio Cassius says he ordered some canals cleared and others dug by soldiers,[10] a traditional action of pharaohs. He cannot in fact have had time to do more than issue the necessary orders, and appoint the necessary officials, starting with Gallus.

Despite the brevity of Octavian's visit the administration of Egypt was altered and improved not long after his visit, and perhaps as a result of it. In particular the *strategoi* appointed to administer each of the forty or so local regions, the nomes, were charged with greater responsibilities in the matter of tax collection.[11] This measure reduced the duties of the governor of Egypt to supervising the major officers in the Alexandrian administration, who in turn were some distance from the *strategoi*. (There was also another administrative layer between the nomes and Alexandria, the *epistrategoi*, four of whom each supervised a large region – Kallimachos had been an *epistrategos* in the Thebaid.)

This new organization is generally credited to Octavian, but just when it was implemented is not clear; and in fact the appointment of Gallus and the swift departure of Octavian argue against any major changes in the earliest Roman years. Gallus fell foul of Octavian after three years, a matter which drew attention once more to the strength of the country, its tradition of independence, and the problem posed by an over-energetic governor. The reorganization probably dates to some later time, after the first three governors, all of whom had major military problems to solve first.

The prefects were rarely in office for more than three years, and could not have imposed any serious changes on what was undoubtedly a resistant bureaucracy. It therefore seems likely that the changes were partly the result of experience gained in attempting to run Egypt using the old Ptolemaic system. This had been generally successful in the last decade before the Roman conquest, judging by the wealth accumulated by Kleopatra, though it had faltered in the 40s because of a series of low Niles, and the wars, civil and foreign, inflicted on the country. However the use to which Egypt was put by the Romans was to be rather different from that imposed by the kings.

It is a notorious fact of Roman imperial history that the entitled Roman citizens in Rome were fed by doles of food, of which Sicily, North Africa, and Egypt were the sources, and the greatest of these eventually was Egypt, though this does not seem to have been the original intention when Augustus set about organizing the country. That is, what the later emperors required from Egypt was both cash and grain. The kings had used Egyptian wealth as diplomatic levers. The Roman emperors required grain to be converted into bread by the recipients of the dole, and the annual arrival of the Egyptian grain ships at Puteoli and Ostia was a major political event. Egypt was not in fact the main source of food for Rome. According to Josephus a century after Augustus, it supplied half of what Africa supplied.[12] But this was a great increase from the time of Augustus, when Egypt had supplied nothing.

The Ptolemaic bureaucracy continued to operate, and some men continued in office during the transition. The bureaucrats' task was above all, from the imperial point of view, to ensure the safety, quality, quantity, and good condition of the grain they collected and dispatched downriver to Alexandria. This was something which had to be done by a responsible official familiar with local conditions, and near the point of production, not by administrators in Alexandria who were all outsiders. The prefects served usually for three years, the heads of department maybe served for longer, but were still not Egyptian. The *strategoi*, on the other hand, were locals, usually Greek Egyptians. They knew how the system worked, and they were the men who kept the great machine operating.

C. Cornelius Gallus, as an experienced general and a friend of Octavian, was an obvious choice for prefect. A militarily competent man was clearly required if there should be trouble in Egypt, which was apparently expected.[13] But another aspect was that Octavian was aggressive and aimed to expand the imperial boundaries. He had already demonstrated this by his war in Illyria and in his annexation of part of North Africa. He had inherited the Republican desire for the expansion of the empire, and wanted the prestige of being an 'imperator'. He spent two years, after returning to Italy, organizing his position within the tattered Roman political system, then set about expanding the bounds of the empire, in Spain, in the Balkans, and in Germany. He added more territory to the empire than any other Roman, and this included Egypt.

Yet Augustus was no general. He tended to be ill at moments of military conflict, as before the battle at Philippi, so he relied on others to command, M. Vipsanius Agrippa in particular, but later his stepsons Drusus and Tiberius. For a man like Gallus, who had been close to Octavian, it would have been obvious that this aggressiveness was something innate in the man. He would reasonably assume that he was expected to take any advantage which presented itself of expanding the empire.

Gallus was operating in a period of transition. He was the first Roman to govern Egypt, and had the title only of 'prefect', while he himself was an *eques*, and all of this rendered his position uncertain in Roman terms. He was the pioneer and his actions could well set the pattern for later governors. Like Octavian, he inherited the Republican predilection for aggression. He began by successfully suppressing a rebellion at Heroopolis, near modern Suez, and another in the south, in the Thebaid, which was much more serious.[14] The cause is put down to the excessive tax demands posed by Octavian, but any rebellion in the south was also fuelled by nationalist anger, not of the loss of Ptolemaic rule, but at the imposition of yet another foreign ruler.

Gallus reported his suppression of the Thebaid rising on an inscription he set up at Philae at the first Nile cataract, the normal southern boundary of Egypt.[15] He claimed that the fighting lasted only fifteen days during which he captured five towns. These are located along a 50 km stretch of the river from Koptos to Thebes, which is the very heart of the most nationalist area of Egypt. This may well have been the area Caesarion was heading for when he was killed; his mother had gone there when driven from power in 49.

Having suppressed both risings with relative ease, Gallus moved on southwards, no doubt being especially zealous in dealing with any lingering dissension. He marched on beyond the first cataract at Philae, and into the Triacontaschoinos – 'Thirty-Mile-Land' – stretching south from Philae.[16] How far south he went is not clear, but he claimed its conquest in his inscription. When he returned to Philae he was met by envoys of the 'King of the Ethiopians', by which he meant the kingdom of Kush, the land ruled from the city of Meroe, far off in the Sudan, whose king claimed to rule from Philae southwards. That is, that kingdom had been attacked and parts annexed by the new rulers of Egypt, who, it became clear later, the king claimed to know nothing about.

There are substantial difficulties over the events between 30 and 20 in the Egyptian south, beginning with the precise political situation beyond Philae before 30 on to the difficulty of interpreting the exact situation as agreed in a peace treaty in 20. In between there is the problem of just what happened to Cornelius Gallus, who were the rulers of Kush at the time, and what policy was pursued by the Roman emperor, none of which can be determined with any precision. On top of all this it is clear that the Roman sources for the events in Egypt are thoroughly contaminated by Roman imperial propaganda. The matter is, in short, controversial.

The Meroitic envoys who met Gallus had presumably two purposes, to investigate who the new Egyptian rulers were, and to negotiate about the Triacontaschoinos. Since they seem to have met Gallus at Philae on his return from his southern march it is likely that they had set out (from Meroe, several hundred kilometres away) well before Gallus' campaign began. It was thus probably an embassy which had been sent to find out what was happening in Egypt, as a result of rumours about the Roman conquest which happened in the autumn of 30. Gallus' whole campaign, and the negotiations at Philae, ended by 17 April 29 according to the date noted in his inscription. This was only seven months after Octavian's victory at Alexandria, so the envoys were not reacting to Gallus' war in Triacontaschoinos.

The information about the death of Kleopatra and the Roman conquest of Egypt probably reached Meroe by way of Thebes, and it would not be surprising if the Kushite king was interested in fishing in troubled waters. Nubian kings had ruled Egypt in the past, and Meroitic culture was heavily influenced by Egyptian, its religion and its gods were similar, its script was an alphabetic version of Egyptian Demotic – though the language is not known. The occupation of Egyptian land could be a dormant ambition in many

Meroitic kings. If anything was inevitable in the new situation it was that an embassy of investigation would come from Meroe.

Gallus' expedition into the south pre-empted any Meroitic action (as opposed to an enquiry). The conquest of the Triacontaschoinos was not something the envoys could contest. Perforce they accepted it, and made an agreement which Gallus interpreted as making the king of Meroe his client, and he claimed to impose a tribute. He organized the Triacontaschoinos under a 'tyrant', and so as another client kingdom. The person whom he appointed is not known, though guesses have been made as to his identity. One suggestion is that he was Akinidad, the Kushite crown prince (and later king); another, more ingenious and perhaps more likely, is that he was in Egyptian called Quper, whose sons were later deified and had a temple dedicated to them by Augustus at Dendera.[17]

Gallus then composed the brief account of his deeds which he had inscribed in three languages on the block of pink granite at Philae. The inscription was headed by a relief of himself as a cavalryman spearing an enemy soldier, though the wording makes it clear that he did all this in the name of Octavian. He must also have sent a written report, perhaps in more detail and less self-laudatory terms, to Octavian in Rome.

The variations between the three versions on the stone have occasioned considerable comment. The thing to recall, however, is that the Latin version was that which had been composed by Gallus himself, and must be regarded as the main one, the original. The Greek version varies from the Latin in the way the new relationship with the Meroitic king is characterized – 'tyrant', is the term used here. But the hieroglyphic version is very different from either of the others. It is difficult to read, partly because the stone has been sawn in two, resulting in part of every line being destroyed, and partly because the extreme hardness of the stone made it difficult for the sculptor to inscribe the hieroglyphs accurately. But for all the difficulty it is obvious that the priests who rendered the Gallus Latin original into Egyptian paid little or no attention to his actual words. They cast the document in traditional Egyptian terms, omitting much of the detail and paying much more attention to the gods. The fighting is mentioned only cursorily: 'he pacified the chiefs of Kush' is virtually the only specific reference to the political events. It is likely that Gallus had no idea of what was in this part of the inscription, nor did any of his people. It is impossible to believe that any of the Romans involved could speak Egyptian, or read the hieroglyphic script, so this third version is of no use in understanding what happened.

This was over, according to the date in the inscription, by April 29. At some point in the next two years, certainly by 27, Gallus was recalled, and was replaced by a new governor, Aelius Gallus. When Cornelius reached

Rome he was accused of some crime whose nature is not clear now, though part of the accusations thrown at him were that he had been too keen to broadcast his achievements in Egypt; one of his colleagues, Valerius Largus, provided such information, perhaps based in part on the vainglorious image of Gallus spearing an enemy shown in the inscription at Philae. As usual with Roman criminal cases all sorts of barely relevant material was drawn in. The crucial point was that Augustus (as he now was) abandoned Gallus, leaving the Senate to pass judgment; he had in fact fallen foul of the changes at Rome while he was in Egypt, by which Augustus claimed to have restored the republic, while actually increasing and entrenching his own power. Gallus' condemnation had probably little to do with his work in Egypt, and more to do with the Senate's momentary revival of its apparent authority and with Augustus letting that happen. Gallus soon committed suicide.[18]

Aelius Gallus suffered for Augustus' policies in a different way. He was sent with perhaps half of the Roman army in Egypt to campaign in Arabia (which will be discussed in the next chapter). The king of Meroe, who may be a different person from the man whose envoys made the treaty at Philae with Cornelius Gallus, took advantage of his removal and of the absence of the Roman troops in Arabia to invade the Egyptian south. An army of 30,000 men, according to Strabo, who was a contemporary of these events (but whose figures are no more reliable than any other ancient historian's), took Aswan and Philae, where the statues of Augustus were overthrown or carried away.[19] To do this they had conquered all the Triacontaschoinos which Cornelius Gallus had taken five years before.

The garrison at Syene (modern Aswan) was not strong enough to withstand the attack. If the Meroitic army had conquered the river south of there, the Roman cohorts in the south can hardly have been taken by surprise, but an attack by '30,000' of the enemy would be overwhelming. The Meroites took Syene, on the east bank of the river, and the two be-templed islands of Elephantine and Philae. A Latin poem inscribed on a pharaonic statue at Philae by Julius Sabinus, the Roman commander of an Ituraean auxiliary cohort, seems to claim that he commanded three cohorts and defeated the attack, though some crucial words are missing, and the tone is vainglorious but unspecific.[20] This Meroitic attack took place as a result, says Strabo, of the reduction of the Roman power in Egypt (because of Aelius Gallus' Arabian expedition), but was countered quickly by the new prefect, P. Petronius. The timing suggests that it had taken a year for the information about the Roman withdrawal of forces under Aelius Gallus (in 24) to reach Meroe and for the attack to be mounted (in 22). Since the round-trip distance from Thebes to Meroe is at least 2,000 km, this is hardly surprising.

The force which Petronius commanded in his counter-attack was '10,000 infantry and 800 cavalry', which sounds like two legions, probably the full remaining Egyptian garrison. His attack was quickly successful in recovering some of the lost land, and the Meroitic forces withdrew to Pselchis, 120 km to the south. Petronius sent envoys, but no agreement resulted, so he attacked again. Strabo describes the Meroitic army as undisciplined, and armed with hide shields and axes, pikes or swords. Any Roman army would have no difficulty trouncing such a force. It was scattered, and the 'generals of Queen Candace' took refuge on an island and were captured.[21]

When asked why the attack had been launched against Philae and Syene, the Meroitic reply was that they were oppressed by the nomarchs, that is, the *strategoi* of the Egyptian administration. This may have been Cornelius Gallus' tyrant whom he set up to administer the Triacontaschoinos, or his underlings. This would explain the ease of the Meroitic conquest, which would thus be in support of a rebellion against the tyrant. (The later deified sons of Quper were presumably killed during this rebellion, hence their honouring by the locals and by Augustus.) This might also explain why the invasion stopped at Syene. Petronius explained that the ruler of the country was Caesar, whose statues they had overthrown, though this does not seem to have been understood. In the same non-comprehension Petronius himself did not understand who ruled in Meroe. The 'Queen Candace' who is said to have ruled was a corruption of 'Kandake', the title of either the wife or the mother of the king. (On the Lion Temple at Naqa, south of Meroe, the queen of the time, Amanitone, is depicted as an equal with her husband, King Natakamani; these two ruled a few decades after the war with Petronius.[22]) So the queen called 'Candace' who is referred to was the king's wife or mother, possibly acting for him. It is clear that the Romans never understood this (any more than do many modern historians).

The generals captured by Petronius at Pselchis probably had no authority to conclude any political agreement. The earlier envoys had done so with Cornelius Gallus, of course, but they clearly thought that he was the new ruler of Egypt. Now there was this 'Caesar'. They may have thought the statues they threw down at Syene and Philae were of Gallus – they probably could not read Greek or Latin or the Egyptian hieroglyphics. Petronius gave them three days to consider matters at Pselchis, but they now knew that he was not the ultimate authority in Egypt, any more than they were in Meroe. No doubt confusion reigned; but one thing was clear – no agreement was possible between the parties present.

Having captured the enemy commanders and scattered their army, Petronius took his forces on south, presumably in search of some authority with whom he could make peace. Pliny the Elder gives a list of the places Petronius captured which begins with Pselchis and goes along the river as far as the second cataract at 'Stadissis', the present Wadi Halfa.[23] This listing has led one student to suppose that Petronius went no further, but Pliny's wording is such that he separates this list of conquests from the next stage in the campaign, which was a march to the Kushite centre of Napata.[24] This journey would most likely follow the desert trail from Korosko, only 70 km or so beyond Pselchis, but north of his extreme conquest at Wadi Halfa. This was the route taken, it is thought, by an expedition of the Pharaoh Psamtik in 591 BC; however, Kitchener's army, building a railway along the way, in 1896–8 went from Wadi Halfa. Despite the assumptions of the Romans there was actually nothing unprecedented in such an expedition. The Egyptians had done it more than once, and of course the Kushites had done so in reverse.

The two main sources for this expedition, Pliny and Strabo, are explicit that Petronius marched his army all the way to Napata. Pliny states that he was at that point 870 (Roman) miles from Syene, which is about right; Strabo, a contemporary of these events, says he reached, captured, and sacked the city. There seems no reason to doubt these statements.[25]

Napata was the burial place of some of their kings and a major religious centre, though the government centre was at Meroe, much further along the Nile. Strabo implies that the Kandake queen was living near Napata, but makes the point that her son, the crown prince, left the place before the Romans arrived; nor was she herself captured. In advance, and presumably to save the city, she offered restitution of those who had been captured and enslaved at Syene, including the return of the statues taken, but Petronius was determined to make his point by capturing the city, which was sacked. He considered marching on, presumably to attack Meroe itself, but was deterred by the distance involved. Without reaching any settlement, presumably because the king was a long way off by then and the Kandake queen refused to treat, he returned northwards.

Petronius' intention at this point was to hold what Cornelius Gallus had conquered, the Triacontaschoinos from Syene to the second cataract. He fortified Qasr Ibrim, some distance north of the second cataract. This was a solid fortress whose original foundation was then at least 1,000 years in the past. He repaired deficiencies in the fortifications, installed a garrison of '400' men – a cohort, presumably – with supplies for two years, and returned to the north with the rest of the army.

The Kushites, no doubt angered by the destruction of Napata, which was a great religious centre comparable in the kingdom with Thebes in Egypt, returned to the attack after some time – again the timing is best accounted for by the sheer distances involved. No doubt this was what Petronius expected, hence the strong garrison at Qasr Ibrim. He had also obviously organized a warning system, and when the Kushite army came north for revenge, he was quickly informed. He reached Qasr Ibrim with an adequate force and further supplies before the attackers, and this clearly deterred an assault. The Kushites realized that militarily they were outmatched. On the other hand, they did have an army on hand to strengthen their negotiating position.

When the Meroitic envoys arrived, this time with plenipotentiary authority, it was Petronius' turn to be unable to negotiate. Augustus was now the only source of diplomacy with external states. The envoys were therefore told that they must go to Caesar to negotiate. Their reply indicates once again the depth of ignorance that separated the empire and the kingdom. They said they did not know who Caesar was, nor how to find him. This is after two wars and almost a decade after the Roman conquest of Egypt. The information passing from Egypt southwards was evidently no more than military, and the Kushite assumption still was that the prefect was Egypt's ruler – something which, no doubt, Cornelius Gallus' conduct had seemed to confirm. It is evident that Petronius' explanation to the generals of the Kandake queen had not penetrated into the royal circles in Napata and Meroe.

In a sense, of course, the interpretation that the prefects ruled Egypt was quite correct. They had waged three wars along the Nile south of Philae in the past ten years: Cornelius Gallus' suppression of the Theban rebellion and his conquest of the Triacontaschoinos; Aelius Gallus' invasion of Arabia, which the Kushites clearly knew about; and Petronius' invasion of their own kingdom and his sacking of Napata. These were all major campaigns, involving marches of thousands of kilometres and the capture of cities and fortresses. Such wars were surely conducted by kings, the Kushites might reasonably assume. Their own campaigns were no more than retaliation.

Petronius presumably explained who Caesar was, and may have had to give them a geography lesson into the bargain. He provided them with an escort who took them through Egypt and across the Mediterranean to Samos, where Augustus was based while he adjusted various problems in the east, including eventually making peace with Parthia at long last. It is in the light of the Roman experiences in Egypt and Arabia and with Parthia that Augustus' negotiations with the Meroitic envoys were conducted.

Augustus was already prepared for the Meroitic ambassadors. Petronius had sent 1,000 of the captives from his Napatan campaign to him (selling others, but many others died of diseases in Egypt). This had been a year earlier, 'when Augustus returned from Cantabria', in 22 or 21 BC. Petronius will also have sent a written report on his activities, and perhaps the escorts carried an updated version – they could deliver one orally if not in writing. The expedition to Napata had revealed something of the size and diffuseness of the Meroitic realm. A campaign of conquest in the Sudan would be never-ending. The expedition into Arabia had also demonstrated the difficulty, even the impossibility, of conquering a desert country. So, although he would no doubt have preferred to add yet another conquest to his rule, Augustus had come to the conclusion that it was not worth the effort. It also would not do to commit a large force to a distant campaign just when he was negotiating with the Parthians: the latest Kushite attack had happened when, and probably because, Aelius Gallus invaded Arabia. The coincidence between events all through the Near East was obvious. The Kushite envoys were lucky: Augustus had to cut his losses in order to gain a Parthian peace.

In the same way that Meroe was seen as a country too far, there is no evidence that the Meroitic rulers were really interested in conquering Egypt. The dynasty was descended from an early group of kings who had been Egyptian pharaohs back in the eighth century BC, but it seems unlikely that ambitions still burned. The competence of Roman legions, demonstrated all too clearly in the past few years, both in Africa and in Arabia, was an effective quencher of any such ambition. So, just as Augustus had evidently come to the decision not to pursue further military adventures along the Nile southwards, the Meroitic king had done the same for the opposite direction.

Agreement was therefore concluded, probably with little difficulty. Augustus agreed to cancel the tribute which had been demanded by Cornelius Gallus (it was probably uncollectable anyway), and to withdraw his forces from much of the Triacontaschoinos. But not from all of it. The northern part, called the Dodekaschoinos – 'Twelve-Mile-Land' – was to be retained, with the southern Roman boundary at Hiera Sykamenos, about 120 km south of Syene. Both sides could therefore claim a victory: the Romans had extended their direct rule south from the boundary accepted by the Ptolemaic kings for at least the previous century; the Meroites could claim to have recovered much of the land taken by Cornelius Gallus.[26]

The Roman force used to garrison the southern territories was light, perhaps no more than one cohort. An inscription from el-Dakkah named the 'cohors Sabini' as positioned there during Augustus' reign – no doubt this was the poetical Sabinus' command. And Augustus sponsored temples. One was at Kalabsha, where a temple to Mandulis (a Kushite god) had originally been built by a Kushite king during the brief independence of the region in the second century BC, and was now enlarged physically and Mandulis himself was now connected with the Egyptian gods Horus and Osiris and Isis, and with the Greek Apollo. This was a state-sponsored syncretism clearly designed to attract and conciliate the local Kushite population. At Dendera he built a temple for the deified sons of Quper. Even if Quper was not Gallus' 'tyrant', his sons were obviously Kushite heroes. So Augustus honouring them was another gesture of conciliation, as well as a reminder that it was the emperor's decision, and his was the power.[27]

The castle at Qasr Ibrim, so recently strengthened by Petronius, and then saved by him in the face of the Kushite threat, was now abandoned and evacuated. Excavations at the fortress have revealed some evidence of the process of evacuation by the Roman garrison. A hollow under a corner bastion had become the repository for unwanted rubbish for decades, even centuries, and one layer of the rubbish dump was Roman. These discards included pottery, 'coins, lamps, parts of woollen cloaks, leather, much sacking ... and sandals of demonstrably Roman type'. The coins provide a date for the deposit in the last century BC and this is confirmed by the pottery and the lamps.

There was also found a number of Greek and Latin papyri, some of the former dated to the 20s BC. One of the Latin papyri, ironically, was a fragment of a book of poems by C. Cornelius Gallus. It had been in the baggage of a Roman officer, perhaps the cohort commander – Julius Sabinus? – a man likely to have been given the book by Gallus himself. But he threw it out, possibly because to possess such a book might be thought politically incorrect by the late 20s, when Gallus had been condemned and abandoned.[28]

But there is another archaeological reference to this story. Archaeologists excavating a temple in Meroe city itself discovered buried in front of it a bronze head of Augustus. This is presumably one of the statues carried off by the army from Philae or Syene in their raid in 24 BC (though some see it of a style later than this). Strabo notes that the return of the filched statues was offered to Petronius when he approached Napata, but there is no sign that this offer was accepted, or that they were actually returned. The precise function of the temple (if indeed it was a temple) is not clear, though it was later decorated with a mural which apparently commemorated the Kushite victory. Whatever the precise dates and details it must have given some satisfaction to the Kushite king and the Kandake queen to be able to walk all over Augustus' head, cut off from its body, whenever they entered the building.[29]

Chapter 9

The Arabian Expedition

Aelius Gallus was appointed prefect of Egypt in the wake of the recall of C. Cornelius Gallus, and arrived in his province in 27. Cornelius' subsequent trial and condemnation by the Senate, and his abandonment by Augustus, were clear indications that the governors of the emperor's provinces would need to do as they were told, no more and no less. Cornelius had behaved in the way a successful Roman general had always behaved under the Republic, boasting and proud and claiming credit for conquests, but now a governor or a general commanded in the emperor's name and did the emperor's bidding – and gave the credit to the emperor.

Aelius Gallus spent a year as prefect in Egypt administering his province. In his first year he sailed up the Nile as far as Thebes. Strabo the geographer accompanied him as did 'his crowd of associates' who at one point got up early to hear the groan which was emitted from the statue of Memnon.[1] The main reason for the voyage was presumably administrative and to sort out any issues left over from Cornelius' time. Therefore for perhaps a year Aelius administered his province as governors were intended to.

Then an order came from Augustus to investigate Arabia. Strabo, who gives an account to the expedition, is rather confused as to its purpose. He says Augustus sent Aelius 'to explore the tribes and places, not only in Arabia, but also in Aithiopia (that is, the Sudan)'. But he then says that it was the Trogodytes who were to be investigated. These lived in Egypt in the land between the Nile and the Red Sea; he comments that the object was to 'win over' the 'Arabians' or subjugate them. It looks very much as though imperial headquarters did not know very much about any of this, and that Aelius Gallus had to persuade them to be more specific. In the end the objective was Arabia, and he ignored both Aithiopia and the Trogodytes.[2]

This episode bristles with problems, beginning, as the last paragraph suggests, with the original purpose of the expedition and going through to its result. There are two accounts of importance, by Strabo and by Pliny – the latter fairly brief – and a mention by Dio Cassius.[3] These have occasioned a range of modern discussions, usually focussed on one aspect only, to the exclusion of other matters. In addition there is the *Periplus Maris Erythraei* (the *periplus* – description and guide – of the Red Sea), written probably a century or so after the expedition (and so after Strabo, before Dio Cassius, and about the same time as Pliny), which gives valuable information about South Arabia which is absent from the other accounts. Only Strabo gives a straightforward account of events, but he was influenced by Augustan propaganda and by his friendship with Aelius Gallus, and this has led to some distortion.

As prefect of Egypt, Aelius had an army of three legions and a dozen auxiliary units at his command. He could also also call on help from the Nabataean king, who was known to have extensive trading contacts with 'Arabia' and volunteered to help, no doubt prompted by Augustus. At this point it became clear that the area of 'Arabia' which interested the emperor was the south, the modern Yemen, a source of myrrh and frankincense and other incenses, and a staging post on the sea-route to India. The land was reputed to harbour much wealth, received because of their sale of precious stones and incenses, but which had supposedly not been spent.

The eventual aim of the expedition is not clear now, and it may well not have been clear to Aelius or even to Augustus at the time. The vague formulation 'winning over' or 'subjugating' the Arabians might mean anything from distant diplomatic contact to brutal conquest and annexation, so it rather looks as though Aelius Gallus was expected to see what could be done, and use his own initiative. The region attracted the Romans because it was reputed to be wealthy. The normal process of Roman warfare was for the victorious army to seize any portable wealth in a conquered city or country. This had been done in Egypt, Julius Caesar had done it in Gaul, Pompey had done it in Syria, Claudius was to do it in Britain, and Petronius was to do it at Napata in a few years' time. This was a well-established and well-understood process, and at the very least Arabia could expect to be looted, even if Roman troops did not remain there to annex the country.

In Egypt the Roman prefects and the department heads had by now investigated the Egyptian government system, and discovered its revenue sources. Cornelius Gallus and Aelius Gallus both spent some time in the Theban region, and Strabo notes that from that region there were several routes leading to ports on the Red Sea.[4] The former *epistrategos* Kallimachos had been '*strategos* of the Red and Indian seas', which meant he supervised those routes and the trade conducted along the Red Sea.[5] Once the Romans were established in Egypt they came to understand that there was a substantial maritime trade from the Red Sea ports with South Arabia and India, a trade which was a major generator of wealth and which they taxed heavily just as had their Ptolemaic predecessors.[6]

Reports about this no doubt went to Rome. By 26 BC the situation in Egypt had been brought under control, the rebellions had been suppressed, and a firm grip had been established on the southern frontier. The revelation of the Red Sea trade excited Augustus' interest, which was no doubt partly mercenary and partly political. The Egyptian Red Sea ports were only part of a much bigger trading system which extended throughout the Red Sea and across the Arabian Sea to India and even beyond. The next major position along the way was South Arabia, the home of the incenses.

There were therefore plenty of inducements for the Roman government to dispatch an expedition there. Possession of the region would give the Roman government a virtual monopoly of the incense trade, from production to sale, and it would allow access to the Indian trade, much of which was in Arab hands; it would be the conquest of an exotic region so as to dazzle Roman opinion, and it might strategically outflank the Parthians, with whom Augustus was considering whether to fight or to negotiate. And then there was India. Alexander had been forced to turn back from a projected Indian conquest; when he died he was preparing an Arabian expedition. Conquering South Arabia would be to outdo even Alexander, which had been the ambition of every conqueror since the great man's death. The collection of reasons, personal, political, financial, exploratory, even romantic, was such as to be irresistible to such a man as Augustus, whose only concession to the fame of the city of Alexandria when he was there was to have Alexander's tomb opened so that he could gaze upon his withered face. (He had been the same age as Alexander at the latter's death, and like him, ruled a large empire; to outdo the great Macedonian was a constant incentive.)

There was another route to South Arabia, by land, whose northern terminus was controlled by the Nabataeans. They received the caravans which marched along the trade route which ran parallel to, but 200 km inland of, the Red Sea coast. At the southern end another community, the Minaeans, organized the dispatch of the caravans from their main city of Qarnaw (called Karna by the Greeks and Romans). There were three other states in the region. Next to the Minaeans was Saba, or the Sabaeans, centred on their city of Marib, the Qatabanians further to the south-east, whose main city was Timna, and the Hadramites (that is, in the Hadramaut region) whose main city was Shabwa. The crucial role of the incenses in all this is indicated by the geographical situations of these main cities, which are all close to the desert edge, and at relatively low altitudes, whereas for comfort in the Arabian heat a city on the higher land would be best.[7]

However, Strabo was quoting Eratosthenes in his description, and so his information was two centuries old. By the time the Romans took an interest, the seaborne trade had changed the political geography of the region. The Greek-Egyptian discovery of the monsoon weather system in the Arabian sea had encouraged the growth of direct traffic between Egyptian Red Sea ports and western India. As a result, in Yemen new ports were developing from which local goods were being exported, and the relocation of economic activity towards the coast also meant the development of new kingdoms in the south and east at the expense of the old inland states. The port at Muza (modern Mocha), almost at the south-east point of the Red Sea, was connected to the city of Zafar in the mountains, which was the centre of the newly important kingdom of the Himyarites ('Homeritae' to Strabo and Pliny). Along the Indian Ocean coast other ports had grown at Aden, Qana and Sahar. Muza and Aden were Himyarite ports, and this state was now pressing on the Sabaeans, and would unite with them a little later. Qana and Sahar were Hadramite ports, and that kingdom was increasing in power as well – the two activities were obviously connected. By the time Roman interest developed, the Himyarite and Hadramite kingdoms were rising, whereas the inland states were beginning to fade.[8]

The development of the sea route between Egypt and South Arabia, and on to India, had concerned not just the inland South Arabian states, but the Nabataeans as well. Nabataean ships had been in the habit of raiding Ptolemaic vessels, but no doubt they had also taken part in the trade as well. It was the land trade which had brought the growth of the desert-edge cities and the inland states, and wealth to the Nabataean kingdom. Seaborne competition brought a relative decline in the land route, though the Nabataeans were adaptable and had entered the sea trade as well, but the land route had by no means been abandoned. The heavy taxation levied at the Egyptian ports on seaborne imports no doubt helped to keep the expensive and slow land transport system going. The Nabataeans could charge lower taxes and export their goods through ports such as Gaza which by-passed Ptolemaic territory. One of the causes of Ptolemaic-Nabataean enmity in Kleopatra's time was that she expanded her control over Nabataean exporting ports, including Gaza and their port at the northern end of the Red Sea.

While the Red Sea trade was limited to Egypt and South Arabia, the Nabataean trade had perhaps not been vitally affected, given Ptolemaic taxes, but once the monsoon system became understood by Greek and Egyptian mariners, from about 100 BC onwards, their maritime enterprise became much more extensive, taking in voyages to India by way of South Arabia. The connection was strong enough, and the quantity of shipping considerable enough, for Kleopatra to have envisaged escaping from the Roman conquest by way of the Red Sea, perhaps to India. The Nabataeans, whom she had made into enemies, had interfered by raiding and burning the ships she had gathered at Kleopatris – near modern Suez – which had earlier been called Arsinoe. Though the Romans probably did not realize it before their arrival in Egypt in 30, the Red Sea was a region of extensive maritime enterprise.

Exactly what Aelius Gallus' instructions were concerning the campaign into South Arabia are unknown, but he may have begun by envisaging a maritime campaign. This was, after all, how Egypt was linked with South Arabia, and it may have seemed logical to use it. Roman commanders would normally, perhaps even instinctively, think in terms of a land campaign, but it is evident that they knew little or nothing about the land approach, other than that it was through desert and was very long. Strabo is quite clear on this, commenting that it was the expedition itself which revealed to the Romans what the land was like – it was, besides being an armed campaign, an exploration. The Nabataeans had clearly kept details of the Arabian routes to themselves, and this was to be one of the problems Gallus was to face later.

The expedition had to be of a substantial size, and in the event Gallus took with him one legion and several auxiliary units. The total Roman force is said to have been 10,000 infantry, which is actually rather vague and no doubt essentially a guess. Gallus also received a contributions of 1,000 men from the Nabataeans, and Herod sent 500 men from Judaea; there were also other small allied contingents which are never detailed. A force this size needed large supplies of food and water, none of which could be guaranteed to be acquired in Arabia on the march, though, as it turned out, there were more local supplies available than expected.

Gallus organized shipbuilding at Kleopatris, which was accessible by canal from the Delta. Naturally the fact that it was a military expedition indicated that warships were needed. Eighty were built, small warships of bireme and trireme size, each of which could carry a number of soldiers, but which would need rowers to propel them. Strabo claims that Gallus had made a mistake, and that he then changed the order, and had 130 other ships – powered by sail – constructed.[9]

Strabo's account of the events of the expedition is suffused with the assumption that Gallus was misled, above all by the Nabataean minister Syllaeus, but he also claims he was deceived over the ships. This has stimulated the modern criticism that the maritime plan was unworkable. Ships packed with soldiers and oarsmen would need to refresh from water supplies every day, so it is claimed, and food and water were simply not available on the Red Sea coast. It is certainly the fact that it was normal for ships in the ancient world to put ashore every night, since night voyaging was dangerous, but later Gallus was able to evacuate the remains of the army by sea.[10] His force, several thousand strong, was carried from the Arabian port of Egra to Myos Hormos in Egypt in eleven days, and then the troops were sent across the Egyptian Eastern Desert to Koptos and the Nile, all apparently without serious difficulty.[11]

So it was clearly possible to shift large forces along the Red Sea, probably in batches, and the argument that it was logistically impossible fails.[12] So we must ignore Strabo's explanations and excuses and consider what Gallus actually did. It seems reasonable to assume that his intention all along had been to take the land route. The ships were therefore for transport from Egypt across the Red Sea. There were dangers in the Red Sea, raiders and pirates, and a convoy of sailing ships would be vulnerable, hence the warships, which could act as protection; they would also subsequently control the whole sea. In that light, the expedition's aim seems to have been conquest.

The army was transported from Kleopatris across to the Arabian shore, camping at a place called Leuke Kome. This place has not been definitively located, but it was probably on the Arabian shore just south of the entrance to the Gulf of Aqaba.[13] This area had contained the Nabataean Red Sea port until Kleopatra persuaded Antony to give it to her, and it was probably the base from which the Nabataeans mounted the raid which burned her ships.

The voyage took fourteen days from Kleopatris, which rather implies that the army was moved in stages. The distance sailed is about 400 km, which, given favourable wind conditions, should have taken a sailing ship five or six days, though Strabo says that the voyage from Egra to Myos Hormos, 500 km, took eleven days. The transport of the army was therefore either very slow, or, more likely, the ships moved the men in batches. (The allies would not need transport, being able to come by land from the north.)

The delay caused to Gallus' expedition by the building of the ships was now compounded by sickness which developed among the soldiers. Strabo indicates two diseases: scurvy, which must have been caused by the diet forced on the soldiers by relying on preserved food and bad water; and infections in their legs, no doubt due to insect bites. Gallus' onward march was delayed for several months. He was joined by the Judaean and Nabataean contingents. The Nabataeans were no doubt concerned to supervise the Roman march, and were expected to act as guides. They would also be useful when the expedition reached South Arabia. The Judaean contingent was Herod's way of stocking up political goodwill at Rome, and he was no doubt interested in finding out the methods and routes of trade which the Nabataeans had used. The Nabataean king, Obodas III, sent his minister, Syllaeus, to command the Nabataean force and to guide the force on the way.

Strabo claims that Syllaeus deliberately took the army along the wrong route and was generally obstructive, but the main reason for Roman difficulty was the size of their expedition. To move an army of 10,000 men along the desert routes of Arabia was probably unprecedented. It would need extreme preparation and a highly organized logistics operation. Acquiring supplies along the route was virtually impossible – 'zeia (a coarse grain), a few palm trees, and butter instead of oil', Strabo says. A slow march, using many of the soldiers to bring up supplies for the rest, is guaranteed.

On the other hand, the journey was about 1,500 km, and was completed in eighty days, which is an average of 20 km per day. The distance was actually greater, and the eighty days is only an estimate, but there cannot have been much in the way of delay and distraction on the march. If Syllaeus really did take the army on unfrequented tracks and no roads, he did not cause much delay. It is difficult to see an army of such size moving much faster in such difficult terrain.

So Aelius Gallus got his men through the desert, with or without local help and supplies. From Leuke Kome he travelled for 'thirty days' through lands ruled by a kinsman of King Obodas called Aretas, who was friendly, inevitably, and provided 'gifts' and no doubt helped out with supplies, though the local produce was not of a quality the Roman troops appreciated. From there they marched through desert for 'fifty days' – these figures are only guesses by Strabo – as far as a city called Negrani, which is the modern Najran.

There was no chance of a surprise arrival. Once the Roman march began it is certain that the word will have spread throughout Arabia with great speed. Certainly the Negrani king knew what he faced, for he had left the city before the expedition arrived, and no doubt many of his people had gone as well. The city was captured instantly. Another march of 'six days' – these smaller numbers are more convincing – brought the Roman forces to a river, though it was probably a dry wadi, where an opposing army was drawn up to stop them. It was of a substantial size, since '10,000 men' died, according to Strabo, and the rest were dispersed. He is probably quoting Aelius Gallus. The men were poorly armed and undisciplined; as with the Kushite forces which faced the army of Petronius a year or so later, Roman military expertise was instantly successful.

It is nowhere stated where this local army, prepared to block the Roman advance, came from, but one must assume it was a coalition of forces collected from several of the local states. The king of Negrani, missing from his city, and the king of Aska, also absent when his city was taken shortly after the battle, were no doubt present at the fight with their troops; other interested parties likely to have provided soldiers were the Minaeans, the Sabaeans, and the Qatabanians. All of these had a direct interest in preventing any further Roman advance, for the approach of a large Roman army was a clear threat to everyone in the region.

As it happens, it was their cities and the geographical situation of those cities which were decisive in turning the Roman force back, not the attempt to fight a Roman army in the open field, which could only be suicidal. Having dispersed the Arab army, and caused the '10,000' deaths, Aelius Gallus captured Aska (modern Nasq) whose king had left, then, according to Strabo, took Athroula (Yatil), where he left a garrison and collected supplies. He moved on to attack 'Marsiaba', generally assumed to be Marib, the main city of the Sabaeans, which is also the name given by Augustus in his *Res Gestae*.[14]

This is the point at which Aelius Gallus' progress halted. For the first time Strabo identified the king – 'Ilarosos' – and tribe, the Rhammanitae, which is presumably his version of the Himyarites, who had by this time established dominance over this Sabaeans. For the first time Gallus here encountered a substantial and well-fortified city whose circuit of walls was said to be 6 miles long (10 km).[15] This was not a place whose capture could be rushed as at Negrani and Aska and Athroula. Gallus laid siege to it.

But here the geography intervened. The cities so far captured were the collecting points for the incenses which were harvested in the near desert, and as such they were situated close to the desert. A besieging army was therefore immediately dependent on the import of food and above all water from better supplied country, but the Roman army did not control that territory; its enemies did. After only six days, Aelius Gallus was compelled to raise the siege.[16]

Gallus by now had time to investigate the local political situation. His capture of Aska and Athroula was of only minor importance, for they were smallish towns. Neither Karna, the main Minaean city involved in the Nabataean trade, nor the city of the Sabaeans (Marib) had been captured. Beyond Marib there were also the kingdoms of the Qatabanians, the Himyarites and the Hadramites, not to mention the seaports through which most of the trade actually went. He had probably been fighting the Qatabanians at Marib, along with the Sabaeans. He had a formidable army, but if opposition to his conquest continued, his forces would rapidly fade away, as casualties in the fighting, to disease, or dispersed into garrisons. He was also out of reach of any reinforcements.

Under the circumstances Gallus decided he could not succeed, and quite probably the vagueness of his instructions was thereby useful, since he had no idea what would constitute success. He abandoned the expedition and, having no doubt collected such supplies as he could and evacuated his garrisons, he set out to march his forces back to the north. Strabo claims Gallus now discovered Syllaeus' treachery, and that he therefore returned by a different route – but in such sparsely supplied land he would necessarily take a different route back, since he had consumed the available supplies along the original route. Gallus therefore headed not for his original starting point at Leuke Kome, but to a seaport called Egra, somewhat over halfway from Yemen to Leuke Kome, where he was able to embark his forces on ships to take them across the Red Sea to Myos Hormos; from there they marched across the Egyptian desert to the Nile.

Strabo's figures confound his accusations of Syllaeus' treachery. He says the march south was eighty-six days from Leuke Kome to the battle at the river – thirty plus fifty plus six days. He spent some time on the campaign, capturing and besieging cities in the south, but perhaps no more than a month. The return march, from Marib to Egra, was completed in 'sixty days'. In giving 'six months' – which would be about 180 days – as the duration of the whole expedition, Strabo is actually saying that Gallus was not delayed in any material way by anyone. Syllaeus continued in office and in power in the Nabataean kingdom for another decade and a half after the expedition. If the Roman government believed he was at fault, he could easily have been extradited.

Gallus had in fact conducted his march and the campaign very competently. He clearly lost a considerable number of soldiers to disease, and probably others to the desert, but Strabo claims that Gallus acknowledged only seven deaths in fighting in the whole campaign. His campaign had made a good deal of sense, and he was not necessarily misled, by Syllaeus or anyone else. He captured a couple of towns and defeated the assembled local army, then marched directly to attack the most powerful city in the region. Negrani, Aska, and Athroula had all been captured without difficulty, and at the first approach. The contrast with Marib is clear. Further, Marib was the key to the joint Sabaean-Qatabanian state, which was also being threatened at the time by the Himyarites. If Gallus could gain control of Marib and the Sabaean state, quite likely the Minaeans and the Qatabanians would fall to him as well. It was also, of course, good Roman military practice to strike at the strongest opposing force on the assumption that its defeat would be decisive.

A variety of reasons have been advanced for Gallus' decision to withdraw: Syllaeus' machinations, recall by Augustus, Aelius Gallus' incompetence, for example – none of which are convincing – but Strabo's report that the army was short of water carries the most conviction. Once it was clear that Marib was too strong to be taken quickly, the position of the expedition became very precarious. Holding the towns he had already captured would not be enough. He had not penetrated very far into the settled area, and this made getting supplies difficult. Defeat at Marib, if it happened, would encourage the rest of South Arabia to become more hostile. The decision to withdraw was therefore sensible, and one must compliment Aelius Gallus on it; it would have been all too easy to dither, to try other means, attack other places, and end with the whole expeditionary force lost. (A further reason may have been news from Egypt, of which he was still prefect, of the trouble on the southern frontier which had been encouraged by his absence.)

We do not know just how strong the Roman force was by the time Gallus decided to retreat. He had lost men in crossing to Leuke Kome, more had died or been incapacitated by the diseases which ravaged the army at Leuke Kome, and we must assume that there had been more casualties on the march. Casualties of seven killed in fighting were alone admitted by Gallus, but that looks very much as though that low figure hid much greater losses

The Arabian Expedition 103

from other causes.[17] It would not be a surprise to learn that he had lost a substantial proportion of his original force, a quarter perhaps.

There is one small further item which had been used to provide one further detail. There is a broken inscription from Baraqish in Yemen, recording, probably, the death of a Roman soldier. His name was P. Cornelius, and he was a cavalryman, though that is all the information on the stone, which is only a fragment of the original. The inscription was in both Latin and Greek,[18] and it is assumed that it was only during Aelius Gallus' campaign that a Roman cavalryman could have reached Yemen, died there, and have had someone skilled enough in making inscriptions to produce the memorial. How he died (if he died) is not known, but the existence of the inscribed stone cannot be directly linked to Gallus' expedition except by assuming a coincidence. It is easily argued that since Gallus' forces were the only Romans to have reached the Yemen, Cornelius must have been one of them. This is not proof, nor is it even a good historical argument.[19] One fact at least operates against it, for Strabo states that the expedition consisted only of infantrymen, yet Cornelius was a cavalryman.[20] There is in fact no reason to deny that other Roman soldiers went to South Arabia in the next centuries, possibly on diplomatic missions, possibly as mercenaries or as exiles. The existence of the inscription cannot prove anything in the absence of a clear connection with Gallus' expedition. It is only interesting.

The history of the whole expedition therefore bristles with problems, and there is yet another. The expedition retired north, reaching Egra after 'sixty days'. This puts the port about two thirds of the way from Marib to Leuke Kome; it has been located at a point roughly opposite the Egyptian port of Berenike. From Egra the surviving troops were taken by ship to Myos Hormos, a voyage Strabo says was made in eleven days. This must have been pre-arranged. The army could not have been left to camp at Egra for very long, since supplies would soon be exhausted. Similarly when the troops were landed at Myos Hormos the same problem arose, and they had to march across the Egyptian Eastern Desert for 200 km in order to reach the Nile. Food and water for several thousand men had to have been stockpiled at both Egra and Myos Hormos, and a considerable fleet had accumulated at Egra to transport the troops. The ships were available, of course, in the fleet which Gallus had built at the beginning of the expedition, and they could be used to bring supplies from the base at Kleopatris to both ports.

This was clearly a well-organized operation, which the sources (and modern historians) pass over in silence, probably because it was successful – only disaster brings out the emotional rhetoric. But on the one hand it destroys the modern theory that it was impossible to move the army in the other direction to invade South Arabia. It is clear that had Gallus wished it would have been possible to move the army in stages the length of the Red Sea and to have invaded South Arabia through the ports. Muza, in Strabo's description, looks like a very suitable landing point. On the other hand it also destroys the interpretations of Gallus' incompetence and Syllaeus' treachery.

The final problem with this episode is to determine whether it was successful on not. Augustus, by including it in his account of his deeds, clearly counted it as a success, though by the time he was composing the document memories will have grown dim, and propaganda claiming it as a success will have had time to work. The determination, of course, depends on its original aims and purposes. If it was either loot or conquest, it was clearly a failure.

The sequel of the expedition was that the kingdoms of South Arabia came into contact with Rome, and remained so for the rest of the existence of the Roman Empire. The *Periplus* comments that a king of the Himyarites and the Sabaeans (and so some time during the first century AD) made diplomatic contact in Rome and sent gifts to the emperor. And in the years following the expedition into South Arabia envoys arrived from India. The coincidence in timing is very suggestive.

The South Arabian kingdoms therefore now swung into the diplomatic orbit of Rome, just as the Kushite kingdom did about the same time. In military terms it was clear that Rome was fully capable of reaching into South Arabia, as it was as of reaching Napata. If the legions could do that, it was equally possible that a determined Roman effort might well move a legion of soldiers as far as India.

So, depending on the perception of the aims of Aelius Gallus' expedition, it was either a military failure, or it was a long term diplomatic success. By the time of Augustus' meeting with the Kushite envoys negotiating peace at Samos in 21/20, Gallus had returned and reported on the situation in Yemen. Relations of a sort had been established therefore with every organized state within Roman reach, from the kingdom of the Crimean Bosporus around to Meroe, and in 20 BC Augustus made peace with Parthians. Aelius Gallus' expedition could be counted as successful.

Chapter 10

The Judaean Problem

Syria was littered with client kingdoms, some of them the size of Roman provinces. Augustus had confirmed Herod in Judaea, and executed the king in Emesa without replacing him. Nabataea was, so the evidence of the Arabian expedition indicated, confirmed as an obedient client. In the north the strategic area of the Euphrates Valley where it cut through the Taurus mountains was controlled by the Kommagenian king from his formidable capital of Samosata. In between these were numerous kings, tetrarchs, princes, free cities, even free villages. Syria was a complex and difficult province, whose governor needed military and diplomatic skills of a high order. He had to watch the Parthians, an active enemy until 20 BC, supervise dozens of princes and kings, oversee the affairs of many proud cities, and command no less than four legions and assorted auxiliary regiments.

The kingdoms were a problem, of course, since their rulers pretended to a legitimacy by inheritance which the Romans could not accept. As a result the death of a king was always a local crisis, when Rome pondered whether to annex the kingdom, or to impose a new king – and in that case which of the family to choose. The fates of the Ituraean and Emesan kingdoms during the Roman civil wars were clear warnings to the various kings, as was Herod's need to go off to Rhodes to seek Augustus' forgiveness and confirmation.

There were many principalities for the Romans and the Roman governors of Syria to be worried about. In the AD 70s, Pliny the Elder compiled his *Natural History* and for Syria he used a survey of Syria produced in Augustus' reign. He listed at least five tetrarchies by name and added that there were seventeen others which he would not even name.[1] There were also the kingdoms of Kommagene, Judaea, Emesa, and Nabataea and others we can detect. The Syrian governor therefore had at least thirty client states to watch. It is a fair guess that any governor would have to deal with at least one royal crisis or succession, possibly more than one, during his term of office.

We do not know much about the minor kingdoms and tetrarchies – many of them no more than a name, and thanks to Pliny, some not even that. The larger ones do make a mark on the sources. Most notably, of course, Judaea, thanks to Josephus, but others pop up from time to time as well. Emesa, for example, was kingless after 30 BC, for kings were killed by both Antony and Octavian. Presumably the kingdom was part of the province from then on, though there were royal family members still around. The most difficult problem, however, at least once Herod's control over Judaea was affirmed, was the old Ituraean kingdom, which Antony had given to Kleopatra.

This had not been destroyed as a political unit, but simply taken over by Kleopatra after the earlier ruler Lysanias was executed. A member of the ruling family, Zenodoros, probably Lysanias' son, had been put in charge. His task seems mainly to have been to collect taxes – Josephus says that he leased the kingdom – and to deliver the product to Kleopatra.[2] He remained in place after Kleopatra's death, and he may have acquired the old title of tetrarch from Octavian – he called himself 'tetrarch and high priest' on his coins – though he was still expected to deliver the cash.[3]

The territory involved included the original principality centred on the southern part of the Bekaa Valley – Zenodoros' high priesthood referred to the temple at Baalbek – and several areas to the east, stretching out towards the desert south of Damascus. There were four sections: Gaulanitis, the upper waters of the Jordan and the Golan Heights, Batanaea to the east, Trachonitis, the modern Leja, the most difficult area, and Auranitis, the modern Hauran or Jebel Druze, an area of upland which is relatively fertile. Much of this was difficult territory. Trachonitis, for example, was largely composed of black basalt and solidified lava, but with pockets of fertile land, and many hollows and caves. It is likely that it was only partly under Zenodoros' control, for he seems to have had only minimal military power at his command. In the early 20s it was the home of gangs of robbers whose target was the rich oasis of Damascus to the north. The city was in fact an old enemy of the Ituraean dynasty, whose members had repeatedly tried to gain possession of the city and its land. Zenodoros, unable to suppress the bandits – or maybe unwilling – nonetheless taxed them, thereby being complicit in their work.[4]

This region, despite its difficulty and relative poverty, had been a region of competition between the surrounding kingdoms. At one time much of it had been under Nabataean control, and the Gaulanitis region had been in Alexander Iannai's Judaean kingdom until it was dismembered by Pompey. It was probably Pompey who handed over these lands to the Ituraeans, who had been settling in them for some time earlier. This, of course, did not prevent their former rulers itching to reclaim them.

The people of Damascus initiated a process of complaint which illustrates how such problems in Syria were dealt with. When the raids became too menacing, or successful, the Damascenes complained to the governor Varro (probably M. Licinius Varro Murena), and asked that he report the problem to Augustus.[5] It is thus evident that in matters concerning the client kings, the governor had to gain permission for action from the emperor. Varro sent the report, and Augustus gave instructions 'to exterminate the bandits', as Josephus says. Varro did so 'and deprived Zenodoros of his tenure', which must have been part of the instructions from Augustus. From later events it is evident that the territories he lost control of were Trachonitis, Batanaea, and Auranitis.[6]

In fact Zenodoros had been blamed by the Damascenes for the raids in the first place. Since he was the tax collector, he had turned a blind eye to the means by which money to pay the taxes was raised. But their behaviour had become so disruptive as to call for an armed Roman expedition into his territory, which implies that they were numerous and dangerous. Rather surprisingly, Zenodoros was allowed to remain in office, only being deprived of the lands to the east, Batanaea, Trachonitis, and Auranitis. After some delay, perhaps a year, during which the lands were no doubt under the control of the Roman army, they were handed on to Herod of Judaea.[7]

This may well have been in part the result of Herod's willingness to participate in Aelius Gallus' Arabian expedition a year or two earlier. He had proved himself reliable as a Roman client, and an efficient ruler of a difficult kingdom. He was more likely than Zenodoros to be able to control the rough lands he was now given, since he was better armed, and was an experienced commander. The task of suppressing the bandits was still unfinished when the Roman forces pulled out.

The Syrian governor also had the more difficult problem of the Parthians to cope with. It was only a little over a decade since Parthian armies had arrived in southern Syria to capitalize on anti-Roman sentiment in both Ituraea and Judaea. This invasion had been provoked in part by continued difficulties for the Romans in Syria. The sooner the Roman forces were re-concentrated in the north, facing Parthia, the safer the empire would be.

Zenodoros did not meekly accept the loss of his lands but went off the Rome to complain, blaming Herod. He apparently got nowhere.[8] Herod meanwhile visited Augustus' colleague M. Vipsanius Agrippa at Mitylene in Lesbos. He was followed there by a delegation from Gadara, a Greek city across the Jordan, who complained of Herod's rule. Agrippa sent them on to Herod in chains. (He let them go, no doubt hoping thereby to disprove their charges of tyranny.[9]) But neither Zenodoros nor the Gadarenes gave up. When Augustus visited Syria in 20 both of them were still complaining, and this time they joined forces. But the Gadarenes were again rejected, and Zenodoros died suddenly about this time. As a result his tetrarchy was dismantled, and Herod was given more of it, so that he now ruled almost all the settled lands from the Jordan eastwards, between the Nabataeans and Damascus.[10] (Gadara was not forgotten and when Herod died it was transferred to the province.)

These transfers of territory between kings were an obvious sign that nothing was politically permanent. The Ituraean kingdom was split into several parts, one of which went to Herod, another was formed into a new tetrarchy centred on the city of Abila in the Anti-Lebanon; the fate of the rest is not known after 20 BC, but the lands in the Bekaa Valley were still being transferred between kings seventy years later so presumably some princeling ruled them after Zenodoros' death.[11]

The surviving principality was small. Some of the lands were taken for the new Roman colony of Berytus, where a large number of Latin-speaking discharged soldiers had been planted. In 15 BC the *colonia*'s territory had been expanded to take in part of the Bekaa, including the temple town of Baalbek-Heliopolis. At some time also the boundaries of Tyre, Sidon and Damascus were expanded so that they took in large parts of Ituraea. This was therefore Augustus' own solution to the Ituraean problem – divide and rule. Not all was taken, however, for the city of Chalkis was the seat of the little principality which lasted for another century or so.

Augustus was therefore busy during his visit to Syria. He concluded a peace with Parthia, dressing it up as a victory because he recovered the legionary standards lost years before. His visit also coincided with royal deaths in Ituraea (Zenodoros) and in Kommagene, where King Mithradates II died soon after killing one of his sons. As a result that son's own son became the new king, Mithradates III, no doubt installed by Augustus who was on the spot. Augustus also arranged his marriage with Iotape, the daughter of the Atropatenian king (who also died in that year). Then, when he reached central Syria, Augustus organized the restoration of the monarchy in Emesa, in the person of Iamblichos II, son of the king he himself had executed a decade earlier.[12]

This was an imperial progress indeed. Augustus had begun at Samos by making peace with the Kushite kingdom, after what he later pronounced to be a successful war, and in Syria he made peace with the great Parthian kingdom. Then he removed or enthroned kings and princes and disposed of their territories from Kommagene to Judaea. Furthermore this turned out to be a successful and relatively stable new system. Of the kings he emplaced or recognized in this tour, Mithradates of Kommagene ruled for two, or maybe three decades; Iamblichos II of Emesa reigned until about AD 5; Herod lasted until 4 BC.

The Nabataean kingdom was ignored in all this, but had developed a grievance against Herod, whose acquisition of Auranitis had stopped a deal which had been arranged between King Obodas III and Zenodoros. Obodas had apparently paid five hundred talents for the region, but it was Herod who had received the grant from Augustus.[13] The two transactions showed a much clearer understanding of power by Herod; simply to buy such a territory was very naive of Obodas. The result was continuation of the old hostility between the two kingdoms.

Whether because of this, or simply as good politics, Herod devoted time and above all resources to polishing his relations with the Roman rulers. Within Palestine he built a new temple at Jerusalem for his Jewish subjects and a new city on the site of Strato's Tower, calling it Caesarea after Augustus. In his new province at Panias, at the source of the Jordan, he built another temple for Augustus. Samaria was expanded, 6,000 settlers were planted there, another temple to Augustus built, and the city was renamed Sebaste in honour of the emperor, and as an inland twin for Caesarea. Fortresses at Masada, at Herodeion, and other places fastened his grip on the kingdom, and new or expanded palaces, often at the sites of earlier Hasmonaean buildings, emphasized his power and wealth. He also 'gave' buildings to many cities in Syria and around the Aegean, paying court to the great Seleukid cities in North Syria and the ancestral cities of Hellenic culture in Greece.

All this was paid for out of the taxation he extracted from the population of his kingdom. Much was spent within the kingdom, but much also went on embellishing outside cities. He pointed out in a speech in 18 BC that this was a period of great prosperity and that the buildings in Palestine were for the benefit of the people as a whole – and that he was about to begin on the Jerusalem temple. But he was also, of course, glorifying himself, and his building program was so extensive that one must assume that he gained much personal satisfaction from it. As with all competent politicians, these actions encompassed several motivations and had several purposes.

His earliest buildings were mainly fortifications in Judaea, which is reasonable since he had had to fight hard to gain his kingdom, and in the 30s threats were everywhere. But the very first example was not military and not even in Judaea, and even before he was king, but was at Rhodes, where he stopped on his way to Rome in 40 BC. He paid there to restore damage caused by a fire, and later he paid for a temple to Pythian Apollo as well. Restoration of damage was also one of the motivations for his work in Judaea, following the great earthquake of 31 BC. Much of Herod's early building was therefore of military necessity or simply repair work. But his new city at Caesarea was in the great tradition of the cities founded by Hellenistic kings, and he was quick to contribute to Octavian's celebratory city of Nikopolis next to the battle site of Actium.[14]

So a second strand in Herod's motivation was to compliment Augustus and Rome. This, given the consistent support he received, was certainly sensible. The new Caesarea began with a smaller area around the harbour, which was called Sebastos and which contained a temple to Augustus – and 'Sebastos' was the Greek version of Augustus; Samaria became Sebaste. Herod was expressing his gratitude in the most permanent way he could imagine, given that it was politically impossible, for religious reasons, for him to do this work inside Judaea.

The dispute between Herod and Obodas of Nabataea over Auranitis continued for several years, becoming gradually worse. The crisis which developed provides much information concerning Roman expectations of their client kings, but also the awkward nature of Roman decision-making where decisions could be appealed and problems continued almost indefinitely. Some of the kings had not fully appreciated the delicate situation they were in. The whole organization of emperor and governor and kings and ministers was liable to constant misunderstanding and intrigue.

Obodas had been foiled over Auranitis in 23 BC, when Herod had been given that land along with Trachonitis, whose banditry-prone inhabitants he was expected to control and discipline. Auranitis was the richest of these regions and had been Nabataean earlier in the century. Certainly Obodas felt he had a claim to it. When he was unable to make that claim good, he did not abandon the intention, though for some years was unable to pursue it.

Strabo describes a Nabataean government system in which a minister – referred to as his 'brother' – acted in the king's name.[15] It seems probable Strabo was generalizing from the peculiar circumstances of Obodas' reign, for such an institution is not heard of before or after, though admittedly the sources are poor. Earlier Nabataean kings had led their armies in battle, and later kings, including Obodas' immediate successor, show no signs of hiding behind a minister. So it is best to assume that Obodas, for whatever reasons, was an inactive king – 'inactive and sluggish by nature', as Josephus says, content to allow Syllaeus to operate for him.[16] It had been Syllaeus who had gone to South Arabia with Aelius Gallus, and in the crisis which developed between Nabataea and Herod, it was Syllaeus who was the authority on the Nabataean side. And later it was Syllaeus who went to Rome, whereas from Judaea it was Herod himself who made that journey.

Syllaeus was powerful and a notable enough man to be able to sue for the hand of Herod's sister Salome. She had been married twice already, and both husbands had fallen foul of Herod and been executed; she was by this time (about 16 BC) almost 50 years old. Salome was apparently keen on the match, perhaps to get away from Herod, but he refused to allow it when Syllaeus refused to be circumcized.[17] As a result of this episode Syllaeus now seems to have become as keen as Obodas in making trouble for Herod, and considerably more effective.

Herod paid much attention to maintaining his Roman contacts. Herod's Roman connections were a major obstacle, however. He visited Agrippa at Lesbos in 16 (and Agrippa returned the visit next year). In 14 he joined Agrippa on a campaign into the Black Sea which must have taken some months, and he saw him again next year as Agrippa prepared to return to Rome. Then in 12 Herod went to Rome again. During this trip the Trachonites rose in rebellion, persuaded to do so by a rumour that Herod was dead. His commanders successfully suppressed the rising, but forty of the diehard survivors escaped from their vengeance into Nabataean territory. Syllaeus installed them at a place called Rhaepta and allowed them to raid back into their homeland, and into the lands of the Decapolis cities and into Judaea. They had thereby returned to their old occupation.

Herod's reaction to this reveals the limits of his powers of action. He first attended to the brigands' homes in Trachonitis. He 'surrounded' the region, according to Josephus, presumably so that any brigands should not escape, as the first group had. Those who were found and caught were killed. These would include any members of the insurgents' families left behind, and those men became still more embittered and increased the range and ferocity of their raids.[18]

His remaining enemies being outside his borders, and Syllaeus refusing to surrender the refugee raiders, Herod approached the governor of Syria, C. Sentius Saturninus. (Saturninus took up the post in 10 BC, which puts these actions into the years 10 and 9 BC.) Herod then increased the pressure on Syllaeus by demanding the repayment of a loan of sixty talents which he had made to the Nabataean earlier. The issues of the loan and the bandits became mixed together, and Saturninus and his procurator came to investigate. The Roman purpose was to restrain both men and to restore peace, or at least to reduce the violence to a level at which it could be ignored. Agreement was reached on the basis that Syllaeus would repay the loan and that each kingdom would expel the exiles of the other. Josephus disingenuously claims that no refugee Arabs were found in Judaea.

Syllaeus, like Zenodoros before him, appealed against this decision to Augustus. He went in person to Rome before the time limit for the agreement expired, so avoiding compliance. This move instantly stopped all proceedings, in theory, but Herod appealed to Saturninus again, and was given permission to recover his debts from defaulters. Whether Saturninus realized what Herod intended is perhaps unlikely, for Herod seems to have deliberately couched his request as if he was merely recovering a few debts. Instead he took an army into Nabataea, attacked and captured Rhaepta, demolished it, and beat off a relieving force of the Nabataean army. In order to control Trachonitis, Herod now transported 3,000 Idumaeans to the region. Saturninus investigated all this, and approved.[19]

Syllaeus in Rome told his story to Augustus, distorting and exaggerating in fine style – 'as was natural', so Josephus revealingly explains. Augustus, utterly taken in, wrote a stinging rebuke to Herod. Syllaeus reported his success to his homeland, with the result that the brigands began their raids again; another rebellion, targeting the Idumaean settlers, began in Trachonitis, and the debts and rents owed to Herod and other Judaeans were not paid. Herod was surely annoyed at the misrepresentation of his actions, especially after Saturninus' approval. It was also a moment of danger, since Augustus was clearly angry, and apparently would not listen to opposing views.

Syllaeus' moment of triumph was brief. Obodas died while he was still in Rome. Syllaeus had apparently hoped for the succession himself, but was foiled by the fact that he was in Rome at the time, and by the action of one of Obodas' relatives, a man called Aeneas, who proclaimed himself king, taking the throne name of Aretas (IV). Abruptly Augustus' anger switched to Nabataea, since Aretas' self-proclamation was a defiance of the emperor's rights of naming successors. Aretas, however, knew what he was doing. Rich gifts for Augustus reached Rome, as did assurances that all was calm, and detailed accusations of a variety of crimes said to have been committed by Syllaeus.

Syllaeus rushed back to Nabataea where he organized some murders and attempted a plot to assassinate Herod. Clearly he had considerable local power. But Herod had sent an envoy, Nikolas of Damascus, to Augustus to explain his own actions, and he did this by accusing Syllaeus. Syllaeus' actions, reported by Saturninus, confirmed this negative impression. Probably because he had had time to reflect, Augustus accepted those explanations. The reports from Saturninus will have helped. And Aretas' gifts were really a request for recognition in due form. Augustus' wrath switched again, and Syllaeus was the one who suffered. He went back to Rome to make his own explanations, and failed. After being detained for a time, he was executed.[20]

The problem of Trachonitis remained. Herod contacted a group of Babylonians who had arrived at Antioch, as political refugees from the Parthians. They were a regiment of 500 mounted archers, plus 100 relatives (and presumably, though they are not mentioned, their families) led by a Babylonian Jew called Zamaris. Saturninus had welcomed them and placed some land at their disposal near Daphne; Herod now offered them a site in Batanaea, a 'city' to live in, and tax-free status. Their task was not to occupy Trachonitis, but to guard against any banditry emanating from it.[21] It would seem that Herod had almost given up on controlling Trachonitis.

This story reveals much about the relationship of the kings and the emperor. Herod was only able to act with the governor's approval, but the foiled opponent swiftly went over the governor's head to complain to the emperor. He, clearly lacking any detailed or neutral testimony, reached a conclusion all too quickly. The items which annoyed him were, first, that Herod had conducted a military operation outside his kingdom without the emperor's permission (though he had that of the governor, who clearly did know the facts of the case), and second, that the accession of a new king in Nabataea did not have his prior approval. That is, and this was clearly directed at Herod as well, the emperor reserved to himself the appointment of a new king, just as he did that of a governor. But the real problem, which Augustus failed to appreciate, was that these decisions were his and his alone, and he was being too easily swayed by an eloquent personal appeal. This was no way to run an empire. If Augustus operated in such a haphazard way, what disasters awaited under inexperienced and even more wayward and incompetent emperors?

Herod's visits to Rome were mainly concerned with the issue which had detonated Augustus' anger over Nabataea – the succession in Judaea. Herod, even more than Aretas, appreciated fully that he would need to have Augustus' agreement if clear and suitable arrangements were to be remade for the Judaean kingdom. (Aretas clearly got Augustus' approval, and ruled for nearly half a century.[22]) Herod was over 60 years old at the time of his last trip to Rome and could not expect to live much longer, but his methods of controlling his family and arranging the succession were disruptive in the extreme, and so the question of the succession arose repeatedly.

He had been married to ten women, who between them had fifteen children, ten of them sons. By 12 BC, when he visited Rome expressly to discuss the succession, one wife had been executed and two divorced (though one of these had returned). So there was a flock of possible heirs to choose from – plus his brother, several nephews, and even grandsons and grandnephews. Herod had quarrelled at one time or another with virtually all of these people, punishing and detaining them. Part of his purpose, of course, had been to keep everyone guessing as to his real intentions.

But it was not Herod's own intentions which were the main element in the decision on the succession; it was Augustus who would decide everything. This had been the burden of his anger in 9 BC when Aretas had seized power in Nabataea; it had been the lesson learned by many in 20 when he came through Syria disposing of kingdoms on every hand. Herod was therefore always careful to include Augustus' wishes in each successive will he made, and in the changes to those wills, but he could never be sure that Augustus would pay any attention to the latest will when he died.

When the elder Pliny listed the kingdoms and tetrarchies in Syria in the AD 70s, he had two lists before him; one was from Augustus' time in which the tetrarchies were named, the other was more recent and included many of the changes more recently made – such as the transformation of Ptolemais-Ake into a Roman colony by Claudius, and Caesarea into a colony by Vespasian. In this list the only tetrarchies he mentions were in northern Palestine, ruled at that time by the descendants of Herod.[23] Most of the tetrarchies of Augustus' time, that is to say, had disappeared by the 70s, annexed into the Syrian province when the various kings had died. This is rarely noted in the sources, but Pliny's lists are evidence, in a negative sense, for their disappearance, and this process had been going on ever since Augustus' tour in 20. Most were small and weak, and our sources' attention is directed elsewhere. This was the possibility, annexation, which Herod had to counter. Augustus was fully capable of extinguishing the Judaean kingdom with an offhand decision, such as that Herod suffered when Syllaeus was being persuasive in Rome. As king he obviously wanted his work to continue after his death. He had to persuade Augustus that this was worth doing.

In fact it is likely that Augustus was never in any doubt that some sort of monarchic system should continue in Judaea. Always amenable to Herod's views, he accepted each will as it turned up, though he reserved to himself the final decision, and the ease with which he accepted each version might be interpreted as indifference, or as a sign that he did not particularly care what Herod's wishes were, because he would make the decision himself. The will Herod presented during his visit to Rome in 12 was a result of Augustus' agreement that he could name his own successor, a mark of confidence which the events of the next years may well have dented. Herod named his eldest son Antipater as his heir, and his next sons, Alexander and Aristoboulos, as Antipater's heirs, or perhaps his colleagues. Augustus accepted this, fully aware that this gave him the ultimate decision.[24]

Over the next eight years Herod changed these arrangements four times. During that time all three of the sons named in the will of 12 BC were executed, while a fourth died in Rome. In the end his final will named Archelaos, his son by the Samaritan Malthake, as his prime successor; Archelaos' brother Antipas and his half-brother Philippos were named as tetrarchs. Herod would probably have changed these provisions had he lived longer. (He had produced three versions in the previous eighteen months.) Archelaos was his eldest surviving son, and Antipas and Philippos were the next eldest and, until their killings, the elder sons had been named in age order as well. Herod clearly had a very strong heredity-impulse in him.[25]

When he died, therefore, in 4 BC – in agony as his enemies assumed and hoped – this was the will Augustus based his decision on. It included handsome bequests to Augustus himself and to his wife Livia, while Herod's sister Salome, one of the more sensible members of the family, was bequeathed three cities. The last will was recited in public. Archelaos took up authority as king, and Antipas and Philippos were allocated Galilee and the northern regions respectively.[26]

Archelaos in fact did the same as Aretas had five years before; he seized power when the king died, though in this case Augustus had known he was named as Herod's heir. Given the turbulence of Judaea, Archelaos' action made sense. But then everyone headed for Rome where they argued for changes and petitioned for themselves, and generally made a great fuss. Augustus got written complaints and suggestions from most of them, and a meeting of the Senate was convened to hear the oral arguments.

With all the disputants in Rome, the absence of all authority in Judaea stimulated riots. There had been at least one celebratory riot in Jerusalem soon after Herod's death; now there were others, in Jerusalem and in the countryside. The initial targets seem to have been Herod's palaces, symbols of his tax-greed and his oppression; that at Jericho was burned by a group from the Peraia led by a royal slave; another at Betharampha was also burned; the Jerusalem palace was attacked; and risings developed in Idumaea and Galilee. In effect the whole country was in turmoil, and in places this took on a clear anti-Roman aspect.

It was hardly surprising. Herod's rule had been brutal and greedy, and his death brought only relief. Responsibility for controlling events devolved upon the Syrian governor, P. Quinctilius Varus, who was already familiar with Judaea and the problems of the Herodian family. Presumably he had been taken by surprise by the speed with which authority collapsed in the south, but he was hundreds of kilometres away and could not react quickly. He had to bring an army from northern Syria to deal with the problem. He had already sent one legion into Palestine, and now he brought two more, with auxiliary cavalry, and the Syrian client kings also provided forces. This last contribution was substantial; the *colonia* at Berytus alone provided 1,500 men, and Aretas contributed substantially. Quite probably half of Varus' force was Syrian.

Varus adopted the usual brutal Roman methods. The first hostile place he came to was Sepphoris in Galilee; he enslaved the inhabitants and burned the city. He moved to Samaria-Sebaste. Here there had been no revolt and the city survived unharmed. The message was clear: rebels would be punished, loyalists were safe. Other places were plundered on the march – Josephus blames the 'Arabs', that is the Nabataeans, getting their own back for earlier Herodian insults. Jerusalem was occupied. The citizens laid the blame for trouble in the city entirely on pilgrims from elsewhere, in the city for the Passover. Varus, who cannot have believed this excuse, but also cannot have relished fighting in the city, accepted this, but he collected many rebels, and crucified 2,000 of them; some of Herod's relatives in Idumaea were also accused of rebellion and were sent off to Rome. Augustus had them executed.[27]

Varus' War lasted ten weeks. It, and the squabbling people in Rome, surely warned Augustus clearly as to the difficulty of ruling Judaea. A new delegation arrived, asking for 'autonomy', which presumably meant the abolition of the monarchy but would be a first step to independence for some.[28] Gadara, which had complained about Herod's rule two decades before, was now released, as was its neighbour Hippos. Augustus also detached Gaza, perhaps for strategic reasons, perhaps to reward Aretas and open up the port for Nabataean trade. Before the fighting in Judaea was over Augustus had made his decisions. He would implement most of the terms of Herod's will, so Archelaos, Antipas, and Philippos were confirmed in their positions, as was Salome in her cities. The three Greek cities were transferred to the Syrian province, and Aretas of the Nabataeans received a part of the Peraia which Herod had taken years before. Archelaos was to be ethnarch, not king.[29]

If anyone in Judaea thought they lived in an independent kingdom, these events surely persuaded them otherwise. Varus' expedition was yet another Roman conquest, and then Augustus broke up the kingdom into half a dozen pieces, in the same way as Pompey had sixty years before. The rebellion, and Varus' War, had contradictory results in the minds of Jews and Romans. The Jews could argue that their rebellion persuaded the Roman to leave them under Jewish rule. One option for Augustus, when Herod died and when the Varus' War was finished, had been to annex the whole kingdom to the province. The rebellion had, it could have been argued, deterred Augustus from doing this. This was a damaging and dangerous thought, which, along with rosy memories of the original Maccabean rebellion in the 160s, could all too easily support the idea that a new rebellion would retain Judaean freedom. At the same time the extent of the rebellion could help the Romans justify the continuation of the client monarchy, which, to Rome, was a useful device controlling a difficult area at second hand. But only if the rulers could do this were they useful.

Chapter 11

Kings and Governors

The eastern part of the Roman Empire was subjected to repeated supervisory visits by members of the imperial ruling family for almost fifty years after Augustus' conquest in 31–30 BC. Agrippa was at Mitylene on Lesbos between 23 and 21 BC, Augustus at Samos and in Syria in 21–19 BC, and Agrippa returned for 17–13 BC. The governors of Syria were thus under the imperial eye for long periods – indeed, it seems that Agrippa acted as Syrian governor himself, using his own legates for the detailed provincial work.[1] After Agrippa's death in 12 BC Augustus was largely pinned down in Rome, but after ten years he had adult heirs who were capable, so he thought, of learning the governing ropes.

In 1 BC Augustus' grandson Gaius Caesar (his adopted son, Agrippa's natural son) went to the east. This is a notoriously difficult episode to understand and, as it happens, the Syrian section is the worst. Gaius arrived in Syria in 1 BC and entered on his consulship *in absentia* in the province two years later. He had already visited Greece, the Aegean, and Egypt. We know nothing of Gaius' activities in Egypt, and in Syria he was occupied with Parthian negotiations, which ended with a meeting on an island in the Euphrates and a modicum of agreement.[2]

During this visit Gaius conducted a campaign in Arabia; exactly where is never stated, though Pliny mentioned it in connection with Aelius Gallus' exploits in South Arabia. Modern conjecture has brought Gaius to the Gulf of Aqaba, or into Nabataea (where one theory is that the kingdom's autonomy was restored by him after an equally conjectural annexation).[3] The term 'Arabia' is never defined. The Nabataean kingdom later became the province of Arabia, but in Gaius' time the term was much looser. It is possible that Gaius' 'Arabian expedition' was conducted either to support or to discipline King Aretas after his unauthorized succession several years before, but there is also a fragmentary notice in Dio Cassius, which mentions trouble in Egypt which was suppressed by a tribune of the praetorian guard.[4] This man was surely part of Gaius' entourage, but, other than that, the connection as well as the location of the problem is unknown.

It is curious that Josephus has nothing on any of this. Aretas IV's army had been used in Judaea in 4 BC by Varus in suppressing the risings and had been especially unpleasant, so that Varus in suppressing the risings had dismissed them early to help calm things down.[5] If Aretas had been deposed in 3

BC or had been the object of a Roman attack in AD 1, it seems probable that Josephus would have noted it. Further, if Gaius had been busy in Nabataea he would also have been in Palestine, and this would have been mentioned by Josephus. The conclusion must be that Gaius was nowhere near Palestine, and that must also rule out a campaign against Aretas.

Archelaos was unpopular in Judaea. He imitated his father in expensive building and oppression, but without his father's ability and panache. He offended the priests by his marriage to Glaphyra, who was the widow of Alexander his half-brother, though she died soon after the wedding. After nine years of his rule a group of Jewish and Samaritan nobles went to Rome to complain to Augustus. Archelaos was then summoned to Rome, interrogated, and, the charges being held to be proved, was deposed and exiled to Vienna in Gallia Narbonensis.[6] The question of what to do with Judaea had now returned.

The possibilities were as before: award Archelaos' kingdom as a whole to another of Herod's relatives, perhaps Antipas or Philippos; divide it between them or with others; or annex it to the province. The decision this time was annexation, in a modified form. Judaea was to become a sub-province of Syria, governed by a prefect of equestrian rank. In this it resembled Egypt, but more to the point, it also resembled other annexed kingdoms, such as Noricum, and later Mauretania and Thrace. It was a neat solution, for the Syrian governor would scarcely be able to attend in detail to Judaea from Antioch, which had to be his main residence in view of his responsibility to watch Parthia. In addition Judaea was being kept separate in the Roman system from the rest of Syria, which may have been a sop to Judaean opinion.

The transfer went off relatively peacefully. The prospect of a census caused apprehension, but the high priest Joazar, committed to cooperation with Rome, calmed things down.[7] The danger was demonstrated in Ituraea where a revolt, possibly occasioned by the threat of this census, occurred just at this time.[8] However at about the same time a new sect of irreconcilables, the Zealots, was founded by Judas of Galilee, one of the leaders of the risings which followed Herod's death.[9] This group later caused much trouble.

Archelaos' property was transferred to the emperor and, in AD 10 when Herod's sister Salome died, her inheritance went to the emperor or to the Empress Livia.[10] Meanwhile Philippos and Antipas were ruling their tetrarchies with considerable success. They both took after their father in their building activities, each founding cities. Philippos was the more considerate ruler, but Antipas had a reputation for deviousness. Philippos' tetrarchy included the difficult Trachonitis; it is curious, and perhaps to his credit, that the trouble Herod had in that area did not, so far as we know, recur, though

Philippos had to compel the obedience to the Babylonians Herod had settled there – and he revoked their tax-free status.[11]

Antipas was married to the daughter of Aretas IV; Archelaos married Glaphyra, the daughter of the Cappadocian king, who was earlier married to his half-brother Alexander and then to King Juba of Mauretania. Even earlier, Augustus had promoted the marriage of Mithradates III of Kommagene and Iotape of Atropatene.[12] This linkage between the several royal families was clearly Augustus' preferred policy, though keeping such families separate also had its Roman advocates. The expedition led by Varus into Judaea in 4 BC had been accompanied by a large force contributed by these kings.[13] If these kings became too closely related and too friendly, their power might become too great, even for the four Roman legions in Syria. This was another matter for the Syrian governors to watch and worry about.

These royal marriages, like the succession, required imperial approval, though for the Judaean royal house, as Syllaeus had discovered, there was another obstacle, in the requirement that the spouse conform to Judaism. This for a time restricted Judaean marriage alliances to the importation of foreign women and the export of Herodian daughters. The row which accompanied Archelaos' marriage with his brother's widow may have been enough to deter other alliances. Antipas married the daughter of Aretas IV, but, after a long marriage he secured a replacement in Herodias, the daughter of his half-brother Aristoboulos. The Nabataean princess, warned of Antipas' intentions, returned speedily to her father; bad blood between Antipas and Aretas followed. The Herodian family, in fact, tended towards intermarriage for another generation.[14]

The marriage of Mithradates III and Iotape produced a son and two daughters, one of whom married the next king of Emesa, Samsigeramos II, the son of Iamblichos II, who had been put on the throne by Augustus in the same year as her father. This marriage probably took place between 5 BC (though this seems too early) and AD 5, quite possibly at about the time Samsigeramos succeeded to the kingship. This is also about the time Mithradates was succeeded by his own son Antiochos III.[15] All these changes were necessarily sanctioned by Augustus.

These kingdoms were safe enough under Augustus, who perhaps enjoyed manipulating them. Tiberius was less indulgent. In Asia Minor he suppressed the Cappadocian kingdom and deposed one of the Thracian kings. In AD 17 Antiochos III of Kommagene died and conflict followed within the kingdom between rich and poor, who both sent deputations to Rome to discuss the future. As in Judaea a decade earlier, the wealthy wanted annexation to Rome and the abolition of the monarchy; the poorer classes wanted the monarchy to continue. The rich got their wish.[16]

Imperial tinkering with the eastern kingdoms became a tradition. When Tiberius died in 37, his successor Gaius Caligula made more changes. In the south the tetrarch Philippos died in 33 or 34. His kingdom was annexed, but put into suspense until a successor could be found. (Philippos had no children.) The revenues of the tetrarchy were held separately from those of the province, so the options were kept open. The governor of Syria, L. Pomponius Flaccus, died not long before Philippos, and Tiberius did not appoint a successor for about a year.[17] The legate of one of the Syrian legions acted as governor in the meantime, but inevitably his authority was less. These non-decisions by the emperor no doubt contributed to the crises which developed in the next few years.

The Parthian king provoked a crisis in Armenia which threatened to grow into a full-scale war, though in the event both sides were fairly restrained, only using proxy forces in the fighting. Tiberius was thus compelled at last to appoint a new Syrian governor, choosing the capable L. Vitellius, consul the year before.[18] He arrived in Syria to discover that the Parthian-Armenian crisis was accompanied by other crises in Palestine. The conjunction of all this helps to explain his actions. In the south the insult Antipas had given Aretas by repudiating his daughter developed about this time into actual fighting.[19] Aretas had waited several years to mount his revenge attack, and the absence of a governor and his successor's preoccupation with Parthia must have seemed his last opportunity – for he was old, having been king for well over forty years.

Vitellius had also to deal with a problem within Palestine. The prefect of Palestine, Pontius Pilate, had got into a fight with a group of Samaritans, who were gathering on their holy mountain, Mount Gerizim. This sort of group activity was always seen as a threat by Roman governors and Pilate dispersed the crowd by force and executed the leaders. The Samaritans complained. Vitellius, faced with Parthian troubles, chose to remove Pilate – he had been in office for ten years, after all, and had accumulated other local antagonisms, though his later reputation in Rome was benign – and so conciliated the complainants.[20]

Then Vitellius had to deal with the quarrel between Antipas and Aretas. Aretas had raided into Antipas' lands in the Peraia, and Antipas' troops were beaten in a battle near Gamala. He complained to Tiberius, who now sent an order to Vitellius to punish Aretas.[21] There must surely be no doubt that they both feared that the Parthians were involved in all this. Tiberius had subsidized his allies in the war in Armenia; the Parthian King Artabanos could obviously do the same in Palestine. The suspicion must be that the recipient of Parthian largesse, if there was one, was Aretas, but it could also be that Antipas had been similarly approached. His nephew Agrippa did in fact make that accusation against him a year or so later.

Vitellius came south with two legions, auxiliaries, and Syrian militia troops during a lull in the Parthian problem. He was intercepted at Ptolemais by a group of Judaean nobles with the request that he not display his military standards on the march through Judaea. He agreed and went further, going to Jerusalem to offer sacrifice, and there he announced a reduction in taxation. He had already handed over control of the high priestly vestments to the temple and had changed the high priest there.[22] All this is clearly a deliberate policy of appeasement of Judaean sensibilities. Given that there is no reason for him to be personally sympathetic to Judaea or Judaism, the best explanation is that he was concerned to prevent trouble while the Parthian problem was still active.

The campaign against Aretas was stopped when news arrived of Tiberius' death. Pausing only to administer the loyalty oath to the Judaeans, Vitellius returned to the north with his forces and soon afterwards he was able to meet with Artabanos at the Euphrates, each man backed by his army. A peace of sorts was arranged. Vitellius had to keep one ear cocked for news from Rome, where the new emperor Gaius might not approve of his actions; Artabanos had just recovered his throne after a brief expulsion, and his kingdom was in an uproar behind him. Vitellius had made certain that there would be no trouble in the south during all this by having Antipas accompany him to the meeting. Antipas no doubt harboured angry feelings at his defeat by Aretas and might well have taken the first opportunity to retaliate. Instead he had to host an elaborate dinner for Vitellius and Artabanos in a tent by the river. Then he spitefully reported the details of the meeting to Rome before Vitellius could do so, a deed which both annoyed Vitellius and raised bureaucratic eyebrows in Rome.[23]

The Parthian crisis, at least in its most threatening aspects, ended with the conference by the Euphrates. By that time the new emperor was firmly in power, and he brought to the throne the friendly relations he had earlier developed with eastern pretenders. He released Agrippa of Judaea from the jail to which Tiberius had consigned him and sent him back to Palestine with the present of his uncle Philippos' old tetrarchy of Panias, Trachonitis, Batanaea, and Auranitis. At some time, perhaps right away, the former territory of Lysanias of Abilene was added to his lands and he was given the title of king.[24]

This is usually described in personal terms, as a result of Agrippa's friendship with Gaius before Tiberius died, but it cannot be separated from recent events in Syria. At the same time or shortly after, but clearly as part of the same policy, the old kingdom of Kommagene was revived, and the son of the previous king, Antiochos IV, now adult and capable, and living in Rome, was installed as king.[25] This took place in 38, at about the time King Artabanos of the Parthians died. The policy of annexation was thus abandoned in favour of a return to the employment of client kings who could better deal with local problems. In Kommagene it was also a defensive measure, since Antiochos was now bound even more closely than his father to the Roman interest and could be regarded as a loyal subject in the face of the Parthian problems which roiled just across Kommagene's eastern border.

The installation of Agrippa in Philippos' old tetrarchy served the same purpose. Indeed Agrippa was so loyal to Rome (and its pleasures) that he could not bring himself to leave the city for his new kingdom for a year and then went back to Rome after only a short visit. But his installation meant there was now a firmer grip on a difficult region, and the responsibilities of the Syrian governor and his soldiers were somewhat reduced; the troops oc-cupying the area could be returned to their units in the north.

Agrippa's promotion to king made his sister Herodias jealous and she nagged her husband Antipas to ask for the same status. When he went to Rome to make the request, Agrippa sent a letter to Gaius accusing Antipas of three anti-Roman crimes: participation with Sejanus in a sedition a decade earlier, conspiracy on behalf of Parthia (and so anti-Roman), and building up an arsenal said to contain equipment sufficient for 70,000 heavy infantry-men. Agrippa's motivation in this is never explained. He received a handsome reward but he could not have counted on this beforehand, nor did he perhaps expect it. When Gaius interrogated Antipas at their meeting at Baiae on the Bay of Naples, he concentrated only on what could be proved, which was the stockpile of weaponry. The old story of Sejanus was hardly relevant to the present situation (which rather tends to support its truth) and the accusation of plotting with Parthia was probably unprovable. But it was only two years since a near-war with Parthia and only three or four since the mutual raiding between Antipas and Aretas. Gaius was already haunted by the threat of plots against him, and a client king with a large stock of weapons could only be seen as a threat. Yet Antipas' punishment was the same as his brother's over three decades earlier: exile in Gaul (or perhaps Spain), in no doubt comfortable circumstances.[26] It looks very much as if Gaius was convinced about the arms, but not of their quantity nor of their purpose. Antipas' guilt seems very likely.

Agrippa's subsequent visit to Rome brought him the reward of Antipas' Palestinian lands, Galilee and the Peraia, to add to those he already ruled. He was present in the city when Gaius was assassinated and helped to hoist Claudius onto the imperial throne. (The two men were of an age, both born in 10 BC.) The murder of Gaius came at a crucial moment for Judaea, for the emperor had plans for installing a statue of himself in the temple in Jerus-alem. This had already caused disturbances in Judaea and Agrippa had exerted himself to dissuade the emperor from the plan, with some success, though he was not the only one. Gaius' death allowed Claudius to abandon the plan, and in order to further distance the imperial administration from Judaean difficulties he expanded Agrippa's kingdom to include Judaea.[27] In only four years, Agrippa had gone from a debt-ridden playboy to being the ruler of the largest of Rome's client states.

At about this time Aretas IV of Nabataea died. He had ruled for forty-nine years and had presided over a kingdom which had become very prosperous. He was succeeded by Malichos II, probably his son. The recent problems with Nabataea may well be one reason for Claudius to resurrect the Judaean kingdom. The attack on Antipas had come when the Roman control over the former tetrarchy of Philippos was uncertain – exiles from there were in Antipas' army and had deserted to Aretas in the fighting – and when Nabataean authorities were intriguing in Damascus. The battle against Antipas also took place near Gamala, which was part of the tetrarchy of Philippos.[28] Aretas had taken advantage of the absence of a governor and of his successor's Parthian preoccupations to encroach on all the neighbours as well as Antipas. Malichos was only just seated on his throne when the Judaean kingdom suddenly reappeared. The coincidence is remarkable.

The internal situation within Judaea became steadily more difficult, even with a king in office. The affair of the emperor's statue was one of a number of incidents which show that relations between the Jews and their Greek neighbours and the Roman government were fraught. Displaying the imperial standards in Judaea had been deemed objectionable even as the soldiers were marching to fight an enemy (apparently this was the first time such objections were raised – some of the Jews were clearly actively searching out ways of being awkward and were devising methods of increasing antipathy towards Rome). The affair of the statue had been provoked by the destruction by Jews in Iamneia of an altar to the emperor. In Agrippa's first year as king in Judaea, a group of Greeks in Dor provoked riots by installing the statue of Claudius in the local synagogue. The Syrian governor P. Petronius – who had earlier shown great reluctance to install Gaius' statue in the temple – reacted swiftly enough to prevent further trouble in this instance.[29] (Petronius was probably the grandson of the Egyptian prefect of the same name of sixty years before; he was a highly successful senator.)

Petronius' successor, C. Vibius Marsus, had trouble also with Agrippa. Perhaps presuming too much on his position and his friendship with Claudius, Agrippa began to build a new city wall at Jerusalem. This was as much a cause of suspicion to the imperial authorities as Antipas' supposed arsenal, and Agrippa should have realized this. Marsus reported the matter to Claudius, who wrote to Agrippa ordering him to stop. In the circumstances Agrippa was lucky to receive only this rap over the knuckles. Claudius could not afford to remove Agrippa so soon after appointing him, but Agrippa was now clearly under suspicion. He went further into Roman black books in 44 when he hosted a meeting with five other kings at Tiberias on the Sea of Galilee. The kings were his elder brother Herod, who had been given the Ituraean remnant kingdom of Chalkis when Agrippa went to Judaea; Samsigeramos of Emesa; Antiochos IV of Kommagene, Samsigeramus' uncle and betrothed to Agrippa's niece Drusilla; Polemo of Pontos, married to Samsigeramos' niece; and Polemo's brother Kotys, king of part of Armenia. This could be claimed to be a family gathering of like-minded, probably bibulous, men, but this is not how it seemed to Marsus, who arrived unexpectedly and ordered the kings home to their kingdoms.[30]

The kings could not really have been surprised at this treatment, though Agrippa, as host, affected to be insulted. After Antipas' secret rearming, and Agrippa's city wall, the hyper-sensitivity of the Romans to any display of independence or initiative by any of these kings should have been clear. Given the recent quarrel between Antipas and Aretas of Nabataea, the absence of the Nabataean king from a meeting so close to his kingdom might provoke further suspicions. Marsus had to watch events in Armenia and Parthia closely and had already had to threaten war to deter Parthian aggression. So a meeting of these kings was especially tactless, even if it was only for dinner and drinks.

Agrippa died in the same year (and before he could commit any more *faux pas*). His son, also Agrippa (II), was judged to be too young to succeed him, and no other candidate seems to have been considered, so the kingdom once again was annexed to the province and put under a new series of procurators.[31] The northern parts of the former kingdom, however, were still regarded as being difficult for the governor to control. In 41 Chalkis had been given to Agrippa I's elder brother Herod, but he died in 48. This was the trigger for further changes. Agrippa II was now twenty-one and adjudged old enough to take charge. He was given the title of king and the tetrarchy of Philippos together with Herod's little kingdom just to the north. Over the next years Agrippa's territories were added to and parts were removed, but he continued to rule his small kingdom for the next half-century.[32] He also had the duty of appointing high priests in Jerusalem. His sisters married into the Roman administration: Berenike to M. Julius Alexander, the son of the second of the Judaean procurators (Ti. Julius Alexander, in office 46–8), and Drusilla to Antonius Felix, the next procurator but one (52–60). These connections no doubt assisted the procurators' work, but all three Jews were firmly in the Roman camp and were recognized to be so, so their influence in Judaean affairs was limited.

The procurators had an extremely difficult task, and all of them struggled to control their restless province. Josephus describes them as decreasingly just, competent only in greed and oppression, though it is in his interest to cast the blame for what resulted onto the Romans, and at Rome it did not seem that there was much of a problem. At the same time it is clear that the population was in a ferment of faction and increasingly anti-Roman. Josephus selects a series of incidents which suggests a spiral of antipathy.[33]

They were several Messiah-events, in which a self-proclaimed prophet claimed to be able to contradict nature and lead his followers into a destruction of Roman power; these were relatively easily dealt with, by brute force, just as Pilate had dealt with the Samaritans and Jesus of Nazareth. Terrorists operated among the Jewish population. They could rarely attack Romans with any success, but pro-Roman Jews were easy targets. The first terrorist group, the Zealots, was largely suppressed by the procurator Antonius Felix in the 50s; they were succeeded by the even more unpleasant and secretive *sicarii* – 'dagger men' – who could only rarely be caught. If they were captured, their fellows took hostages to gain their release.

Several events could be characterized as rebellions. Roman military power was sufficient to suppress them, but the violence involved stimulated further resentment. The Roman authorities tried their best to avoid inflaming Jewish religious sensibilities – one soldier who tore up a Torah was executed – but the heart of the matter was not religious. The aim of the anti-Roman groups – the prophets, the Messiahs, the Zealots, the *sicarii*, and increasingly much of the Jewish population – was political separation. They harked back to earlier Jewish history, when a small band of Jews took on the might of the Seleukid kingdom and won – at least that was how it was interpreted. The situation in the period after Herod's death appeared to be similar. The old Maccabee methods had required the subjugation of fellow-travelling Jews by terrorist methods; these methods, adjusted to circumstances, were being employed again, in order to eliminate the pro-Romans and so mobilize the population to rise against Roman rule.

This was a political aim, though it was (and is) often dressed up in a religious guise, which allowed the Romans, seen as clumsy infidels, to be blamed, and the Jews to claim righteousness. But the precise and immediate Jewish aim was political independence. The kingdom of Herod could have been considered as approximating to an independent state, and its restoration under Agrippa I clearly calmed down the problems which the procurators had faced before 41. Had Agrippa II been old enough to rule when his father died (or had Agrippa I lived longer), this might have deflected anti-Roman hostility, though it seems fairly unlikely.

However, independence was not the only aim, any more than it had been that of the Maccabees. The ultimate aim was empire. The Jews of Judaea looked to their brethren in other parts of the world to provide the political and manpower foundation for it. Their aim may not have been articulated quite so blatantly as this, but for an indication of the extreme Jewish thinking on the issue, one only has to read the Book of Revelation. Beneath all the nonsense of numbers and beasts, it is a vision of the destruction of Rome and its replacement by a new Jewish ruling city, a new Jerusalem. This book was written in or near Asia Minor, probably in the 70s, after the Jewish war had ended in Jewish destruction; it reflected the agony of Jews elsewhere, and the undercurrent of political ambition they all felt.

The increasing problem in Judaea does not seem to have impacted in any serious way in the rest of the empire (which suggests that Josephus' account is tendentious and exaggerated). Roman governors were assumed to be able to deal with such matters as minor rebellions without much trouble. Several groups of rebels or terrorists or opponents were sent to Rome by the procurators for investigation and/or punishment, and judgements between disputants were usually more or less fair, though in the political atmosphere in Judaea any dispute between a Jews and Greeks (or Romans) was judged locally in political terms, not on its merits. An example is the dispute which developed between Jews and 'Syrians' in Caesarea.

The argument was about the precedence of Jews or Greeks ('Syrians') in the city. It was an argument which was unending and unsolvable, because the two sides based themselves on contradictory premises, but the general unrest fed into this perpetual argument so that the two sides came to blows. A first outbreak of violence was suppressed by the city council, but a second produced greater violence and injuries. The procurator Felix used soldiers to stop the fighting, but effectively took the side of the Syrians. His soldiers looted several wealthy Jews' houses before he recalled them. Both sides sent delegations to complain to the emperor (Nero by this time) and this coincided with the replacement of Felix by the next procurator, Porcius Festus.

Josephus claims that bribes were liberally handed out by both groups in Rome and that Felix, about whose conduct the Jews complained, was protected by his brother Pallas, one of the emperor's secretaries. He also claims that the judgement about the city government was that of Beryllos, Nero's Greek secretary. (It was obviously the task of such a man to prepare his recommendations, and in this sort of dispute it is unlikely that the emperor – any emperor – took much notice of the details.) Whether all this is true is perhaps irrelevant, and bribery is so often claimed by Josephus that one comes to doubt it. The emperor's decision (whether or not it was actually Beryllos') was in favour of the 'Syrians'. This presumably actually means he supported the authority of the city council, which is what one would expect. Similarly expected is the continued dissatisfaction of the Jews with the ruling, for they were not concerned with 'justice' but with power in the city. The quarrel therefore continued, and having reached the stage of violence once, easily did so again.[34]

The essential point, of course, is how the two sides so easily resorted to fighting each other. The authority of the city council was thus defied and weakened, and the procurator had to intervene. There were similar disputes in other places, including, repeatedly, Jerusalem. A new dispute in Caesarea is located by Josephus as the spark which began the subsequent rebellion, but the tinder was well prepared beforehand. A dispute over land next to the synagogue brought insulting behaviour by both sides. The violence could not be suppressed by the troops, who were probably under strength because the procurator Gessius Florus was out of the city at the time. The Jews complained to Florus, taking their copy of the Torah with them. He arrested them, perhaps out of antipathy, perhaps to stop them raising further complaints or spreading the dispute, but the arrest itself raised complaints in Jerusalem.[35]

Florus claimed seventeen talents from the temple treasury for the imperial service, a payment of tax arrears. A riot ensued, which was put down with considerable violence. In order to reinforce his control Florus then required them to organize a ceremonial and friendly greeting for two cohorts of troops which were on their way from Caesarea. The notables of the city, who included Queen Berenike, Agrippa II's sister, and the high priests, contrived to organize the greeting, but the soldiers were clearly apprehensive and when they arrived they failed to respond to the apparently friendly greetings. Insulted by the crowd for their stern demeanor, the soldiers retaliated with violence. Florus decided now that it would be better to withdraw. He left just one cohort in the city, handed over responsibility for public order to the city, and went to Caesarea.[36]

It is easy to blame Florus, as Josephus does. He was no doubt not very competent, greedy, and unsympathetic to the Jews – but this merely made him a normal Roman governor. None of such men had any formal training or qualifications for their posts, and all were expected to enrich themselves in office. But it required an exceptional, not an ordinary, man to control Judaea in the 60s, and Florus had no immediate support from either Rome or the Syrian governor. Indeed the governor, Cestius Gallus, had already undermined Florus' authority earlier by promising a rioting crowd that he would get Florus to be better behaved.[37]

So it was not solely Florus' fault that a rebellion began. In fact, by withdrawing with most of the soldiers from the city, Florus was appeasing the anger of the population. The city notables, including the high priests, were normally able to impose their control. But the anti-Roman groups took Florus' withdrawal as a sign of weakness and were buoyed up by their apparent victory.

The danger of a full rebellion was clear. King Agrippa, with Berenike beside him, pointed out that it was not Florus who was the problem, but Rome itself. He made an eloquent speech (eloquent in Josephus' version, at least) during which he appealed to those who were neutral or pro-Roman, declaring that the recent events could already be seen as rebellion. Damage to the Antonia fortress, tax arrears, as well as the violence against Roman soldiers, were all going to be reckoned up in Antioch and Rome against the people of Jerusalem. He was persuasive, and convinced enough people that the danger was real. The taxes were collected, and repair of the damages begun.

This, of course, did not suit the anti-Roman group. Agrippa also pointed out, once the reparations were being organized, that it was necessary to continue to obey Florus. This insistence swung opinion back towards the enemies of Rome. A group of Zealots, led by the grandson of Judas of Galilee, took the opportunity of this brief episode of good will towards them to seize control of the old Hasmonaean and Herodian fortress of Masada in the Judaean desert, killing the Roman garrison in the process. By itself this could have been brushed off as the work of a group of brigands, who could have been suppressed with little difficulty, but they also enlisted the high priest's son on their side, who persuaded his father Ananaias to cease the sacrifices made daily for the emperor. This was much more serious, and a defiance of the whole empire. This was the declaration of rebellion, a proclamation of independence.[38]

Chapter 12

The Jewish Rebellion: Campaigns in the Country

The capture of Masada by the Zealots and the defiance of refusing the temple sacrifice made it clear to pro-Roman Jews and neutralists that revolutionaries were in the process of gaining control over affairs in Judaea. The killing of the Roman garrison at Masada made it certain that the Roman army would arrive sooner or later, if only to retake Masada, though such an expeditionary force would have to march from northern Syria, and would therefore take some time to arrive. The Jewish establishment in Jerusalem – the chief priests, the nobles, members of the Herodian family, and their followers, a substantial and wealthy group – made an attempt to pre-empt the Roman attack.[1]

They were also concerned to prevent the revolutionaries from gaining wider power and so putting into effect the social revolution which some of them espoused. This is only attested by the enmity of their Jewish and Roman enemies, but the actions of at least one of their leaders, Simon bar Giora, in attacking the houses of wealthy Jews suggest an equalitarian set of beliefs.[2] If this was widespread amongst the revolutionaries in Jerusalem as early as 66, this would be another reason for those of wealth and property to both oppose them and welcome Roman help. But first they attempted to suppress the anti-Roman party themselves.

For this they needed troops. The prefect Gessius Florus had left only a single cohort of Roman troops in the city, which was not enough to be more than a symbolic presence when much of the city population was hostile. Nor were the other cohorts he commanded at Caesarea and elsewhere enough to retake the city. But King Agrippa was a fellow spirit, pro-Roman, intelligent, the senior Herodian, and he commanded a substantial armed force, which he needed to control his difficult kingdom. They called him in and asked for more troops from Florus at the same time.

The obvious aim was to suppress the anti-Roman element in the city before the Roman governor Cestius Gallus arrived and then hand the leaders over to him. Gallus would presumably have to deal with such places as Masada, but the morale of the captors of that fort would surely collapse if their Jerusalem followers were crushed by other Jews. And since the revolutionaries had resorted to force first, the pro-Romans could claim to be justified in calling for help.

Agrippa sent 2,000 cavalry, not the most suitable soldiers for street fighting and conducting a siege, but they were probably the best troops he had, since his large, sparsely populated kingdom needed a mobile force above all. And cavalry were very useful, even in constrained places, for intimidating foot soldiers, especially poorly armed and untrained men. Florus was apparently unable to send any troops; his first priority would be to safeguard his position in Caesarea, which was almost as disturbed as Jerusalem, and to maintain control over the cities along the coast; it appears later that there was a Roman unit in Ashkelon, and this no doubt was also the case in such places as Gaza.[3]

Together with the Roman cohort and with the assistance of the wealthy in the city, Agrippa's men gained control of the Upper City, roughly the western half, though the insurgents continued to control the temple and the Lower City. The fighting lasted a week, by which time the insurgents were winning. The soldiers withdrew to Herod's fortified palace on the west of the city, and the Antonia fortress north of the temple. The Antonia was then captured by the insurgents in no more than two days' fighting, and the soldiers there, mainly Romans, were massacred (as at Masada). The royal troops in the palace were not prepared to continue the fight and agreed to leave; they were allowed to go, apparently with their weapons. The Roman troops there held out longer but then agreed to leave after surrendering their weapons. They were massacred after doing so.[4] There could be no clearer demonstration that one major element in the insurgency was hostility to Rome: Roman soldiers, even protected by solemn oaths, were killed; Jewish soldiers were allowed to leave unharmed even with their weapons.

In the process the insurgents had begun to turn upon each other. One of the leaders, Menahem, had brought weapons from the stores at Masada and on the strength of this had assumed a quasi-dictatorial position which grated on many of the others. He and many of his followers were killed in a riot, and the palaces of Agrippa and his sister Berenike were burned; at the other extreme, the high priest Ananaias was found in the palace when it fell and was murdered.[5] The revolutionaries gained control of the building holding the archives and burnt the records of debtors, hoping thereby to gain their support. (But, having destroyed these records, there was no real reason why the debtors should support them.) For the time being the revolution hung between the extremes of conservative reaction and revolution, but uneasily.

The news from Jerusalem sparked violence in the surrounding region. Josephus gives a survey of what happened, though it is not by any means accurate or complete, merely a schematic account. He claims the first outbreak was at Caesarea, which is quite likely, for there had long been tension between the Jews and the 'Syrians' there. But he also claims that 20,000 Jews were murdered in one day, and the rest were expelled from the city. One can believe in the expulsion, and in a massacre, but not in the numbers, nor that the city 'was completely emptied of Jews'. Other places in Palestine were certainly the scenes of similar conflicts between Jews and Greeks. Josephus singles out the massacre of Jews at Skythopolis for a detailed description, but the Jewish reprisals and attacks and expulsions of 'Syrians' are scarcely referred to. He also contradicts himself: Ashkelon is said to have been burned and razed at one point, yet it is later the scene of a massacre of Jews, and later still (and presumably all along) it had a Roman garrison.[6]

The problem for the Greeks (or 'Syrians', as Josephus tends to call them) was that they did not know if what had happened in Jerusalem was likely to spread elsewhere. It could have been an internal Judaean matter, with which the Greek cities were not unfamiliar, or it could have been the prelude to an attempted revival of the Jewish kingdom and its extension. The Jews living in the cities of Palestine and Syria might be planning similar coups. This certainly helps explain why in many cases the Jewish population was imprisoned. Where their numbers were relatively small they were clearly not dangerous. At Gerasa the Jews of the city were protected, and those who wanted to leave were escorted to the border. In the great cities of North Syria, Antioch and Apamea, no trouble developed. Phoenicia illustrates the varied approaches. At Sidon no action was taken, either to kill or expel or imprison the Jews; at Tyre, however, some were killed, and most were imprisoned – the Jews from Galilee had attacked a Tyrian village, which had long been disputed between Tyre and Galilee, so the situation in the area was clearly tense.[7] (Tyre, of course, had a tradition of enmity towards the Jewish state, and this is likely to have been at the basis of the action.)

Josephus is obviously attempting to give an impression of widespread uncertainty, with outbreaks of violence by both Jews and Greeks. It is unlikely that his catalogue is complete or wholly accurate – Ashkelon is the test – and he clearly indulged in his penchant for numerical exaggeration. Yet the overall insistence of a chaotic situation, and a breakdown of order in much of the countryside, can be accepted; it had happened before, of course, as in the case of Varus' War. The cities were generally able to control their internal situations, however, usually by violent means. Of course, the previous generation of Jewish disorder and agitation had increased intra-communal tensions throughout Palestine to such a point that events at Jerusalem could easily set off these social explosions.

The great cities of North Syria saw no trouble, partly because the city councils were able to prevent it, partly because the numbers of Jews were relatively small, but perhaps mainly because the region was heavily garrisoned by Roman soldiers. Yet this latter consideration did not prevent trouble in Egypt in Alexandria. There were two legions stationed close to the city, but with detachments throughout Egypt. The real difference is that there were ancient hatreds between Jews and Greeks in Alexandria which had caused riots before.

The revolutionary outbreak in Jerusalem – only a few days' journey away – brought another bout. It is significant that the Macedonians and Greeks of the city now called the Jews 'enemies' and 'spies'.

It may not have helped the situation that the prefect of Egypt was Ti. Julius Alexander, of a wealthy Jewish family, though he no longer observed the religion. He had had a notable civil career, and had been prefect of Judaea twenty years before. But his ancestry made him the target of abuse from both sides, as a Jew by the Greeks, as an apostate by the Jews. As both sets of rioters failed to heed his orders to desist, Alexander turned the legionaries on the Jews, whom he clearly identified as the most violent – though he was also following the general Roman imperial policy of favouring the Greeks in eastern parts of the empire. The soldiers were then joined in despoiling the Jewish quarter by the Greeks of the city. Josephus' estimate of the dead is 50,000, but his figures can never be believed; what is certain is that the Jewish insurrection in Alexandria – if that is what it was – was crushed.[8]

Amid these events certain items indicate that those in control in Jerusalem were taking measures to prepare for the Roman reply which all knew would come. The fortresses built by Herod were seized, notably Kypros in the Jericho plain, and Machaerus across the Jordan in the Peraia.[9] From later events it is clear that all Judaea came under the rebels' control, if rather precariously. Neighbouring areas, meanwhile, reacted by controlling or driving out their Jewish inhabitants so that the cities of the Syrian province, including the cities of the Decapolis, remained loyal to Rome.

In North Syria the governor Cestius Gallus organized his reply. He marched an army south along the coast road to Ptolemais. He brought one legion, XII *Fulminata*, which had been stationed at Raphanea, along with vexillations of 2,000 men from each of the other three legions in his province (X *Fretensis*, VI *Ferrata*, and III *Gallica*), six auxiliary infantry cohorts, and four *alae* of cavalry. XII *Fulminata*'s base at Raphanea made it the southernmost legion in North Syria, and this was presumably the collecting place for the other legionary forces. The auxiliary forces amounted in numbers to the equivalent of half a legion. So Gallus at Ptolemais had about 15,000 Roman and auxiliary troops. In addition he had called up forces from the client kingdoms: 2,000 cavalry and 3,000 infantry were provided by Antiochos of Kommagene; 3,000 infantry and about 1,500 cavalry from King Agrippa; 4,000 soldiers, of which perhaps 1,500 were cavalry, from Sohaemos of Emesa; more were taken from the city militias.[10] In total he had thereby doubled the size of his force.

The force Gallus brought with him to the Judaean war was not perhaps overwhelming, but it was certainly considered adequate. Gallus was an experienced governor, having been in post in Syria for three years already. We do not know of his earlier career, other than that he had been consul in 42, but it can be assumed that he had governed other provinces, and had commanded Roman forces elsewhere. He had greater responsibilities than simply governing Syria and suppressing trouble in Judaea. He was also in the front line if Parthia should attack. In Rome the emperor (Nero) was preparing to travel to the East with the intention of conducting an expedition into Armenia where Roman forces have been fighting Armenians and Parthians for several years. One legion was based at Seleukeia-Zeugma, the crossing point of the Euphrates; it also was on the front line. It is not surprising that Gallus let Judaea alone for some time before marching south, or that he left three of his legions on guard in Syria. (Another legion, V *Macedonica*, was in the region as well, left there after the recent warfare, and was no doubt intended for use in Nero's campaign.[11]) These legionary and auxiliary forces had recently been involved in a war with Parthia, so the troops were battle-hardened. But the conduct of some Roman forces had been less than inspiring in that war; perhaps news of defeats in the north had encouraged Jewish rebels in the south.

Gallus' campaign was directed against Jerusalem, for if Roman control of the city was regained, he knew that the rest of the rebel area would either fall quickly, or be relatively easily conquered piece by piece. He moved methodically, as is shown by the care he had taken to collect what must have seemed a very powerful overwhelming force. Having reached Ptolemais he first cleared his landward flank by capturing the fortified town of Chabulon, on the border of Galilee. It will have pleased him to find that the population had fled, but it was ominous that they later returned to attack the small force he left to hold the town. Nevertheless the demonstration had made it dangerous for the relatively few rebels in Galilee to attempt anything further for the moment. Galilee, however, was notorious for its brigands and its rowdy inhabitants, and Gallus clearly expected further trouble from the region later.

Gallus moved on south to Caesarea, which became his new headquarters. Presumably Florus was still there, and still prefect, but he now completely vanishes from the story, though all sides, Josephus and Cestius Gallus, were happy to heap the blame for the war on him. Gallus sent a combined land and sea expedition to capture Joppa, taking the inhabitants – it was a Jewish city – by surprise. A massacre followed, so Josephus says. This was an important conquest for Joppa, along with Caesarea, was the most important port on the coast and the preferred port for Jewish trade; in Roman hands it prevented any Jewish maritime expansion. (Contact with the insurrection in Alexandria was thus blocked.) Gallus also sent a cavalry force inland from Caesarea against Narbatene, on the way towards Sebaste. The centre of this area, the town of Narbata, had been the place to which the Jews from Caesarea fled when attacked by their neighbours earlier in the year; it was evidently an important

Jewish centre and no doubt a town firmly on the side of the insurrection. The area was ravaged, its inhabitants killed or driven out. Meanwhile it appears that the thrust into Galilee provoked the rebels there to coalesce into an army of sorts, so a detachment under the command of L. Caesennius Gallus, the legionary commander of XII *Fulminata*, was sent to deter any attack. He accepted the surrender of the peaceable Sepphoris, the main urban centre in western Galilee. The contrasting fates of Chabulon and Narbata and of Sepphoris carried the usual message: surrenders meant peace, while resistance brought destruction. He then located and defeated the armed gathering of Galileans in the hills nearby. The survivors dispersed and Cestius Gallus assumed that any insurrection in Galilee had been contained.[12]

These easy victories made it clear that the Jewish resistance in the open country was incompetent, and that the fortified towns could be captured without serious difficulty. This was all that Cestius Gallus needed, and he could only have been encouraged in his aim to bring the war directly to Jerusalem. So the obvious thing was to attack the city at once. He took the direct route. From Caesarea the army marched south by way of Antipatris and Lydda, protected on the right by the Roman control of Joppa, and on the left by the destruction in Narbatene, while Sebaste, like Sepphoris, wanted nothing to do with the rebellion. Only a single point of resistance was encountered, at a tower, which was speedily captured. Lydda was almost empty of its inhabitants, except for fifty people, who were killed. From there the army turned south-east to climb the Beth Horon pass to the Judaean plateau.

This pass had been the scene of a major Maccabean victory over two centuries before, a fact certainly well known to the Jews if not to the Romans (though Agrippa II, who accompanied Cestius Gallus, could have told them). This time the invading forces got through without being opposed, which is a powerful indication of the lack of organization and planning by the rebels. This march took place on the Jewish Feast of Tabernacles, perhaps not by coincidence. Josephus attributes the desertion of Lydda to its population having gone to Jerusalem for the festival; with Agrippa's advice Gallus could have deliberately timed his march for the festival on the assumption he would not be opposed.

Gallus camped at Gibeon, about 10 km north of Jerusalem, and here at last he was faced by a substantial Jewish army, which attacked impetuously. The numbers and excitement of the Jewish attackers gave them a brief success, but they were quickly defeated by the ability of the Roman army to manoeuvre. In fact exactly the same manoeuvre – the movement of one wing of the Roman army to take the Jewish forces in the flank – had caused the defeat of the Galileans. It was so elementary a move that it merely exposes the inexperience of the Jewish forces and perhaps their lack of imagination. Their impetuosity, however, also allowed them to escape quickly back into the city. At last, rather late in the day, a party led by Simon bar Giora ambushed part of the supply train in the Beth Horon pass, but Cestius Gallus had reached a position from which he could attack Jerusalem.[13]

Gallus moved his camp from Gibeon to Mount Scopus, close to the northern wall of the city. He was now facing difficulties. His army could clearly defeat a Jewish army in the open field, but such a battle was no longer likely; on the other hand the city before him was large and populous and well fortified, and he did not have a serious siege train. His line of communications from Caesarea and Joppa was long, and, at Beth Horon, vulnerable, as Simon's ambush had shown. There, Jewish skirmishers and guerrillas (adopting the old Maccabean tactics) had occupied the heights on either side of the pass, and Gallus was beginning to feel the pinch over his supplies. Also it was now late in the year (November in our calendar), and local supplies were exiguous enough and could only get fewer; Roman foragers collected what they could.

After three days Gallus attacked the 'First Wall' – the north wall – of the city. He was using the same approach as every other commander who has attacked Jerusalem, for the other three sides of the city were protected by the steep slopes of ravines. The city is therefore fortified by a single wall on those sides, but by three successive walls on the northern side, called by the Romans (and archaeologists) the 'First', 'Second', and the 'Third' or 'Old' walls. The northernmost of these walls was fairly easily penetrated, and the Roman forces broke through, capturing the northern suburb called Bezetha, which burned during the assault.

This brought the Romans against the Second Wall, anchored by Herod's palace on the west, and by the Antonia fortress and the temple on the east. For the next week this wall was attacked. Josephus claims that there were groups in the city who would have let the Romans in, had the Romans responded to their plots – no doubt quite true – but that the insurgents succeeded in blocking all such approaches. Quite probably the Romans also did not notice them. But Josephus' explanation of divisions within the city's population is undoubtedly correct, and this was known to Gallus. Yet neither internal plots nor external assaults succeeded. After attacking the city with only limited success for ten days, Gallus withdrew his forces.[14]

Josephus, our only source on all this, was in the city during this attack and claims that the city was about to fall when Gallus decided to withdraw. This is, however, in defiance of what he has already said. Gallus could see clearly enough that resistance was as strong as ever – the capture of the northern suburb had made no serious dent in the defences – and that his enemies were more numerous than the troops under his command. They had been outnumbered even in the Gibeon battle, which may not have mattered very much in a set-piece battle, but in the enclosed spaces of the city the Romans' deficiency in numbers would be critical. Further if he stayed longer on the exposed Judaean plateau he would endanger the whole expedition. He had made no real preparations for a long siege, and this was what was now in prospect. He would need more men, many more supplies, and a bigger siege train. It was by now November and winter was arriving; at 6,000 ft winter in Jerusalem can be very cold (as British soldiers attacking the city in December 1917 discovered). He may also have felt that by relieving the pressure on the city those inside who were still pro-Roman (who had tried in vain to contact him during the attack), or those who simply wanted peace, might be able to secure control from the fighters. Whatever his reasons, and he had good ones, Gallus withdrew his army from the city.

He must also have known that the withdrawal would be difficult. His communications with Caesarea were, if not cut, then under guerrilla attack, especially in the Beth Horon pass. The Roman retreat was harassed from the moment they left the city. After staying for a night at the camp at Mount Scopus, the Roman army marched away, once again harassed by men whom Josephus calls 'brigands' (though he was on their side at the time). The army rested for two days at the old camp at Gibeon (which had presumably been continually manned). Josephus suggests that Cestius Gallus was uncertain about what to do, but his actions make it clear that he was in full control. Gallus divested himself of much of the army's impedimenta, killing unneeded animals, and so, despite Josephus' highly coloured description, the army was able to get through most of the pass in a single march. It is simply wrong to claim that 'Cestius and his entire army were, indeed, within an ace of being captured'. By the time night fell (about 5.00 pm at this season) the Romans camped ('found refuge') at Beth Horon, by which Josephus must mean the village at the foot of the pass. Then, leaving a rear guard of just 400 men to delay any pursuit, a stealthy night march broke contact with the Jewish pursuers, and the army reached Antipatris next day. The rearguard is said to have been 'rapidly dispatched', but it is virtually certain many will have escaped, and absolutely certain that the Jewish forces had been hoodwinked.

Josephus implies that the Romans had carried their battering rams and artillery all the way through the pass, only to abandon them in their 'flight' from Beth Horon to Antipatris. Certainly the Jews secured some of these machines and took them to Jerusalem, but it is more likely that they were taken at Gibeon. If the Romans actually did carry them all through the pass, the Jews' harassment cannot have been very serious. That is, Josephus was wrong in several significant details concerning this flight, or he was inventing them. He also claims that there were Roman casualties of 5,300 infantry and

480 cavalry, but one can never trust his figures, especially when boasting of a Jewish victory and accounting for the enemy dead who were spread over a distance of tens of kilometres.[15] Even if his figures can be accepted, they would only constitute a sixth of Gallus' army. The destruction of a legion, as sometimes assumed, did not take place.

The insurgents believed they had won a victory. Their city had withstood a major assault and the Roman army had retreated. But this was a victory which was heavily qualified. It was not decisive by any means, and to call it a victory without recognizing its strong limitations was to delude oneself. Gallus' retreat from the city to the lowland had been managed very well. He clearly knew what he was doing, above all by moving quickly – the Roman army had marched 40 km (Gibeon to Beth Horon to Antipatris) in two days while under attack. This was a considerable achievement, and might be counted as a defensive victory in itself. The army had lost only part of its strength, and none of the conquests in the lowlands had been lost.

Nevertheless even if the Jewish victory was less than complete, to the Romans it really was a clear defeat. This was something which Roman armies were not accustomed to, and would obviously need to be redressed. Cestius Gallus disappears from the record, either sacked or expired, and it was clear that both a new commander and more troops were needed. Gallus in his report to the emperor had laid much of the blame for the whole trouble on Florus. Nero was in Achaia, touring Greece and enjoying himself winning crowns at the Olympic Games and other festivals. This was in a sense his personal preparation for the planned Eastern expedition. But the news from Judaea spoiled the party, though he acted quickly enough to appoint a new commander at once, choosing T. Flavius Vespasianus, another old ex-consul with military experience. Vespasian was given two more legions, one of them already in Syria but apparently out to the governor's control, V *Macedonica*, and one taken from the Egyptian garrison, XV *Apollinaris*, command of which was given to Vespasian's son Titus.

Cestius Gallus was also replaced as governor, by L. Licinius Mucianus. There was at once a certain conflict between the authorities of Mucianus in Syria and Vespasian in Judaea, which was not surprising, for when Vespasian took two legions (V *Macedonia* and X *Fretensis*) from Syria, and most of the auxiliary regiments as well, and other forces from the client kings and the cities. But eventually the hard fight in Judaea and bad news from Rome drove the two men into alliance.[16]

Chapter 13

The Jewish Rebellion: Vespasian's Approach

The new Roman measures took time to implement. Vespasian had to travel from Greece to Syria through Asia Minor in winter, arriving at Antioch on 1 March, and Titus had to sail to Egypt, also in winter. These winter journeys, though slow, did indicate the urgency with which the Judaean War (as it now clearly was) was seen by the imperial government. However, once he reached Syria, Vespasian seems to have had to act as Syrian governor for a time. Gallus died, by suicide or otherwise, before Mucianus, the new governor, could arrive, and Tacitus implies that Vespasian was Gallus' immediate successor. Mucianus, who will have had to come out from Italy, seems to have arrived in the autumn.[1] So Vespasian had time to sort out the forces he was to use and it was probably May before the Roman army was ready to take the offensive.

Meanwhile, during the period of about six months between Cestius Gallus' retreat and Vespasian's advance, the Jewish rebels made significant territorial advances and set about organizing their territories for both expansion and defence. They also perpetuated and worsened their internal disputes.

There were serious consequences from both these developments in Judaea. The expansion of the rebellion's power brought memories to the Jews' neighbours of the same process which had taken place from the time of the Maccabean revolt in the 160s BC, in which one aspect had been a powerful anti-Greek sentiment. This had expressed itself in the destruction of a number of Greek cities – Pella, Gadara, Gaza, Ashdod amongst others – and attacks on many more. These cities had been restored by Roman rulers, notably Pompey, and their present inhabitants could not fail to recall all of this history, and it put them firmly on the side of the Romans. Indeed Josephus remarks that the Greeks recruited from the cities to back up the legions were especially keen to fight.[2]

The internal disputes within the rebellion produced several layers of argument. The basis, perhaps, was a widespread feeling amongst all the Jewish population in Judaea that it should be an independent state. This had been the root of the reluctant acceptance of the Herodian kings, who were generally personally unpopular but who at least were Jewish rulers and so kept the Romans at arm's length. But the next layer up from this attitudinal base divided the proponents into monarchists – which at this time could only mean a Herodian king – and republicans. But the Herodians, fully aware of Roman power and determination and their own personal unpopularity among the

Jews, were united in opposition to this movement towards independence, as Agrippa II had already shown by his speech to the people of Jerusalem several months before. Then again, the 'republicans' included both those who saw the state as a theocracy, in which the head of state was the high priest, with religion as the state's *raison d'être*, and others who were less than happy at that prospect. But the fact was that it was their religion which made them Jews, so a theocratic element was necessary.

Another layer of argument, or division, among the insurgents was personified by the men who are best described as revolutionaries – men like Simon bar Giora, Eleazar bar Ananus, and John of Gischala. They probably began as men who believed that Judaean society was blighted by a division between rich and poor. The outbreak of the rebellion, with which they had little to do originally, allowed them to develop ideas which were partly anti-monarchist, partly anti-rich, but wholly anti-Roman. This last element in their programme – if such it may be called – was the main fuel for their fanaticism, and the goad which made them such vigorous, not to say unscrupulous, fighters, and was the foundation of such popular support as they had. But this set of political beliefs also alienated many of the Jews who were as anti-Roman as the revolutionaries, but who had no wish to be reduced, as they might have put it, to equality with the poor. The whole set and variety of attitudes and hopes, together with the expansion, political and military which was soon manifested after Cestius Gallus' defeat, made the surrounding non-Jewish communities as adamant in their opposition to the rebellion as the revolutionaries were in promoting it.

This last is important, since there was undoubtedly a widespread anti-Roman sentiment among the ordinary populations of the empire. In this same period there were rebellions in Britain, Germany, Gaul, and Pontos, together with imperial usurpations emanating from Spain, Germany, and the East. The empire was clearly unstable. In Syria in particular there there were the several client kingdoms, all of which resented in various degrees their subordination to Roman rule, and, like Judaea, hankered after full independence.

(In counter-factual mode for a moment, a degree of moderation by the Jewish rebels might well have allowed them to spread the rebellion throughout Syria; further, Egypt was always resentful of non-Egyptian rulers; and there were client kings in Asia Minor as ambivalent at Roman control as those in Syria. It might not have taken much to bring down the whole Roman structure east of Greece.)

But it was the sets of beliefs and attitudes revealed and developed in and by the rebellion which was too alienating to bring any support from people outside the Jewish community in Palestine. Anti-rich, pro-independence, and pro-expansion, exclusively Jewish – these qualities decisively offset the general anti-Roman feeling which existed, and which was the only possible basis for rebellion to spread outside Judaea. And in the face of Roman military power and expertise it was only by gaining wider support and enlisting other communities that the Jewish rebellion could hope to succeed in maintaining its independence. The alliance of non-Jews (Greek, Syrians, Egyptians) with Roman power was overwhelming. It was typified in Alexandria where the alliance of the Greek citizens, the Roman legions, and the Roman government put down the Jewish insurrection. In Syria the Greeks of the cities and the Semitic kings of the client states joined together with the Romans in fighting the Jewish rebellion, and this was because the rebels seemed to be even more unpleasant than Roman rule.

The defeat of Gallus' army meant that a new Roman attack was inevitable. As a result many of those who opposed the war left Jerusalem (including, it seems, the Christians).[3] The victory by contrast convinced others that the rebellion was successful, and the high priests contrived to assume command, using the Sanhedrin as their governing instrument, supported by a popular assembly. That is, the Jewish aristocracy had managed to gain, or re-gain, a precarious control.

This did not please the extremists, such as the leader of the guerillas who had fought at Beth Horon, Eleazar son of Simon, a former *sicarius* who is now termed a 'Zealot' by Josephus. He had kept control of the weapons and treasure taken in the battle, and this gave him considerable authority. He was, however, carefully shut out of the formal structure of command.[4] This was obviously a mistake and allowed him an independent demagogic power which set the Sanhedrin at naught.

The new government, assuming perhaps that the war was over, but more likely attempting to convince everyone of its legitimacy, created the institutions to perform the normal government functions. A mint was organized to produce distinctively Jewish coins, in both silver and bronze – silver coinage was the prerogative of the Roman imperial government – which omitted the head of the emperor in favour of such slogans as 'Jerusalem the holy', with pictures of natural or religious objects on the reverse.[5]

Defence was the other main priority for the new government. The wall which Gallus' forces had so easily broken through, the 'First Wall', was repaired and strengthened and heightened. The rest of the country was provided with a defence organization of six military regions, plus Jerusalem: Idumaea in the south, in the east the Jordan Valley was divided lengthwise, the Peraia across the Jordan, Jericho on the west; Galilee was the northern command; the northern part of Judaea was divided into the north-west based at Thamna, and the north-east, around Akrabaeta. Some of these areas were as much notional as actual. For instance in north-west Judaea John the Essene's region included, besides Thamna in the hills about Mount Ephraim, the towns of Lydda, Joppa, and Emmaus, all of which were still in Roman control.[6]

The appointed commanders were obviously expected to extemporize both a local civil administration and an army, and to attend to other matters as they arose. One of these duties, as it appears, was the expansion of the independent Jewish state, and John the Essene did extend his authority into the lowlands. Joseph bar Matthias (Josephus the historian) was appointed to command in Galilee and had to establish a civic administration, recruit an army, and exert control over large areas which had been effectively abandoned by every authority.[7] In the south the city of Ashkelon was garrisoned by a Roman force under Antonius, presumably put there by Florus or Gallus. A rash Jewish attack had already been rebuffed, suffering heavy casualties.[8]

The initial intention of the new government in Jerusalem, even if it was a socially conservative group, was therefore to expand Jewish territory in every direction – so it was committed to at least part of the rebel cause, if not to the social revolution of some of the rebels. Joppa was occupied, having been left unguarded and unpopulated after its early capture by Cestius Gallus; true to their guerrilla origins, the Jews in Joppa took to the sea and raided along the Syrian coast.[9] In Galilee Josephus recruited an army (which he claims numbered 100,000 men) and fortified many of the more prominent places, including Sepphoris, which had so quickly joined Gallus earlier, and Tiberias, which was in Agrippa's kingdom. Tiberias' mixed Jewish and non-Jewish people were not at all keen on finding themselves included in the revolutionary state. Both of these places were thus subject to conquest by the rebels, and Josephus also spread his forces east into Gaulanitis, Agrippa's territory again, where the key post was Gamala.[10]

The disputes within Jerusalem between the 'moderates', who now controlled the government through the high priest and the Sanhedrin, and those such as Eleazar bar Ananus, who were social as well as political revolutionaries, had been one of the motives behind this new provincial organization. Several of the wilder elements were given command posts outside the city, no doubt in the hope that they would expend their energies on enemies rather than the government. At the same time the revolutionaries were placed under the command of area commanders who were usually of a more conservative bent; no doubt it was hoped that this would help control and direct them. This was only marginally successful. John the Essene was in command of the north-west and it was some of his men who became the 'pirates' based at Joppa – the term, is, of course, that applied to them by their enemies. In the north-east Simon bar Giora, originally from Gerasa, was technically under the command of John bar Ananaias, but he used his forces to conduct a campaign against the wealthy Jews of the area, looting their houses, until driven out by forces sent by the Sanhedrin. Both of these were acting to extend the area of the Jewish state, as was Josephus in seizing parts of Agrippa's kingdom. Simon took refuge in Masada, while he used it as his base from which to continue the social revolution. In Idumaea the command went to Jesus bar Sapphias and Eleazar bar Neus, but the local hero was Niger, one of the commanders who had led the attack on Ashkelon. He was a kindred spirit to Simon, and recruited a band of Idumaean revolutionaries; the south of Judaea was not under any sort of control by the government in Jerusalem. In Galilee Josephus faced the same problem, his revolutionary opponent being a local man John of Gischala. John was unconvinced of Josephus' ardour for the cause – quite correctly if he was thinking of a social revolution – and repeatedly intrigued and plotted to get rid of him. Josephus was, however, quite as competent an intriguer as John. They were still both active in Galilee when the Romans came.[11]

Vespasian's forces collected at Ptolemais, where he was joined by Titus with the force from Alexandria. He adopted the same initial strategy as Gallus. From Ptolemais it was obvious that it was necessary first of all to ensure control of the coastal towns and Galilee, since from those areas his communications would be vulnerable when he moved against Jerusalem. The successful defence of Ashkelon had allowed Titus and the XV *Apollinaris* legion a relatively easy march from Alexandria, while three cohorts which Cestius Gallus had left in Ptolemais had blocked any Jewish sorties out of Galilee into the region between Galilee and the west. Thus Vespasian had three legions (XV *Apollinaris*, X *Fretensis* and V *Macedonica*), and he brought eighteen auxiliary cohorts and five cavalry *alae* from the north. Five more cohorts and a cavalry *ala* had been left in Caesarea by Gallus; there were also the three cohorts at Ptolemais, the two at Ashkelon under Antonius, and smaller forces in other places in the lowlands. The client kings supplied a total of 6,000 infantry and 3,000 cavalry, and King Malichos of Nabataea had been called on to contribute another 1,000 horses and 5,000 infantry; he had not been involved in the earlier campaigns, but the expansion of the rebels' control into the Peraia and Gaulanitis posed a threat to his territories. Josephus claimed a total Roman force of 60,000, but if his account of the units included is correct, it was more like 40,000 to 45,000, half as much again as Cestius Gallus had commanded.[12]

At Ptolemais Vespasian was met by a delegation from Sepphoris. Josephus' work to strengthen the town's defences had warned the rulers there of the possibility of being involved in the war. They asked for support from Vespasian against the rebels and he sent troops under a tribune called Placidus, who used the place as a base for cavalry raids into the rest of Galilee.[13] They found various places better prepared for defence than the year before. Vespasian, appreciating the need to control Galilee before he could attack Jerusalem, turned to a full campaign of conquest.

Josephus sent a force to attack Sepphoris when its defection became clear, but was foiled by the fortifications he himself had made, and the attackers dispersed on the news of the Roman approach. Josephus was unable to collect a field force capable of facing the Romans and had to rely on his fortified towns. Vespasian made preparations to attack Jotapata by having his troops begin the construction of an approach road. Josephus went into the town to direct the defence and then found himself trapped there when the siege was formed. This may or may not have been Vespasian's intention but he was surely pleased to have ensnared the enemy commander. This siege was the equivalent in Galilee of that of Jerusalem in Judaea: once Jotapata was taken, the rest of Galilee would fall easily. Josephus describes the siege in boastful detail, so much so that one is surprised that the Romans succeeded, so ingeniously conducted was the defence. But a deserter reported to the Romans that the night guards slept at their posts, so Josephus' command style was careless. Titus led a silent storming party over the wall, and the town fell. Josephus escaped into a cave, where he persuaded his forty companions to commit suicide while he and one other survived, or so he claims.[14]

He was taken to Vespasian, where he boldly predicted that the general would become emperor.[15] This was an extremely dangerous prediction for both the prophet and the general, since to even voice the thought would be regarded by Nero as treason, if he heard of it. Josephus (who had spent some time in Nero's Rome) obviously knew this. Vespasian threatened to send him to Nero, which would probably mean his execution; his motive for the 'prediction' was therefore to avoid this. Vespasian's reaction should have been to kill Josephus at once, but others had heard his words. His life was spared, and he was kept him in chains – which Josephus claims was his own suggestion.

Vespasian's reaction is illuminating. The thought of his elevation was clearly neither alien to him nor was it perhaps the first time it had occurred to him. He commanded the largest army in the empire. The last time a general had command of a similar force was two years before, when Cn. Domitius Corbulo campaigned successfully in Armenia. After his victory he was compelled to commit suicide by order of the emperor. Corbulo had been a friend of Vespasian's – they were of an age – and later his second son Domitian married Corbulo's daughter. No doubt Vespasian expected to receive the same treatment from Nero after his victory he would win in Judaea, since the unmilitary Nero could not abide a subordinate who had military glory. This small episode with Josephus indicates that suicide would not be Vespasian's answer to an imperial summons after victory.

Assuming that Josephus did not really have powers of accurate and detailed prediction concerning a man he had only just met, this episode also suggests that the idea that Vespasian, as a successful general, would then claim the position of emperor, was fairly widespread. People in the empire were finely attuned to the interpretation of such events as the killing of Corbulo only two years before. The choice of a man of nearly 60 years of age to conduct a difficult campaign was also a clear sign that Nero, a sprightly 30, assumed that Vespasian was too old for such an ambition. However, faced with a probable order to kill himself, Vespasian was apparently already determined to challenge Nero's decision. He could not allow Josephus to be sent to Nero to repeat his dangerous prediction, as Josephus undoubtedly calculated; at the same time he needed to take his time over the reconquest of Judaea, in order to mature whatever plans he had already conceived.

After Jotapata Vespasian assumed that Galilee was conquered and moved his army south to Caesarea, sending XV *Apollinaris* to garrison Skythopolis, then visited King Agrippa at Caesarea Philippi, supposedly for a holiday.[16] But generals in the midst of a war do not spend three weeks resting and feasting out of touch with their troops. The meeting with Agrippa can only have had a political purpose, or rather, several such purposes. Josephus' forces had made military thrusts into Agrippa's territory, and Agrippa had to lay a siege to attempt to recover Gamala in reaction, but in the end he had to withdraw from the siege and lost control of Gaulanitis. If Josephus' surviving Galilean forces (now, of course, all the more liable to be directed by John of Gischala) should expand that move, Agrippa's whole kingdom might fall. One aspect of the meeting was therefore to discuss the defence of the rest of Agrippa's kingdom further north. One wonders also if Vespasian happened to mention Josephus' prophecy. Certainly Agrippa later came out in support of Vespasian's imperial ambitions, and he had strong connections with the other Syrian client kings. It would be dangerous to be too open, but nods and winks could be exchanged.

There was also the consideration that Josephus had been hoping that Agrippa could be detached from the Roman side. While in control of Galilee, Josephus had taken several measures whose object was clearly to establish links with the king. One of Agrippa's overseers, Ptolemy, was ambushed and robbed by Josephus' men, but Josephus took control of the spoil intending to return it to the king; the Sanhedrin in Jerusalem ordered the destruction of Agrippa's palace at Tiberias because of the sculptures there, which were held to be against the second commandment, but Josephus saved many of the art objects for Agrippa; two of Agrippa's man from Trachonitis attempted to defect to the rebels, but Josephus sent them back.[17] Needless to say, this policy was disliked by many Galileans, but it made political sense if Agrippa could be induced to join the rebellion. At the very least Agrippa might intervene if Josephus was captured. From the Roman point of view, however, these contacts were suspicious. Hence another reason for Vespasian's visit to Caesarea Philippi: it was as much a threat as a reinforcement of their alliance.

The immediate result of this meeting was a new campaign in Galilee, directed against the towns which had not yet fallen. Since Vespasian seems to have assumed Galilee was dealt with after Jotapata, this can only have been to assist Agrippa, and, of course, it consumed more time. The objects of Roman attack in this campaign were all on the east – Tiberias and Taricheai on the Sea of Galilee, and Gamala in Gaulanitis – and so one of the aims was to prevent any revolutionary attack from there or from the south on Agrippa's lands. If his kingdom was in danger he would need to hold back his forces for its defence; clearing Galilee completely would not only prevent such attacks and restore Agrippa's authority over his whole kingdom. It would also prevent raids on Vespasian's communications and release more of Agrippa's forces to assist the Roman campaign.

So the army was brought from Caesarea once again into Galilee. Tiberias, deeply divided between Jews and Gentiles, and content enough under Agrippa's benign rule, surrendered without resistance, and Titus achieved the same quick result at Taricheai, another of Agrippa's towns. Vespasian was careful to distinguish between Agrippa's subjects and the rebels at both Tiberias and Taricheai. Agrippa's people and the towns were returned to the king, while the rebels caught at both places were killed or enslaved.[18] A siege had to be mounted at the extremely difficult site of Gamala, but after a month the place fell. Archaeological evidence shows that some of the fighting, as Josephus says, was bitter. The first Roman assault was beaten back, but a second succeeded, with many casualties on each side. Meanwhile the last points of resistance in Galilee fell to Roman detachments, Mount Tabor during the Gamala siege, while John of Gischala escaped from his home town when it was threatened, despite having vowed to fight to the death, as Josephus maliciously points out.[19] He led a large crowd of supporters and refugees to Jerusalem.

The conquest of Galilee revealed clearly enough to the Romans that the majority of the Jewish population was unwilling to resist, and that any place which defied the Roman forces probably did so because local power had been seized by the revolutionaries. Only occasionally did a majority fight strongly. In the Galilee campaign only Jotapata and Gamala put up serious resistance; otherwise most places had surrendered as soon as the Roman forces arrived, or as soon as the revolutionaries had escaped.

This was clearly encouraging, as was the easy recapture of Joppa. The 'pirates', as the Romans called the Jews who had retaken the town and then conducted a destructive maritime campaign against Roman communications and supply routes, got wind of the attack. They left the town in their ships, no doubt intending to seize another base (or return to Joppa if the Romans left), but they were caught in a storm and the fleet was wrecked. Having taken the town, the Romans demolished it, destroyed any remaining ships, and left a garrison there.[20] (It is clear that there was no Roman fleet available to combat the Jewish ships.)

From the main base at Caesarea Vespasian now took a force south to secure the lowlands along the coast. In this area several places were already under Roman control, such as Joppa and Ashkelon; others had been taken by Cestius Gallus but may well not have been held on to. The example of Joppa indicated the need to prevent Jewish access to the sea, and Vespasian campaigned as far south as Ashdod; Iamneia and apparently Lydda and Antipatris were garrisoned and Jewish refugees were resettled there.[21]

One of the results of the defeat and rejection of the wild men in Galilee and elsewhere had been that they had gathered in Jerusalem, which destabilized the political situation there. During the winter of 67/68 a vicious internal war went on in the city. John of Gischala, who was clearly a very competent survivor, became the Zealots' leader, and a terrorist campaign against the rich and powerful in effect put the Zealots in control of the city, so much so that they elected their own high priest. The Zealots, despite their quasi-religious name or nickname, were thus less than respectful of the practices of the Jewish religion, and this caused a revulsion of feeling in which the moderates, led by Annas, a former high priest, drove the Zealots into the inner courts of the temple. In the face of imminent defeat they called in help from their like-minded colleagues in Idumaea. Annas prevented the entry of these forces by shutting the gates in their faces, but Zealots let them in during a storm. These reinforcements enabled the Zealots to recover control of the whole city. Annas was killed and they followed this up by a bloodthirsty purge of other prominent moderates. This, as it turned out, was not pleasing to many of the Idumaeans, who also took note of Vespasian's coastal march, which brought a major Roman force close to their homeland. Most of them then left the city, but it remained in Zealot control.[22]

Vespasian's army was in winter quarters during these events, which he and his commanders regarded as being useful to their cause.[23] The revolutionaries' control of the lands outside core-Judaea was being whittled away while the Zealots fought to gain control of Jerusalem. Vespasian's strategy had not really changed, though it had taken longer than perhaps expected to secure all these preliminary conquests, not that he was concerned to hurry. It was always necessary to gain control of the coastlands before tackling the uplands, and the expansion of Jewish control by way of their military provinces made it necessary to apply that policy elsewhere. As the campaign in Galilee and the case of the Joppan 'pirates' both showed, Vespasian was extremely sensitive about his rearward communications.

In the spring of 68 Vespasian moved to ensure that he in turn cut the remaining contacts the rebels had with the outside world, a lesson perhaps reinforced by the need to separate the rebels from Agrippa's territories. Part of the Roman army marched through the Great Plain to the Peraia; Gadora was captured and a detachment was left in the area to complete the conquest of the region – it appears to have been an even easier and more straightforward task than Galilee. Another march took part of the army southwards. A garrison was put into Antipatris, and a major base was established at Emmaus for V *Macedonica*. Raids were sent into Idumaea, where the rival Jewish raiders, Niger and Simon bar Giora, had been drawn into the fighting in Jerusalem. It may have been news of this Roman advance which pulled many of the Idumaeans out of the city. Another march to the east through the Great Plain secured Roman control of the west bank of the Jordan valley, at Koreai and Jericho. Another major camp was established at Jericho, and then a third at Adida, just in front of Beth Horon. These fortified camps blocked the main exits from the Judaean plateau.[24]

These marches and camps had finally isolated Judaea, and their establishment obviously presaged a new Roman attack on the city. Vespasian's methodical approach was clearly successful, and similar but probably more strenuous preparations were now made at Caesarea for the siege of Jerusalem which was going to be necessary. This will have included stockpiling food and weapons, and the construction of a siege train – lessons learned from Cestius Gallus' experiences. It was while this was being done that the news arrived that Nero was dead, most suitably by his own hand (more or less), and that there was a new emperor, P. Sulpicius Galba. No doubt Vespasian felt mingled relief – at not having to defy Nero when the time came – and chagrin – that someone else had beaten him to the imperial punch.

Military operations now ceased until Vespasian could receive instructions from the new emperor, though he clearly kept up his guard and maintained the positions he had reached. Titus went off to Rome to pledge his father's allegiance to Galba, and to get new orders. He got as far as Corinth, where he learned that Galba himself was now dead. He returned to Caesarea.[25]

Chapter 14

The Jewish Rebellion: Jerusalem

The preoccupation of the Romans with events in Rome continued throughout 68 and into 69, with the result that few operations against the rebel regime in Judaea were undertaken for a year and a half. In Rome Galba was killed on behalf of Otho in January, and this led to a civil war in which Vitellius, the son of the Syrian governor of twenty years before, succeeded in removing Otho.[1] So by the middle of 69 the fourth emperor in a year was on the throne, and from the point of view of many the quality had steadily declined.

In the eastern part of the empire, whose armies had taken no part in events so far, the most significant figure, Vespasian, was meanwhile organizing his own usurpation. He may well have accepted subordination to a man like the stern unbending Galba, or even to Nero, who had an hereditary right to be emperor, but he could hardly be expected to obey such lacklustre and uninspiring near-incompetents as Otho and Vitellius.

Just when Vespasian determined to make an attempt to seize the throne is not clear, if there ever was a precise moment of decision. His reaction to Josephus' 'prophecy' of his elevation suggests that the idea was neither new nor unwelcome, but the death of Nero and his replacement by the more acceptable Galba would certainly have pushed any tentative plans to one side; after all, Vespasian was unlikely to be ordered to commit suicide by Galba, and he readily tendered his allegiance to the new ruler even while Galba was still in Spain.

Probably the decisive moment, or period, was when Titus reached Greece on his way to bring his father's greetings to Galba and to solicit new instructions. There he heard the news of Galba's murder, which was bad enough, but his replacement, Otho, was another Nero-type. (Indeed Otho had been married to the Empress Poppaea before Nero stole her from him.) But the news was still worse, for the challenger to Otho was A. Vitellius, whose personal reputation was as bad as Otho's. Vitellius had been marching against Galba at first, but now he had the easier task of fighting Otho.[2]

Titus stopped and discussed matters with his fellow travellers. One of these was King Agrippa, others were confidential friends of Titus and of Vespasian, men who probably knew of Vespasian's half-formed ambition. The decisions they reached make it clear that Titus had decided that his father would now make a bid to become emperor – and so that father and son had already discussed the matter in some detail. It is obvious that nothing could be done in

Italy while Otho and Vitellius were fighting it out, if only because Vespasian had much preparation still to do and he was too far away to influence events. But he would need information about events, and here he had considerable resources.

The second decision made at Corinth was that King Agrippa would go on to Italy, from where he would be able to send information back to Syria and Judaea. He could also contact three members of Vespasian's family who were in Rome, his teenage son Domitian, his brother T. Flavius Sabinus, who was prefect of the city, and his nephew, also T. Flavius Sabinus, who had been designated consul for part of the year 69. These men, including Agrippa, were obviously well placed to send detailed information to Vespasian. The family were generally loyal to each other, and they could quietly promote his cause when the time came.

Titus himself did some canvassing on his way back to Caesarea. From Corinth, after parting with Agrippa, he went to Ephesos, where he met the governor of Asia, C. Fonteius Agrippa. The governorship of Asia always went to a senior senator, a consular, who therefore had much influence over the neighbouring governors in the other Asian provinces. Fonteius was agreeable, so it seems, to the notion of a Flavian emperor, though how explicit such an agreement was is not known. Titus then sped up, calling on his way only at the oracle of Paphos in Cyprus, and once again he was reassured. In a superstitious age it began to seem as though the gods, as revealed by oracles (Paphos) and prophets (Josephus), were on the side of the Flavians.[3]

Titus reached Caesarea and his father about the beginning of March 69. From then on they waited for news from Italy. Vespasian had already heard the news of Otho's accession and had pledged his allegiance to him. This, if Otho won the war with Vitellius, would have been the end of the matter, for Vespasian could never have broken his word. But then in April Vitellius won the battle at Bedriacum and Otho committed suicide. Vespasian will have heard the news by the end of May, and from then on he was free to act, for Vitellius had attacked both of the emperors to whom Vespasian had pledged allegiance. One of his motives in his rebellion was to avenge these two men. The mint at Antioch had produced coins for Galba and Otho, but none for Vitellius. This must have been on governor Mucianus' instructions, and it suggests that he and Titus had already made plans. Titus, who was not quite so constrained as his father, had been free to make quiet preparations even earlier; as with Fonteius, so with Mucianus.[4]

The prefect of Egypt, Ti. Julius Alexander (the son of the Judaean procurator of twenty years before) was also brought into the plot. This, along with his own forces, gave Vespasian command of two more legions, a total of least eight. He made contact with the III *Gallica* legion, which had recently been transferred to Moesia from Syria, and which apparently remembered Vespasian with pleasure. Other legions in the Balkan frontier were alienated from Vitellius by the arrogant behaviour of Vitellius' troops who had won the fight for the empire at Bedriacum. This was scarcely enough to induce them to rebel, but they were thus open to be persuaded against Vitellius, and the men of III *Gallica* were well placed to spread the word about Vespasian, and to point out that he was giving a lead.

Vespasian also had the goodwill of others who had been alienated by the various emperors so far, though, as with III *Gallica*, this was a passive support only. He would need to be active and decisive to gain the empire. He was encouraged by another prophecy of his good fortune, this time by the Baal of Carmel. This was widely publicized, unlike Josephus' prophecy, for it was always helpful to have the gods on your side.

The plot emerged into the open in the near simultaneous proclamations of Vespasian as emperor in Judaea and Egypt and Antioch in the first week of July, and then by the swift adhesion to his cause of virtually all prominent Romans in the East, including Fonteius Agrippa and his governing colleagues in Asia Minor.[5] Abruptly Vitellius discovered that half of the empire defied him.

The effect of all this on the war in Judaea was to halt Roman attacks for a full year from June 68 (the capture of Jericho) to June 69, but the Jews were largely unable to take advantage of the lull, though it is difficult to see what they could have done. Vespasian's troops may well have been halted and encamped, and may well have been looking over their shoulders at events in Italy, but their disposition and strength made it impossible for the Jewish fighters to break out of their territory of Judaea. Their apparent military incapacity may well have been one of the reasons they turned on one other so viciously.

The triumph of the Zealots in the city was followed by a split in their ranks. First, a large part of the Idumaeans left to go home, though some did remain in the city. Then the behaviour of John of Gischala angered the original Zealots, who were led by Eleazar bar Simon. John, like Menahem before him, had arrived in the city from outside, gaining or giving the impression that he had saved it by his presence, and had now acquired inflated ideas of his own importance and capability. He seemed to Eleazar's men to be setting himself up as a dictator, and he had a large enough following (he had brought several thousands of his people with him from Galilee) that his pretensions seemed credible. The Zealots broke with him, which blocked his ambition, though the two groups did not actually fight each other.[6]

Meanwhile, in the Judaean countryside the *sicarii* who had established themselves in Masada carried out raids against anyone of whom they disapproved, usually other Jews. They had been joined by Simon bar Giora when he had been ousted from northeast Judaea, and he brought a wider ambition with him, and perhaps a reinforcement. He recruited more people, especially from the refugees who had escaped from the Zealots in Jerusalem. Some of these took refuge with the Romans, but any who did not do so were clearly both anti-Zealot (or perhaps anti-Eleazar and anti-John of Gischala) and anti-Roman. Simon's manpower grew. From Masada he made raids widely over Judaea, effectively establishing a loose control over much of the countryside outside the city. He regained some control over his old command area, and invaded Idumaea in the south, where he and the Idumaeans fought a drawn battle. He withdrew, the Idumaeans went home, then Simon returned and overran their country. He turned on Jerusalem, where the Zealot regime was so unpopular that he was let into the city.

The aim of his allies in the city was to relieve themselves of the Zealot domination, and Simon seems to have been appointed to some sort of official position courtesy of the former high priest. The Zealots maintained control of the temple, however, and Simon's egalitarian instincts meant that the remaining elements of the wealthy in the city suffered once again. There were thus three armed groups controlling different parts of the city: Eleazar and his Zealots in the inner court of the temple; John of Gischala's people held the outer court and part of the city south of the temple; Simon's people held the rest of the city. Simon's forces were the largest in number, but the others were behind powerful fortifications.[7]

All this took place during the twelve months the Romans were at a stand-still. The time and energy of the Jews in Jerusalem was thus spent by the several factions in the city in attempting to gain full control of the city for themselves, and all of them failed. In the process the extremists alienated those moderates who remained and either killed them or drove them out. Vespasian, because of the refugees who went to the Romans, was well informed of the conditions in the city, and so the delay imposed on him by the simultaneous upheavals in the west did not damage his military position in Judaea. Particularly satisfactory must have been the news that, in the fighting in the city, large stores of grain were burnt.[8] (When he was proclaimed emperor in July 69, one of the first actions Vespasian took was to ensure his control of Egypt, which gave him control of that part of the corn supply which the province exported to Rome.)

Roman operations in Judaea resumed in June. This can be seen as a preliminary to the siege of Jerusalem, but the proclamation of Vespasian as emperor came so soon after this campaign that it is more likely a tidying-up of affairs in Judaea before he headed off to Rome. Vespasian cleared Jewish authority out of northeast Judaea, where Simon bar Giora had been active, thereby denting his authority in the city to some extent. Roman forces were also pushed up onto the plateau, where Bethel and Gophna were taken, and Roman cavalry roamed almost to the city walls. Another expedition, commanded by Sex. Vettulenus Cerealis, the legate of V *Macedonica*, went into Idumaea and captured Hebron, one of Simon's main achievements and where he had taken a large food supply. The country was ravaged, which again damaged Simon's reputation, but also significantly reduced the resources available to the city. The rebellion held only the city and the small area around it by this time.[9]

Once Vespasian's bid for the empire was launched, the Jews gained another respite. The size of the forces arrayed against them was reduced, though Vespasian had so well entrenched and positioned those who remained that, even if they had tried, the Jews were unable to break the ring around them (though they do not seem even to have made the attempt). Vespasian went to Egypt to oversee the imperial campaign, and Titus remained in command in Palestine. It was Mucianus who commanded the army which was directed against Vitellius (though he was pre-empted by the Balkan legions, who invaded Italy before Mucianus and his Syrian forces could get there.)

Of the legions in the Syrian command, Mucianus took only one full legion, VI *Ferrata*, with him, but he also took large vexillations, amounting to half the legionary manpower, from each of the others: IV *Scythica*, V *Macedonica*, X *Fretensis*, XII *Fulminata* and XV *Apollinaris*.[10] His legionary troops were therefore the equivalent of three and a half legions, and he knew he would be able to collect III *Gallica* on the way, and perhaps others. This was a large enough force to overwhelm any possible Roman enemy met with before Italy; Vitellius' only hope was to consolidate his forces, but this would strip the frontier, something he could not afford to do. One of Vespasian's strengths was that he maintained the Jewish war even while his army marched on Rome – defending the empire all the time. Titus was left with five legions at half strength and many of the auxiliary regiments; he had also two fairly small vexillations from the Egyptian legions which he had brought up two years before. He would not do much attacking with this force, but the Jewish war was not abandoned.

This depleted force was required not simply to conduct the war in Judaea but also to control all Syria and to stand on guard facing Parthia. It was therefore useful that the armies of the client kings, and the militias of the cities, were in camp facing Judaea, so that there was no ready force available for rebellion in North Syria. It was perhaps surprising that the Parthian king, Vologaeses I, had not taken advantage of the Romans' problems so far. Of course he had just had to fight a hard war against Corbulo, and neither Cestius Gallus nor Mucianus had so far seriously reduced the Roman military presence in North Syria. But now it was necessary to send much of that presence to the West, and

Syria was clearly now much more vulnerable. It was time to contact Vologaeses to try to ascertain his intentions, if any, and those of his brother Tiridates, who had just been installed as king in Armenia by Nero; both may have felt aggrieved by the Roman changes, and fearful that a new emperor might revoke the peace agreement Nero had made. In another way Vologaeses was probably relieved, since it was no secret that Nero had been planning a new Parthian war.

Envoys were sent to interview Vologaeses, and maybe to Tiridates. It took some time to make the journey and to receive a reply, so that most of the action was over by the time the missions were completed. But if envoys were travelling it was very unlikely that any action would be taken. And when Vespasian did receive a reply it was to the effect that Vologaeses could offer him 40,000 mounted archers to help.[11] Such an offer was, of course, ludicrous, and Vologaeses must have known it would be refused, as in fact it was, with thanks. He also failed to address Vespasian as emperor, so there could well be grounds on both sides for feeling insulted. But Vespasian, as Vologaeses surely knew, was in no position either to accept Parthian troops for use in a civil war or to take offence while his legions in Syria were at half strength and entangled in a Jewish war. But the tactical deployment of envoys and the use of slow travel and exchange of letters did mean that, if Vologaeses intended anything, it was too late. Vespasian's diplomacy had been successful.

The reduction in military manpower in Syria therefore did not persuade Vologaeses to attack, but at the same time it prevented Titus in Palestine from being able to mount a serious attack on the Jewish rebels. He and his father could not afford a defeat at such a crucial time, nor could they afford to lock their forces into a siege; it was best therefore not to attack at all until overwhelming strength was available. (The number of fighters in Jerusalem is put by Josephus at about 25,000 – far too many for five half-strength legions.)

Once Vitellius was dead (in December 69) and Mucianus had reached Rome, the surplus troops he then had were quickly sent to the frontiers where there was trouble. So III *Gallica* was sent back to Syria in January and was in Moesia fighting a Sarmatian war in February;[12] probably other vexillations of the Syrian legions were returned as well. What was now required, after the civil war, was a clear military victory over a non-Roman enemy, and Judaea, having been the new emperor's own command, was the most important of these frontier wars. The Syrian garrison was thus revived, the danger of a Parthian attack was obviated, and the Jewish war was prosecuted to the full.

Vespasian gave Titus command of the returned troops, together with XII *Fulminata*, which had now presumably recruited its numbers from the losses in the defeat under Cestius Gallus – and was no doubt keen to gain revenge. More vexillations of 1,000 men from each of the two legions in Egypt also arrived. The contingents of troops from the client kings were increased, with Agrippa and Sohaemos of Emesa commanding personally; militia from more cities were embodied and brought south. Josephus also mentions '3,000 guards from the Euphrates', who are otherwise not known; possibly this was half of the legion which was based at Seleukeia-Zeugma, the bridge over the river, or it may have been an otherwise unknown force which was scattered along the the river to prevent smuggling. This was as big an army as Vespasian had started with, a clear sign of the need of a new emperor to gain an early, clear, and decisive victory to help legitimize his rule.[13]

Titus organized the advance on Jerusalem from three directions. V *Macedonica*, camped at Emmaus, advanced along the Beth Horon route; XII *Fulminata* climbed the steep road from Jericho; the other legions, under Titus himself, marched due south from Samaria. Titus, with two legions on the Samaria road, scouted on ahead with his bodyguard of cavalrymen as he came near Jerusalem. He and his bodyguard were ambushed by a sortie from the city. He survived, but the capture of a Roman horse seems to have elated the defenders. Another sortie disturbed X *Fretensis* while the soldiers were preparing their camp, but had more effect in the city than on the Romans. These minor near-successes persuaded the city's defenders, whose internal disputes had stilled when the legions arrived, that they had little to fear from the Romans; their mutual disputes revived. Eleazar, in the inner court of the temple, was eliminated by John of Gischala in a surprise attack at Passover when the gates were opened for worshippers to enter. John thereby gained control of Eleazar's forces and of the temple, but his forces were still outnumbered by those of Simon.[14]

Titus moved his forces close to the north wall and to the northern part of the western wall, and began to batter at both of them. When the Romans broke through, after about a fortnight, the Jews abandoned the whole of the northern suburb of the city (which Gallus had also taken earlier). The increased threat to the city again persuaded the leaders in the city – John and Simon by now – to cease fighting each other, but they did not trust each other enough to join, and could not accept, a unified command; instead they simply agreed to defend their own sections of the city. The Romans stormed the Second Wall, west of the Antonia fortress, after only five days, but this led them into a part of the city with numerous narrow streets and tall buildings and they were quickly driven out with considerable casualties.[15]

Titus' forces retook the Second Wall and then demolished a long section of it, so gaining control over the area where his earlier attack had been beaten back. The key to the rest of the city was the fortified temple, and the key to the temple was the Antonia fortress which occupied the north-west corner of the temple platform. The Jewish defenders had mounted artillery there, machines captured from Cestius Gallus during his retreat, and used these to harass the Roman forces attacking both the fortress and the wall to the west. Most of this work involved building earthworks to allow battering rams to get close to the wall and so permit an assault, and building these took two months. In the city, famine was spreading, and desertions (as the Zealots called them) increased, at least among those who had not been killed by fighters for complaining. A sortie by John of Gischala's men against the earthwork which was built to attack the Antonia succeeded in collapsing it; two days later a sortie by Simon bar Giora's men burnt some of the Roman rams and artillery at other points.[16]

Titus' men set to work to prepare a new attack on the fortress and to build a circumvallation wall to isolate the city completely, and so prevent food supplies from getting in. After three weeks the wall of the Antonia was breached (at a point, ironically, where it had been weakened by a tunnel dug by the defenders earlier). The attackers found that a secondary wall had been built by the defenders just inside the breach, but the sentries were asleep (as at Jotapata) and another silent escalation organized by Titus took the fortress next night. After an unsuccessful attempt to capture the courts around the temple by a sudden rushed attack, Titus called off the operation and turned to demolishing the fortress, which would allow better access to the court.[17]

Titus had repeatedly offered to negotiate, usually after one of his successful operations. Josephus claims to have been his main mouthpiece, though it is difficult to imagine a man like John of Gischala responding favourably to his old enemy. After gaining control of the Antonia, and learning that the daily sacrifice in the temple had been suspended for lack of victims, Titus tried again to initiate negotiations – but only for a Jewish surrender, not for any sort of compromise or agreement. Josephus and a group of wealthy man who had escaped the city were used in this appeal. They pointed out that more fighting would almost certainly damage the temple itself.[18]

This message had less impact than expected. The revolutionaries were perhaps less concerned about such damage than many of the people in the city or than these 'deserters'. They had already killed several former high priests, deposed the serving high priest and elected their own, a man who knew nothing of the rituals; they had discontinued the sacrifices; they had fought each other within the temple area for the last two years, in which fighting it had no doubt sustained damage; John had seized the moment when Eleazar had opened the gates at Passover to murder him and seize control. So when the negotiators threatened some sort of sacrilege this had little effect on the leaders in the city, though the more devout of the inhabitants were certainly affected.

Josephus is clear that these exhortations only had the effect of stiffening resistance by those in the city doing the fighting. No doubt the fact that the exhortations came from the very men whom John and Simon had been attacking and pillaging for their wealth merely angered them and played against their ideological leanings. Titus probably had few hopes of success in these appeals. He knew about conditions in the city from people who were still escaping from the city despite the surrounding walls. This was not necessarily to the defendants' disadvantage since by definition any 'deserters' were less than enthusiastic fighters, while if they stayed they would also consume scarce food. The fewer who were inside the city the longer the exiguous supplies would last, and the more fanatical would be the resistance to the Roman attacks. At least Titus let the refugees out and sent them to safety rather than forcing them to starve to death between the lines.

Titus concentrated all his forces on the walls of the temple platform. Both sides demolished parts of the portico giving access from the north into the outer temple court. When many Roman casualties were caused by a Jewish ambush, the Romans replied by burning all the porticoes. A six-day bombardment of the western side of the platform had no obvious effect, so the battering rams were moved into position on their earthen mounds. Titus tried a surprise assault, assuming the defenders would expect more ramming. For once the Jewish sentries were alert, but the Romans did manage to set fire to the wooden gates. The fire spread to other porticoes, leaving relatively easy access for the Romans at many points into the outer court.[19]

The Jewish fighters withdrew to the inner court, almost as well fortified as the rest of the temple. It was only a small area, but one from which they could make sorties in a variety of directions. This they did early in the following morning, so that Titus had to bring up reinforcements, only defeating the sortie in the end with a cavalry charge. He resolved to finish the fight with a full-scale assault by the whole army next day, but the Jews anticipated him with another sally. In this fighting, which was clearly much more difficult and even more confused than earlier, the wall of the inner court was partly burnt down – presumably there were wooden buildings arranged along the wall for this to happen. The Romans thereupon broke into the area of the temple itself, and the flames spread, either accidentally or deliberately, to the buildings beside the temple. Josephus implies that much of this was accidental, in line with his interpretation that Titus was a humane and discriminating, even devout, commander. But Titus and his staff were fully prepared for a swift raid into the temple in order to seize – 'rescue' – the treasures there.[20]

The temple burned. The defenders were killed by Roman soldiers who were exalted by the victory, or they died in the flames. Josephus suggests that Titus tried to prevent the burning of the temple and the massacre, but both assertions are unlikely. He would know how soldiers behave in such a situation, and his men had built up a substantial body of hatred of their enemies during the siege. It is unlikely that he or they would have cared much for the temple after the long siege, except, as he is reported to have said, as an architectural monument, though it was already badly damaged. Seizing the treasures kept there was an automatic response, a proof of his victory, and they were exhibited in the triumph at Rome. It is more likely that the destruction of the temple was the Roman intention from the start, or at least had become an aim once it was seen that the building was one of the main inspirations and centres of the resistance. Left standing it would have been a symbol of martyrdom and defiance, as well as being a powerful fortress, as the recent fighting had just proved. Of course, its destruction also made it a symbol, but at least it did not physically exist to provide a rallying point. Later the legions conducted a thanksgiving sacrifice before their own standards, which involved sacrificing a pig, possibly intended as a further insult of triumph aimed at the Jews' superstitions, though it is equally possible that the idea never occurred to the soldiers – and pork was the main meat eaten by Roman soldiers. Titus, who surely understood the symbolism of the pig, did not object.[21]

But the fighting was not yet finished. John of Gischala and Simon bar Giora and many of their people escaped from the massacre in the temple – John's second escape. They still had control of the Upper City, the western section of the city, and they set up their headquarters in Herod's fortified palace. An attempt to persuade Titus to let them leave and go 'to the desert' was predictably and scornfully refused. Titus then let his forces invade the Lower City, which was sacked. Meanwhile, the Zealots' commanders did much the same in the Upper City, killing and expelling those who had opposed them. Titus had his men construct another wall of circumvallation to isolate this last refuge, and set his men to building more approach mounds as a preliminary to either a bombardment or an assault.

Refugees escaped out of the Upper City in a steady stream, including a batch of relatives of King Izates of Adiabene, who was a Jewish convert: they had been present all through the siege, and not surprisingly Titus kept them as prisoners. (Adiabene was a Parthian client state; killing these people, even though they were clearly active Roman enemies, could be a dangerous move.)

The battering of the wall of the Upper City had immediate results. This was the old wall, or First Wall, which is likely to be have been in poorer condition than those attacked earlier. The determination of the rebels was weakening. One group of Idumaeans had already attempted to surrender separately, but were foiled and kept thereafter under guard. The wall was breached almost at once, and the towers began to collapse. At last the rebels' morale collapsed and they fled. Some may have got way into the surrounding country; most of them died in the city, as the Roman troops looted and burned what was left.[22]

John and Simon fled into the tunnels under the palace (another of John's escapes). They had a few people with them, but, not surprisingly after the famine in the city, they had little food. It seems clear that despite having burnt the city, the Romans carefully watched and searched it for some time afterwards and one of their motives for burning sections of the city was obviously to drive out the last resisters. John of Gischala finally surrendered; Simon tried to dig his way out, but was captured. They were reserved for Titus' triumph.[23] (John here made a final escape: Simon was executed, but John was imprisoned for life.)

Much emphasis is laid on the Romans' behaviour in the hour of victory, burning, looting, and massacring, but large numbers of the city's inhabitants clearly survived. Of those killed it seems likely that the rebels had accounted for as many as the Romans. The survivors who worth selling were sold, the old and sick killed.[24] Josephus attempts a count of the dead, but his figures are as wild as ever. Thus, as usual, the Romans made the war pay for itself.

Chapter 15

The Jewish Rebellion: Aftermath

The city was destroyed, its population driven out or killed or sold into slavery. Jerusalem, as a community, had ceased to exist, its buildings ruined and reeking with the stench of death and fire. The surrounding country was ravaged, though some forts remained in Jewish control. But the people in none of these can have had any hope of achieving their aspirations to independence now that Jerusalem and its fighters were gone.

So the fighting was not over, though the war was. A new Roman administration was put in place, not just in Judaea but in Syria as well. A prefect for Judaea had been appointed, probably by Vespasian, since he worked closely with Titus, and probably his main task was to take some of the administrative weight off Titus' shoulders while he fought the siege. This was M. Antonius Julianus, whose presence is attested once in Josephus' account, where he is described as one of Titus' chief officers, along with the legates of the legions, though he is nowhere mentioned as participating in the fighting.[1]

In Syria, in the absence of Mucianus in Europe, the senior legionary legate Cn. Pompeius Collega, of IV *Scythica*, acted as temporary governor.[2] It was not until some time in 71 that the new governor arrived. This was L. Junius Caesennius Paetus, who had been one of Corbulo's legionary legates in the Armenian war, and one of Cestius Gallus' legionary commanders in his Judaean campaign. His appointment was no doubt in part due to his relationship with Vespasian, whose niece he had married.[3]

The Syrian governor's geographical responsibilities had been both extended and restricted. In the south the prefect who had governed Judaea was now replaced by a man of senatorial rank, and the area was made into a separate province, with a legionary garrison, so the Syrian governor had no responsibility there (though the Decapolis remained his for the time being). Legion X *Fretensis* was established in a fortress in the western part of the ruins of Jerusalem, using Herod's palace as its base, probably because this building had largely survived the fighting.[4] Detachments of the legion and its associated auxiliary regiments were placed in various sites in the country, though for a few years there were still rebel forts to be captured.

Vespasian sailed from Egypt to Rome in early 71, leaving Titus to tidy up in Palestine and Syria. During the winter of 70/71 Titus made a progress through Syria accepting praise and presumably imposing decisions. This was done before Paetus arrived to take up the governorship. He could anyway hardly be appointed before Vespasian reached Rome, and perhaps it was deemed best for Titus to implement the more difficult decisions and conduct the necessary diplomacy before the new man took office.

It took some time to restore a semblance of order in Palestine. Jerusalem was finally completely conquered early in September 70, though there were still rebels at large in the city, and, as it turned out, under it. Disposing of the dead and of the survivors no doubt took some time. John of Gischala and Simon bar Giora were not captured until October. The remaining structures in the city which might have been useful as military bases if a new rebellion happened had to be demolished, including all the city's walls, and the wall around the temple.[5] The temple platform was left, not merely a flat place without the wall, perhaps because it was so well built that destroying it was too difficult – it is, of course, still there.

Titus spent a month or more on this task. Then he dispersed the army. Given the threat implied by King Vologaeses' offer of '40,000 mounted archers' to 'assist' Vespasian's campaign for the imperial throne, it was urgent to re-establish the garrison of North Syria. The vexillations of the legions which Mucianus had taken to Italy began to return early in 71, but it would take time to return all the legions to their full strengths. A powerful force was needed in Palestine until the final resistance was removed. Titus sent XII *Fulminata* back to its old Syrian base at Raphanea, and X *Fretensis* was to finish the campaign in Judaea; V *Macedonica* and XV *Apollinaris*, neither of which had been part of the original Syrian garrison before the war, went to Caesarea. Ostensibly they were to guard the great number of prisoners and the spoil which had been gathered there, but this posting also awaited a decision on where they should next be stationed.[6]

Titus spent the winter of 70/71 travelling about Syria. He spent some time with Agrippa at Caesarea Philippi. (Agrippa had earned Flavian gratitude by his assistance in Rome during the war, and had been got out of the city in time to avoid an unpleasant fate at Vitellian hands.) Titus was also involved with Agrippa's sister Berenike, who had some hopes of marriage. But no imperial prince could afford marriage with an Oriental queen after Kleopatra, and she had to settle for being Titus' mistress for some years. As Tacitus, in his ruthless way, says, 'the young man's heart was not insensible to Berenike, but his feelings towards her proved no obstacle to action'. Titus' focus was always on power.[7]

Just as with his father's visit to the same place earlier, Titus' sojourn with Agrippa was not merely pleasure, and was probably never intended to be anything but a working visit, with pleasure attached. (The trees and waters of the region would be a pleasure in themselves after the dusty Judaean plateau.) News of the capture of Simon reached him there, and of finding other rebels hiding in the tunnels. The need for a powerful garrison in Palestine was thereby reaffirmed. But we have no hint of what Titus and Agrippa discussed, though at the least the future of the Palestinian administration would be on the agenda. It is also probable that the subject of the client kings came up. Agrippa had been of great assistance both in the war in Palestine and in the usurpation; he also governed a land which was as awkward as ever, so he was probably safe for the time being. The other kings, however, though they may have been of assistance, had less call on Flavian gratitude, and (as will be discussed later) were geographically in a much more delicate position. In Nabataea King Malichos II died in 70. He had been helpful in the latter part of the war in Judaea, but to call in too many Nabataean Arabs would only have provoked greater Jewish ire. It would seem that his successor, Rabbel, was quite acceptable to the Flavians, who must have approved his accession. Rabbel claimed to have brought 'life and deliverance to his people'; possibly it was deliverance from Roman annexation which he had accomplished.[8]

Titus returned to Caesarea for a time where he celebrated his brother's eighteenth birthday (24 October) with a gory spectacle in which many Jewish prisoners died in the arena. Others had already been sacrificed in an amphitheatre at Caesarea Philippi, and he went on to Berytus to kill off still more. Berytus *colonia* was a Latin-speaking island in the Greek east, and regularly provided 1,500 men from its militia for imperial expeditions. They were treated to an extravagant display in celebration of Vespasian's birthday (17 November). From there, Titus reached North Syria. At Antioch a crisis had arisen between Greeks and Jews, when a fire was blamed on the Jews. The temporary governor, Cn. Pompeius Collega, clamped down to prevent violence and made a careful examination, finding that the accusations against the Jews were false. When Titus arrived he was nevertheless petitioned to expel the Jews from the city. He refused, but his decision only came after some time.[9]

His main purpose in visiting North Syria, and perhaps in spending so long in the region, was to meet a delegation from Vologaeses at Seleukeia-Zeugma on the Euphrates. The meeting went well, the main purpose, at least in public, was for the Parthian delegation to pass on Vologaeses' congratulations and to present Titus with a golden crown to mark his victory. Josephus is at his most narrow and exasperating in this section of his book. He merely mentions Titus' visits to Caesarea Philippi, Berytus, and Seleukeia-Zeugma, but spends pages on the dispute at Antioch, and says nothing of substance about Titus' discussions with Agrippa or the Parthians. We can only go on assumptions based on what happened in the next few years to find out what it was all about. For example it is likely that the fated of the members of the Adiabene royal family, captured in Jerusalem, was discussed – but Titus, even so, took them to Rome as hostages for the behaviour of the king. He was not going to release them without a fairly substantial concession on Vologaeses' part.[10]

The decisions on all the problems which are identified by Titus' travels in the winter of 70/71 were, of course, not his alone to make. One of the reasons why he stayed over the winter in Syria – for Josephus' reason, that the winter season was dangerous for travel, is not good enough, considering that Titus had at least twice travelled by sea in the last two winters, and Vespasian had sailed to Italy in January – was to await instructions from his father, who would need some time in Rome to consider all his options, and find a new governor. The matter of Judaea could be safely left to Titus, but the future of the client kingdoms and relations with the Parthians were issues for Vespasian to decide. So were the dispositions of the legions, an imperial responsibility which was also involved with the Parthian problem, and, as it turned out, also with the issue of the client kingdoms.

The new governors were appointed by Vespasian in 71 and took up their posts during the year. Titus moved back to Judaea in the spring to inspect his conquered land for the last time. He went up to examine Jerusalem, which had now been cleared of rebels. The city had been ransacked for personal and public treasure which had been abandoned, sometimes buried by the inhabitants. He decided that X *Fretensis* was a sufficient garrison for the country and was capable, along with auxiliary forces, of capturing the last forts. Just how many of these auxiliaries were posted to Judaea is not known. In 86 there were at least two cavalry and four infantry regiments there, but immediately after 70 it seems likely that there were more. It was a substantial garrison for a small province with no external frontiers (apart from one with Nabataea) – at least 10,000 men and perhaps more at the beginning – but not for one so recently so heavily disturbed.[11]

The first governor was Sex. Vettulenus Cerialis. He had commanded V *Macedonica* all through the war, and had been entrusted with independent commands more than once; he may have taken over as legate of X *Fretensis* as well as governor. His main task, of course, was the reduction of the remaining forts, though he was soon replaced as governor by Sex. Lucilius Bassus, who had been a Flavian ally in Italy during the usurpation. This may be the deliberate choice – by Vespasian, where Cerialis may well have been Titus' choice – of a man who had no earlier connection with Judaea and had not been involved in the war. So perhaps it was a conciliatory gesture towards the surviving Jews. He would not have built up any local hatreds – except for being a Roman, of course – and could maybe take a clearer view of matters than the men who had been fighting there for several years.[12]

Titus went from Judaea to Egypt. Josephus (and most historians) then moves him on board ship for Rome.[13] But he could have done that from

Caesarea, or Ptolemais, or Berytus, so his visit to Egypt had a purpose other than to catch a ship. Alexandria, of course, had been the scene of a Jewish insurrection in 66, put down with much killing by the legions stationed close to the city. Legion XV *Apollinaris* had been sent there at first, but when all was seen to be quiet Titus had brought it to Palestine, and later he was able to call up a thousand men from each of the remaining two legions for the war in Judaea.

Since then matters had changed. Some of the prisoners from Judaea had been sent to work in the Egyptian quarries as slaves, and it is possible that some at least had been bought out by wealthy Egyptian Jews. (There is a biblical injunction to do this.) Any redeemed Judaean slaves are likely to have been desperately anti-Roman, and by 72 they had been joined by some *sicarii* who had escaped from Judaea after the fall of the city and the forts. (This is generally attributed to escapes from the forts, but escapees from the city are as likely to have got to Egypt earlier.) Their stories and their propaganda were infectious.[14]

Investigations into the situation in Egypt are thus a likely reason for Titus' visit. In Alexandria the Greek inhabitants were still virulently angered by the Jews and asked, as had the Antiochenes, that Titus punish them – he again refused. He no doubt made the position clear to the Jewish council and could hold before them the demands of the Greeks as an incentive to root out the subversives. He also attended a ritual ceremony of the Apis bull at Memphis, where he is said to have worn a diadem, thus emphasizing the imperial succession to the earlier Ptolemaic and pharaonic kings. And, having seen the situation in Egypt and judged that it was containable, he ordered the two legions still at Caesarea to go to their new provinces, XV *Apollinaris* to Pannonia, V *Macedonica* to Moesia. (He had not, despite Josephus words, taken the legions to Egypt.)[15]

The prefect of Egypt during and after Titus' visit was Ti. Julius Lupus. He was the man responsible for dealing with the problem of the arrival of the rebels. No doubt Titus' visit gingered him up, and the Jewish council in Alexandria was properly alarmed at their agitations. Presumably at the request of the prefect, they handed over 600 to the Roman authorities. The refugee *sicarii*, finding themselves opposed by the Jewish establishment, had characteristically resorted to murder, which gave the councillors an even more personal motive for removing them. The initial attraction and sympathy felt by many Jews for the refugees was countered quickly enough when they were reminded of the fate of the refugees' fellows in Palestine, not to mention the death toll in Alexandria several years before.

Some of those who escaped from the Roman net in a city fled south, some as far as Thebes, before being caught. All are said to have been tortured to death, refusing to acknowledge Caesar as their lord.[16]

Other refugees headed for Cyrene, where they also stirred up support, largely among the poor. A gathering they organized was broken up by the forces of the governor, Catullus, who captured the leader Jonathan. He in turn accused those who had opposed him of equally subversive behaviour, and Catullus turned on them as well. (Josephus' figures in all this are as unbelievable as elsewhere.) Vespasian investigated when Catullus brought Jonathan to Rome and concluded that Jonathan had lied.[17] He would, however, be quite pleased that in both Alexandria and Cyrenaica the Roman governmental weight had been brought down on potential as well as actual subversives.

Vespasian reacted to the trouble in Egypt by ordering the destruction of the Jewish temple at Leontopolis in Egypt, presumably just in case it became the focus for more trouble, maybe as a substitute for the temple in Jerusalem his son had destroyed. In a way the sequel showed that the emperor was right. Lupus closed the temple, but let local Jews continue to use the precinct; when it was evident that some had kept up the cult, Lupus' successor stripped the building of its fittings. The building was not yet destroyed, possibly because to do so might inflame feelings again.[18]

All this activity in Egypt and Cyrenaica resulted from the arrival of men driven from Judaea by the fighting; only the initial fighting in Alexandria was simultaneous with the fighting in Judaea. On the other hand, the fears of both Greeks and Jews, and the apprehensions of the imperial government at that possibility of a much wider insurrection, are clear. The readiness with which the poor in particular responded to a few inflammatory speeches by the *sicarii* indicates quite clearly that there was a community of aspiration to either independence or empire, or both, common to Jews everywhere. And the events in all these places created suspicions on both sides which fuelled further Jewish wars in the next seventy years.

In Judaea the governor Cerealis does not seem to have had time to attend to the forts still held by the Jews. There were three of these: Herodeion, south of Jerusalem, Machaerus across the Dead Sea in the southern part of the Peraia, and Masada. It was not until his replacement arrived that serious attacks were made on them. This delay may have been due in part to the many tasks Cerealis had to undertake first, including the construction of a secure legionary base, the distribution of detachments and auxiliary regiments to strategic places, and the construction of their own forts. There were also other areas where rebels had taken refuge and from which they could emerge to conduct raids; the caves above the Essene settlement at Engedi on the shore of the Dead Sea, which had been destroyed by a *sicarii* raid from Masada, were likely places in which to hide. And there were plenty of other similar places throughout Palestine.[19]

When Lucilius Bassus arrived, late in 71, all this preparatory work had been done, and he was able to get on with attacking the forts. He took the nearest and apparently the most vulnerable first. Herodeion had been held against Simon's attack the year before by Jews who were shocked by his pretensions. This suggests that they were not the type of social revolutionaries who had followed John or Simon. Josephus simply says that Bassus reduced the fort to surrender. It was a substantial fort, not easy to capture without a major operation, yet it seems to have fallen quickly. One must conclude that the garrison did not put up much of a fight. Bassus is said then – after its capture – to have gathered the detachments and auxiliaries and brought up the legion to attack Machaerus. This means Bassus had taken Herodeion with a relatively small force – again the implication is of a fairly easy task and little opposition.[20]

The whole of the Roman force was needed, however, for Machaerus. Its situation was isolated. Some of the troops were needed to guard communications, and others had to hold the rest of Judaea. The castle was well fortified and, rather like Jerusalem, was defended naturally by steep ravines, a physically formidable proposition for the besieger. It was, however, vulnerable because of its inhabitants and garrison.

There were two groups holding the place, both prepared to fight, but one consisted of stricter Jews than the rest, and they seized control of the acropolis. The rest of the population, whom Josephus refers to as their 'alien colleagues', was left to defend the lower town. Since these 'alien colleagues' were clearly willing to fight, it would seem that they were also Jews, the term 'alien' presumably referring to their doctrinal differences. Josephus suggests that the main fighting was done by those in the castle, but his story also shows they were no more determined than those in Herodeion.

Bassus set his soldiers to work on constructing a mound which would let him bring his machines close to the wall. This involved filling in one of the ravines and was clearly going to take some time. The working soldiers were harassed by the Jews in the castle, but when one of them, a young man called Eleazar, was captured, scourged, and then threatened with crucifixion, his fellows quickly surrendered in exchange for their own freedom. Those in the town were thus abandoned. They broke out that night – therefore demonstrating that they were more determined fighters than those who had held the acropolis, who are Josephus' apparent heroes – but only some of them got away. The rest were captured, the men killed, the women and children sold. This, of course, implies that they had been doing a good deal of the fighting as well. Josephus' source in all this was presumably someone who had survived, that is, a man who had been in the acropolis group. Hence the bias in his account towards them, and hence also that we must be very sceptical of his account. The acropolis group, the purer in their own estimation, were the less determined, and gave in the more easily.[21]

The captures of Herodeion and Machaerus had therefore been relatively easy, more engineering work than fighting. Bassus may well have felt that capturing Masada would be similarly straightforward, but first he had to clear out other bands of rebels. One group, which included some of those who had escaped from Machaerus, was hidden in a forest called Jardes, whose location is not known, though it was probably in the Jordan Valley. The operation was fairly straightforward. Bassus surrounded and isolated the forest with his cavalry, and the infantry began felling the trees. (It cannot have been a very big forest.) The Jews, rather than be driven into an ever smaller area, came out to fight – as no doubt Bassus had always wanted – and they were largely killed.[22]

Bassus died at some time between this fight and the spring of 73. He was replaced by L. Flavius Silva Nonius Bassus, who arrived in 73. Overlapping with both governors was the procurator, the financial administrator, who was L. Laberius Maximus, who had been in office since at least 70. He received instructions from Vespasian during Bassus' regime to begin the process of regularizing land ownership in Judaea, where land owned by rebels had been confiscated, and was now regarded as imperial land. This was to be leased out to those who could use it. A colony of veteran soldiers was established at Emmaus, which had been a legionary camp during the war. And a tax was laid on Jews everywhere, equivalent to what they had been expected to contribute to the temple.[23] It was not just legionary sacrifices of pigs which carried a sting. The imperial government's grip was also strengthened by the foundation of a new city near Sebaste, called Flavia Neapolis (now Nablus). Its foundation date of 71/72 indicates that much of the work was done by the first two governors. Joppa, ruined by the fighting during the war, was re-founded as a city, again with the name Flavia, no doubt in part in order to keep the government in non-Jewish control, and to make use of its port. In addition Caesarea was promoted in status.

While the campaigns against Herodeion and Machaerus were on, and the new cities were being founded, another imperial policy was being revised. Vespasian was the first emperor since Augustus to have first-hand experience of the situation in the East, and Titus in his tour in 70/71 had been able to examine the land and its political system as the dust settled after the Jewish rebellion. Both had also encountered the Parthian power. The offer of 40,000 mounted archers to Vespasian by King Vologaeses was a not-too subtle reminder of the power of the Parthian king, and to an experienced politician the award of the golden crown to Titus might have seemed to be an attempt to lull his suspicions. The Roman Empire was also suffering invasions and rebellions along the Danube and the Rhine frontiers, and two of the legions in

Palestine went to reinforce the Danube line (where Fonteius Agrippa had died in battle earlier in 70). In the east it was clearly necessary to be fully on guard with respect to the Parthians, and this raised the issue of the client kings.

During the fighting in Palestine the client kings had been very supportive, providing substantial numbers of troops for the campaigns, but this only emphasized the size of their armies. There had been substantial Roman military casualties in the fighting and, at the same time, the client kings' armies had gained valuable fighting experience. Titus could report to Vespasian in 71 when he returned to Rome that the Parthians seemed dangerous, that there was still fighting in Palestine, that the kings' armies were large and battle-experienced, and that the Roman military presence in Syria was being reduced by the removal of two of the legions which had fought in the Judaean war.

This was the situation which the new governors for Palestine and Syria faced. Lucilius Bassus' task was clearly to finish off the war in Judaea, while Caesennius Paetus was given the task of making it clear to the Parthians that Rome was alert to their threat. Titus had surely already done so in the meeting at Zeugma, but Paetus would be able to reinforce the message. Two measures were to be taken: two of the client kingdoms were to be annexed, and another legion was to be pushed forward to the frontier in Cappadocia. This would be XII *Fulminata*, formerly stationed at Raphanea. Pushing it forward to the frontier was clearly a broad hint to the Parthians.

Paetus' immediate task when he reached his new command in late 71, therefore, was to prepare for the annexation of two of the client kingdoms, Kommagene and Emesa, each of which had an army larger than a Roman legion. Since it seems that many of these measures were directed at impressing, or perhaps deterring, Parthia, the first kingdom to be dealt with was Kommagene, occupying a stretch of the Euphrates between the two empires. King Antiochus IV owed his throne to Rome, had held it loyally for thirty-four years, and he had contributed forces to all Rome's wars in the region. But his kingdom was now in the way, interrupting communications between Syria and Cappadocia; his capital Samosata was a notoriously strong fortress; and his sons were ambitious. Corbulo's war had ended with the Parthian Tiridates as King of Armenia. Apart from the communication problem, the real nightmare for the Syrian government was that a Kommagenian rebellion would clearly tempt the Parthians to invade, and coming through Kommagene the Parthian forces would arrive in the midst of North Syria, only a couple of days' march from Antioch. Josephus produced some justifications along these lines, but they look mostly to be *post facto* reasoning.

Paetus had been given authority to act as he thought fit, but this presumably only applied to his methods, not his task. (No Roman provincial governor would annex a client kingdom without the emperor's instructions.)

Using VI *Ferrata*, auxiliary regiments, and contingents supplied by Sohaemos of Emesa and Aristoboulos of Chalkis, Paetus marched into Kommagene. Antiochos, who may well have known what was coming, and who was now an old man, and knew full well to whom he owed his throne, signalled his surrender. His sons, however, Epiphanes and Callinicus, took command of the local army and confronted the Roman invasion. Just the fact that the army had been mobilized, and that the king was present, implies that Antiochos intended at first to fight. But then he left his sons to conduct a competent defence for a day, which only proved to the Romans just how necessary the conquest had become. Antiochos went to Kilikia, where he ruled a separate small kingdom, but he was arrested by a centurion and sent on to Rome. His army gave way once it became clear he had left, and his sons escaped the battle (the casualties were therefore merely ordinary people). They crossed to Parthia where they were welcomed as royalty by Vologaeses. Once it was clear that the Roman annexation was accomplished they were induced without difficulty to return and live in Rome.[24]

Sohaemos of Emesa was probably also on the list for annexation, and his participation in the Kommagenian war did not save his kingdom. He had been king since 54 and may also have been old. This war is the last time he is heard of in our sources, and no other members of his family – of whom half a dozen are known of his own generation, and as many of their successors – bore the royal title. (Sohaemos had been 'Great King', not a title likely to be abandoned, and he had been granted consular rank.) The Emesan kingdom was annexed, probably in 73, and probably after Sohaemos' death. Paetus, however, who seems to have been a clumsy and tactless fellow, may well have simply gone from Kommagene to deprive him of his throne.[25]

Emesa, like the other kingdoms, could do nothing to prevent Roman annexation when that had been determined on. Its geographical position, like Kommagene's, had been its protection so far, as perhaps was its original poverty, but now it had become dangerous in Roman perception – and also rich. The city controlled a major route along the upper Orontes River, which led south into the Bekaa Valley, and north to the great city of Apamea. Another route ran west, by way of the legionary base at Raphanea, to the Mediterranean coast between Arados and Tripolis. A fourth route, and perhaps the crucial one for the Romans, went east to the oasis city of Palmyra in the desert, whence several other routes continued to the Euphrates River, in the Parthian Empire.

Palmyra had been developing as an increasingly important trading community for the last century. It had probably had a small Roman garrison since Tiberius' reign, perhaps only intermittently, but it was essentially self-governing, though during his governorship in Syria, Mucianus had regulated the city's taxation system, a fact recorded in a damaged inscription. The city had extensive contacts in Parthia and beyond, but it was also a self-consciously Arab community.[26] And this is the point, for Emesa was also Semitic, in its royal house's origins, its fundamental language, and its connections; it was also the transit point for Palmyra's exports into the Roman Empire. As such, like Palmyra, it had become rich in the last century. Though its wealth and connections – Sohaemos was related to Agrippa II and to Antiochos IV of Kommagene – made it far more important by the AD 70s than it had been when the dynasty was replaced by Augustus in 20 BC.

Rich cities close to Roman territory always excited Roman imperial cupidity. (One of the Romans' motives for conquering Jerusalem had been to seize the treasure reputed to be in the temple – it had been looted by Romans more than once since Pompey's time, but it was still a very wealthy institution.) Vespasian was notoriously tight-fisted with money, a fact which is partly personal to him, but largely the result of the destruction of wealth in the civil war and the expenses brought in by the subsequent fighting. Roman motives for annexing Emesa were therefore somewhat different from those applying to Kommagene, partly financial and only partly strategic, but just as compelling. By directly controlling Emesa the empire would collect its own taxes, and could exercise greater influence (that is, more control) over the desert city.

The annexation of Emesa may not have been accomplished by Paetus. Like Bassus in Palestine he died soon after his victory, and his successor A. Marius Celsus was in post by the middle of 73. Given the time needed for travel between Syria and Rome, this suggests that Paetus died in the winter of 72/73. Celsus was a former commander of XV *Apollinaris*, consul in 69, and had been in post as governor of Germania Inferior until the spring of 73; he was thus transferred very urgently to Syria before he had completed his tour in Germany. But then he was in office in Syria only for a few months. Either he died (still in 73) or his appointment was only intended to be temporary. He was replaced later in 73 by M. Ulpius Traianus.

Traianus had been a legionary commander (X *Fretensis*) in the Judaean war, was consul in 70, and was a close colleague of Vespasian. Whatever it was that killed Paetus and Celsus – and it seems reasonable to blame a local epidemic – Traianus was apparently immune, or perhaps acclimatized. He governed Syria for five years, which would seem to be the remainder of Celsus' term and a full three-year term of his own in addition.[27]

One of these three men annexed Emesa, in 73 in all probability. In 75 Traianus' name is recorded on milestones marking out the new Roman route from Palmyra to Sura on the Euphrates, and others in the desert roads west of Palmyra. Roman control over the roads implies control over the termini of these roads – Emesa, Palmyra, and Sura. Traianus also appears to have been responsible for beginning a major development of a naval base at Seleukeia-in-Pieria, as recorded in another inscription. This, suitably enough, was to be one of the assets used by his son Trajan in his Parthian war forty years later. All this made it quite clear to Parthia that Rome was fully prepared for any hostilities. In fact a minor war was conducted by Traianus, though the details escape us.[28]

While these annexations were being accomplished in North Syria, the final resistance of Jewish rebels was being brought to an end. Flavius Silva replaced Lucilius Bassus in 73, and had just one major task to accomplish, the capture of the last fort in rebel control, Masada. Masada appeared to be a formidable fortress, a steep-sided rock crowned by a defensive encircling wall, and stocked with water and provisions sufficient for several years' defiance. However, the Romans were well prepared for such a task. As at Jerusalem and Machaerus, a siege ramp was constructed, while camps for detachments were established to block all possible exits. The people in the fort expected to be attacked from a different direction and can only have watched helplessly as the ramp rose inexorably towards them. When it was high enough a tower was erected to overtop the wall and a heavy bombardment broke it down. A wooden barrier was hastily built to block the opening, but this was easily burnt, and the Romans could invade the fort. The whole process, from the arrival of the Roman forces to the breaking of the wall is calculated to have taken no more than a few weeks.[29]

Josephus has a description of events inside the fort which can only have happened in his imagination, since he claims that the only survivors of the people in the fort were two women and five children who had hidden themselves away and so could not see what was going on. He claims that the commander, Eleazar bar Jair, persuaded all those in the fort to commit suicide, so that only death met the Romans as they entered. However, since he claims that they were all dead, Josephus cannot have known what happened. (His own earlier account of the mass suicide at Jotapata must also be suspect.)

When the site was excavated in the 1960s a number of skeletons was found in a cave, but only twenty-five people were represented – three more were found elsewhere. The Jewish garrison was supposed to number 1,000 people. It is highly unlikely that their bodies would have been removed. The best solution to the puzzle is to discard Josephus' fantasy of mass patriotic suicide, and to presume that, as at Herodeion and Machaerus, the garrison surrendered when it became obvious that the Romans could get inside the fort. The whole siege had taken only a few months and very probably was over by April or May of 73.[30] The Jewish rebellion was over.

Chapter 16

The Desert Frontier

It may well be that the death of the Nabataean king in 70, and his succession by Rabbel II in that year, which was recognized by Rome, was the one event which allowed the kingdom to continue in existence for the next generation. The recognition of Rabbel as king must have come from Vespasian during his time in Judaea (or Egypt) while he was preoccupied with organizing his usurpation. Had he lost, no doubt Rabbel would have fallen with him, but since Vespasian made good his claim to be emperor, Rabbel was safe. Indeed, had his predecessor died a year or two later, the kingdom might well have been annexed at the same time as Kommagene and Emesa.

In the event the kingdom survived, increasingly anomalous, until 106. The kingdom of Agrippa II was taken over at his death sometime in the 90s, and that of Chalkis had probably gone earlier, so that the Nabataean was the only one left by the time the new imperial dynasty, in the person of Trajan – son of the Syrian governor in the 70s – seized power. The delicate situation of the kingdom eventually produced its annexation in 106, probably after a brief military campaign, in time to ensure that it did not threaten the flank of Trajan's intended campaign of conquest into Parthia.[1] Instead it was the Jews who provided the threat with a widespread rebellion in Egypt, Cyprus, and Cyrenaica in 115. And twenty years later Hadrian was forced into another four-year campaign of extermination in Palestine by another Jewish rebellion.

With the annexation of Kommagene and Emesa in 72/73, the Roman eastern frontier lost its cushion between the province and the Parthian territories. Until 70 Rome and Parthia had been separated by the client kingdoms which both empires had maintained: Kommagene faced Armenia-Sophene and Osrhoene, which also faced the province across the Euphrates at Seleukeia-Zeugma. To the south the desert states of Palmyra and Emesa interposed between them as well. But from 73 only Osrhoene on the Parthian side, and Palmyra and Nabataea on the Roman, remained.

From 72/73, therefore, the Romans had developed a new and formal frontier system. The legions, which had been mainly stationed within Syria until Vespasian's reign, were largely shifted closer to Parthia. One result was that Trajan was tempted into his ultimately disastrous Parthian war. Another result was the construction of lines of forts ever further eastwards to block or interrupt any Parthian encroachment, or, after the annexation of Nabataea, to control the desert tribes.

This sort of system had, of course, also developed in Egypt, on the southern Nile frontier which was stabilized by Petronius in the 20s BC, and in the deserts to east and west of the river. The basic reasons were, as in Arabia, defence against attacks by the desert nomads, but the method was different in the three directions in which Egypt faced Africa. In the south, as discussed in Chapter 8, the enemy was an organized state, Kush, based at Meroe, but one which was largely peaceable. So the defensive system consisted of a number of forts along the river, fairly lightly manned. To the west, all the nearby oases – Siwah, Kharja, and others, were occupied, with a stern fort in each, to control the people, to tax them, to protect them, and to act as a forward defence for the Nile populations.[2]

To the east, on the other hand, the priority was less defence than economics. There were a line of ports along the Red Sea coast – Myos Hormos and Berenike, mentioned in connection with Aelius Gallus' Arabian campaign in Chapter 9 – were the most important. These were connected to the Nile Valley by a series of roads which were fortified and patrolled. The desert was also an economic resource in itself, for there were quarries of much-prized stone there, such as porphyry, and also gold mines. The quarries were worked by slaves (such as the Jewish rebel prisoners) and they had to be guarded and controlled; gold mines were an imperial resource and similarly had to be controlled. The main resource, however, was the Indian and Yemeni trade which came through the ports. Each port had its garrison and its fort, or forts.[3]

In Egypt, therefore, the Nile Valley was only lightly garrisoned, but the surrounding lands were, by comparison, subject to a considerable military presence. As time went on, the original garrison of the country was reduced and redeployed in the light of the growing Roman understanding of the country. (The reduction in manpower was, of course, one of the reasons that the Jewish rebellion in 115–17 had been fairly successful.)

In Syria the situation was different. The gradual expansion of Roman control eastwards, marked especially by the annexation of the major client kingdoms in 72/73, was also the result of considerable economic development. Some of this was the product of the peace imposed by Roman control, and of the increasing trade passing through the Syrian ports, but mostly it was the result of an improving climate. The borderlands of the desert retreated before slowly expanding agricultural colonization. This was partly peasant enterprise, and partly investment from the products of trade. Within the old settled area there was also an internal colonization, which also brought much agricultural specialization, for once a peaceful future seemed guaranteed, olive trees could be planted, vineyards expanded – both of which might take decades to become fully productive. Each of these was thus was a long-term investment and required peaceable conditions to be undertaken. By the late first century North Syria was a major producer and exporter of olive oil and wine.[4] Palestine, constantly disturbed until halfway through the second century, was less productive, but as a relatively well-watered land its basic agricultural system endured, and could recover quickly. Its time of prosperity came later.

There were limits to the physical expansion of an agricultural regime, however, and this seems to have been reached by about the time the Nabataean client state was annexed. From then on the static frontier became increasingly well guarded. The legions moved east, forts were built, particularly, as in Egypt's Eastern Desert, along the roads. The old King's Highway along the plateaux east of the Jordan was studded with forts, whose distribution and history is being investigated by archaeologists now.[5] The roads to Palmyra were guarded later – the main road became called the Strata Diocletiana – but the merchant princes of that city guarded their own caravans themselves beforehand, and, of course, they had good contacts among the desert tribes.

So, having beaten down local resistance, Rome became the guardian of the survivors. The army gradually shifted its bases to face the desert Arabs and the Parthian empire.

Conclusion

The wars Rome waged in Egypt and Judaea – and Arabia – tended to be fairly brief, but could be particularly brutal. This, of course, was the Roman method, practicing terror methods in order to get the fighting over as quickly as possible, and to deter any later fighting. It did not always work, of course, as the repeated conflicts with the Jews shows. It is also the case that frequent victories led to Roman over-confidence. The Arabian campaign of Aelius Gallus is a clear example. To expect a single legion and some auxiliary regiments to conquer a large territory 1,000 miles beyond the Roman frontier was over-confidence of a high degree, and it was only due to the skilful command of Aelius Gallus himself that a complete Roman disaster was avoided. Augustus, of course, called it a victory, but it was a victory only in the sense that most of the troops were evacuated successfully – an ancient Dunkirk, in fact.

Similarly the attempts to penetrate south into the Sudan had to be called off after two expeditions had revealed the size of the enemy territory and the enormous distances involved. Of course, both the Meroe and the Yemeni expeditions coincided with constant problems with Parthia, and Augustus needed to have peace everywhere in order to convince the Parthian king that Rome was strong, undistracted, and able to concentrate on him. So the greater problem of Parthia demanded the abandonment of the Sudanese and Yemeni adventures. Perhaps conquest could have been made if Rome had concentrated its armed strength in the right place, but this was never possible.

The conquests of Egypt and Judaea therefore marked the real terminus of Roman expansion. Occasional conquests away from the eastern frontier were possible – in Britain, Germany, Dacia – but the brooding presence of a rival empire effectively blocked any more expansion eastwards. The connection was clearly made even in 40 BC, when Parthia sponsored the replacement of one Jewish king by another while other client kings in Syria deftly shifted allegiance. The message was clear; if Rome was weak in Syria, Parthia could conquer. It was necessary to concentrate a powerful Roman army in North Syria as a constant precaution against this.

Why therefore did Parthia not take advantage of the great Jewish rebellion in 66–70? There were probably two reasons: one was the war Rome and Parthia had recently fought ('Corbulo's War') which had been concluded by a peace agreement between the Parthian and Armenian kings and the Emperor Nero. While Nero lived, that peace was secure by the normal diplomatic practices of the time. By the time Nero died, the nature of the Jewish rebellion had become clear, and it is likely that the Parthians wanted nothing to do with it. They had a large Jewish population of their own in Babylonia, and they had seen how quickly the infection of rebellion could spread, particularly in what happened at Alexandria. It was easier to establish amicable relations with the pretender Vespasian than to act to take advantage of his difficult situation.

So this was the second reason why the expansion of the Roman Empire came to a halt at the Euphrates and the Arabian desert and the first cataract of the Nile. The Roman government could never be certain of the loyalty of its conquered and subject peoples. The Jews were the most notorious case of persistent internal enemies, but were by no means the only people who had to be watched. Some or all of the legions stationed in Syria were inside the province, and when forces were pushed forward to the Parthian frontier, others took their places. Egypt might be peaceful, but only because it had a powerful and occupying garrison. The Roman Empire, faced with the need to constantly watch its subjects and to hold on to the land it had seized, was paralyzed into a condition of constant tension and unable to expand further.

Notes

Chapter 1: Judaea: Pompey's Conquest

1 Appian, *The Mithridatic Wars* 106; cf Seyrig (1950) 11–50.
2 Josephus, *Antiquitates Judaicae*, 13.49–420.
3 Appian, *The Syrian Wars* 49–50; Plutarch, *Life of Pompey* 38–9; Dio Cassius, *History of Rome* 4 37.7a (Xiphilinos' epitome, highly misleading); Downey (1951) 149–63.
4 Strabo, *Geography* 16.18.
5 Chad (1972).
6 Josephus, *Antiquitates Judaicae* 14.39.
7 Josephus, *Antiquitates Judaicae* 14.29.
8 Myers (2011).
9 Bowersock (1983).
10 As for example in 88, the defeat of Antiochos XII (Josephus, *Antiquitates Judaicae* 13.39).
11 This is due, of course, above all to the works of the historian Josephus, though he has to be scrutinized carefully, being biased, above all, in his description of the great revolt, in which he took a prominent personal part.
12 Josephus, *Antiquitates Judaicae* 14.4.28.
13 Josephus, *Antiquitates Judaicae* 14.30–3.
14 Josephus, *Antiquitates Judaicae* 14.41–5.
15 Josephus, *Antiquitates Judaicae* 14.47–9.
16 Josephus, *Antiquitates Judaicae* 14.49.
17 The survival of this dynasty until the 60s is not certain; a member ruled both cities in the 70s and it is very probable that this continued ten years later. The two cities had united in the face of Judaean hostility, and that did not end until the Romans arrived and reduced Judaean power.
18 Josephus, *Antiquitates Judaicae* 14.50–1.
19 Josephus, *Antiquitates Judaicae* 14.75; Demetrios, since he was a freedman, had no doubt been enslaved and sold by Alexander Iannai in his conquest of Gadara. One's sympathy is entirely with Demetrios.
20 Josephus, *Antiquitates Judaicae* 14.52.
21 Josephus, *Antiquitates Judaicae* 14.57–60.
22 Appian, *The Mithridatic Wars*, 114; Josephus, *Antiquitates Judaicae* 14.35 seems to be a different, earlier, contact.
23 Pliny the Elder, *Natural History* 39.16.
24 Josephus, *Antiquitates Judaicae* 14.61–70.

25 Josephus, *Antiquitates Judaicae* 14.73, 79.

26 Josephus, *Antiquitates Judaicae* 14.74 – 76; Jones (1971) 258–61.

27 Head (1911) 787.

28 Pliny the Elder, *Natural History* 5.74; Jones (1971) 250–1.

29 Josephus, *Antiquitates Judaicae* 14.79; Dio Cassius, *History of Rome* 37.20.1; Plutarch, *Life of Pompey* 42.

30 Josephus, *Antiquitates Judaicae* 14.80–1; Bowersock (1983) 32–3.

31 Pliny the Elder, *Natural History* 5.81–2; see also Jones (1971) 262–5.

Chapter 2: Gabinius

1 Dio Cassius, *History of Rome* 36.48.2; Brunt (1971) 458.

2 Appian, *The Syrian Wars* 51; Bowersock (1983) 33–4.

3 Cicero, *De Domo sua* 23, 55, and *Pro Sestio* 4; Brunt (1971) 461.

4 Josephus, *Antiquitates Judaicae* 14.82; it is clear from Josephus' words that the insurrection had begun before Gabinius arrived, *contra* Smallwood (1981) 31.

5 So Marcus in the Loeb edition of Josephus, *Antiquitates Judaicae* (at 14.82), following a suggestion by Schalit. There is actually no evidence for this; all Josephus says is that he was stopped by 'Romans'.

6 Josephus, *Antiquitates Judaicae* 14.83–7; *Bellum Judaicarum* 1.163.

7 Josephus, *Antiquitates Judaicae* 14.88; Josephus, *Bellum Judaicarum* 1.166; Jones (1971) 259.

8 Josephus, *Antiquitates Judaicae* 14.89–91.

9 Josephus, *Antiquitates Judaicae* 14.92–7.

10 Sherwin-White (1983) 271–2.

11 Justin, *Epitome* 39.5; Livy, *periochae* 70; Cicero, *De Lege Agraria* 2.5.1; Appian, *The Civil Wars* 1.111.

12 Holbl (2001) 222.

13 Plutarch, *Life of Crassus* 13.2; Cicero, *De Rege Alexandrinum*.

14 Cicero, *De Lege Agraria*, and *Ad Atticum* 2.1.3.

15 Diodoros, *Library of History* 1.83.8–9; Suetonius, *Life of Caesar* 54.3 and others; Caesar, *Civil Wars* 3.107; Cicero, *Pro Rabirio* 3, and *Ad Atticum* 2.16.2.

16 Dio Cassius, *History of Rome* 39.12; Plutarch, *Life of Pompey* 49.7, *Life of Cato* 34.7; Livy, *periochae* 104.

17 A good account of all this is in Whitehorne (1994) 182–5.

18 Dio Cassius, *History of Rome* 39.15.1–3, and 16.3.

19 Plutarch, *Life of Pompey* 49; Cicero, *Ad Quinto* 2.2.3; *Ad Familiares* 1.1.3 and 7; Dio Cassius, *History of Rome* 39.12.

20 Josephus, *Antiquitates Judaicae* 14.99.

21 Dio Cassius, *History of Rome* 39.58.1.

22 Strabo, *Geography* 17.1.11.

23 Dio Cassius, *History of Rome* 39.58.

24 Plutarch, *Life of Antony* 3.2–6; Huzar (1978) 31–2, exaggerates Antony's part, even inventing events.

25 Dio Cassius, *History of Rome* 39.58.3.

26 Caesar, *Civil Wars* 3.4.4; Plutarch, *Life of Pompey* 78.

27 Cicero, *Pro Rabirio* 22–8 and 38–45.

28 Bagnall and Derow (2004) no 62 (SB 22, 15203).

29 Dio Cassius, *History of Rome* 39.59.2.

30 Josephus, *Antiquitates Judaicae* 14.100–2.

31 Josephus, *Antiquitates Judaicae* 14.104; Bowersock (1983) 35–6.

32 Josephus, *Antiquitates Judaicae* 14.103.

Chapter 3: The Emergence of Antipater and Kleopatra

1 Josephus, *Antiquitates Judaicae* 14.77.

2 Josephus, *Antiquitates Judaicae* 14.121–2.

3 Josephus, *Antiquitates Judaicae* 14.121; *Bellum Judaicarum* 1.181.

4 Josephus, *Antiquitates Judaicae* 14.81.

5 Josephus, *Antiquitates Judaicae* 14.101–2.

6 Josephus, *Antiquitates Judaicae* 14.127 and 139.

7 Josephus, *Antiquitates Judaicae* 14.372.

8 Josephus, *Antiquitates Judaicae* 14.120.

9 Josephus, *Antiquitates Judaicae* 14.105–9; Josephus as usual provides figures (10,000 talents) which are by no means to be believed.

10 Josephus, *Antiquitates Judaicae* 14.119–20.

11 Dio Cassius, *History of Rome* 52.35.4; Caesar, *Civil Wars* 3.108.4–6, and *Alexandrian War* 33.1.

12 Holbl (2001) 231.

13 Maehlers (1983) 1–16.

14 Dio Cassius, *History of Rome* 50.30.1–2.

15 Valerius Maximus, *Memorable Deeds and Sayings* 4.1.15; also mentioned by Cicero, *Ad Atticum*, 5.3 and Caesar, *Civil Wars* 3.110.

16 Holbl (2001) 231–2 giving references.

17 Malalas, *Chronicle* 9.279; this is not a very reliable source, but he must get something right at times, and this item is so curious that it can be accepted.

18 Discussed by Will (1982) 529–30.

19 Plutarch, *Life of Antony* 27.4–5, though he spoils the point by adding a whole series of other languages for her.

20 Holbl (2001) 231–2.

21 Brett (1937) 452–63.

22 Dio Cassius, *History of Rome* 42.12; Caesar, *Civil Wars* 3.40.

23 Lucan, *Pharsalia* 5.58–64.

24 Josephus, *Antiquitates Judaicae* 14.123–5.

25 Josephus, *Antiquitates Judaicae* 14.126.

26 Smallwood (1981) 36 note; the date of the marriage is uncertain.

27 Caesar, *Civil Wars* 3.88.

28 Caesar, *Civil Wars* 3.82 and 102; Plutarch, *Life of Pompey* 74 and 77; Dio Cassius, *History of Rome* 42.2.3–3.1; Appian, *Civil Wars* 2.88; Lucan, *Pharsalia* 8.120–30.

29 Caesar *Civil Wars* 3.102.

30 Plutarch, *Life of Pompey* 77; Dio Cassius, *History of Rome* 42.3.1; Caesar, *Civil Wars* 3.103; Appian, *Civil Wars* 2.84.

31 Caesar, *Civil Wars* 3.103.

32 Caesar, *Civil Wars* 3.104; Plutarch, *Life of Pompey* 77–8; Dio Cassius, *History of Rome* 42.3.3–4.1; Appian, *Civil Wars* 2.84.

Chapter 4: Caesar

1 Caesar, *Civil Wars* 3.106; Plutarch, *Life of Caesar* 48; Dio Cassius, *History of Rome* 42.8.1.

2 Plutarch, *Life of Pompey* 80.

3 Caesar, *Civil Wars* 3.106.

4 Plutarch, *Life of Caesar* 48; the total sum he claimed was 17½ million *denarii*; Gelzer (1968) 247.

5 Plutarch, *Life of Caesar* 48.

6 Caesar, *Civil Wars* 106–7; Appian, *Civil Wars* 2.89; Lucan, *Pharsalia* 10.14–19.

7 Caesar, *Civil Wars* 108.

8 Plutarch, *Life of Caesar* 49; Caesar does not mention her arrival, or her presence in the palace.

9 Dio Cassius, *History of Rome* 42.35.1–6.

10 Dio Cassius, *History of Rome* 42.36.1–2.

11 Caesar, *Civil Wars* 3.109; Dio Cassius, *History of Rome* 37.1–2.

12 Caesar, *Civil Wars* 3.110–12; Dio Cassius, *History of Rome* 42.38.2, 39.1–2, 40.1.

13 *Alexandrian War* 2–3 and 5–8.

14 *Alexandrian War* 10–16.

15 *Alexandrian War* 17–21; Dio Cassius, *History of Rome* 42.40.4–5; Appian, *Civil Wars* 90; Plutarch, *Life of Caesar* 49.

16 *Alexandrian War* 23–6; Dio Cassius, *History of Rome* 42.40.6.

17 *Alexandrian War* 9.

18 *Alexandrian War* 26; Josephus, *Antiquitates Judaicae* 14.127–9.

19 Josephus, *Antiquitates Judaicae* 14.130; *Alexandrian War* 26; Dio Cassius, *History of Rome* 42.41.1–2.

20 *Alexandrian War* 27; Dio Cassius, *History of Rome* 42.43.1.

21 Josephus, *Antiquitates Judaicae* 14.131–2.

22 Holbl (2001) 280.

23 *Alexandrian War* 24; Dio Cassius, *History of Rome* 42.43.2.

24 *Alexandrian War* 30–2; Appian, *Civil Wars* 2.90; Josephus, *Antiquitates Judaicae* 14.136; Dio Cassius, *History of Rome* 42.43.4.

25 Beginning with Appian, *Civil Wars* 2.90.

26 *Alexandrian War* 33; Dio Cassius, *History of Rome* 42.44.1–45.1; Appian, *Civil Wars* 2.90.

27 Strabo, *Geography* 16.2.10; Jones (1971) 261; Seyrig (1950) 20–1; Sullivan (1980) 198–9, does not agree about Arethusa.

28 Josephus, *Antiquitates Judaicae* 14.137, 140–4, 202–10; *Bellum Judaicarum* 195–200; Smallwood (1981) 38–41.

Chapter 5: Herod

1 Josephus, *Antiquitates Judaicae* 14.158–9; Richardson (1996) 46–7, for the children.

2 Josephus, *Antiquitates Judaicae* 14.159–60.

3 Josephus, *Antiquitates Judaicae* 14.167–70; McLaren (1991) 67–79.

4 Josephus, *Antiquitates Judaicae* 14.180–94.

5 Josephus, *Antiquitates Judaicae* 14.268; Dio Cassius, *History of Rome* 47.26.3–7; Appian, *Civil Wars* 3.77.

6 Dio Cassius, *History of Rome* 47.27.1–5; Josephus, *Antiquitates Judaicae* 14.268 (presumably Phasael and Herod, but Josephus does not identify them); Cicero, *Ad Atticum* 14.9.3.

7 Appian, *Civil Wars* 3.77.

8 Appian, *Civil Wars* 4.58; Dio Cassius, *History of Rome* 47.28.1.

9 Josephus, *Antiquitates Judaicae* 14.272–6.

10 Josephus, *Antiquitates Judaicae* 14.277–9.

11 Josephus, *Antiquitates Judaicae* 14.281–4.

12 Josephus, *Antiquitates Judaicae* 14.285–93.

13 Josephus, *Antiquitates Judaicae* 14.294–6.

14 Josephus, *Antiquitates Judaicae* 14.297–9.

15 Josephus, *Antiquitates Judaicae* 14.301–5.

16 Josephus, *Antiquitates Judaicae* 14.324–9.

17 Dio Cassius, *History of Rome* 38.24.3–26.1; Appian, *Civil Wars* 5.65; Plutarch, *Life of Antony* 30.1.

18 Josephus, *Antiquitates Judaicae* 14.330–9; *Bellum Judaicarum* 1.248–9.

19 Josephus, *Antiquitates Judaicae* 14.353–62.

20 Josephus, *Antiquitates Judaicae* 14.366.

21 Dio Cassius, *History of Rome* 48.24–6, 39–41, 49.20–2; Plutarch, *Life of Antony* 30, 33–4; Appian, *Civil Wars* 5.65; Livy, *periochae* 127–8.

22 Josephus, *Antiquitates Judaicae* 14.370–8.

23 Josephus, *Antiquitates Judaicae* 14.378–89; *Bellum Judaicarum* 1.285.

24 Josephus, *Antiquitates Judaicae* 14.390–3; Dio Cassius, *History of Rome* 48.41;

Silo's *nomen* is not certain.

25 Josephus, *Antiquitates Judaicae* 14.394–400.

26 Josephus, *Antiquitates Judaicae* 14.402–11.

27 Josephus, *Antiquitates Judaicae* 14.412–18.

28 Josephus, *Antiquitates Judaicae* 14.420–1.

29 Josephus, *Antiquitates Judaicae* 14.434–47.

30 Josephus, *Antiquitates Judaicae* 14.448–61.

31 Josephus, *Antiquitates Judaicae* 14.465–86, 490.

Chapter 6: Kleopatra

1 Plutarch, *Life of Caesar* 49.10; Holbl (2001) 28.

2 Van 't Dack (1988) 185–213.

3 Ricketts (1980).

4 Meuleraera (1959) 1–25; *Prosopographia Ptolemaica* 1.194, VI, 16277 and 17147; Thomas (1975).

5 Suetonius, *Life of Julius* 52.1.

6 Suetonius, *Life of Julius* 52.2; Dio Cassius, *History of Rome* 47.3.5; Plutarch, *Life of Caesar* 49.5.

7 Josephus, *Antiquitates Judaicae* 15.89.

8 Dio Cassius, *History of Rome* 47.31.5; *Stele Serapeum* 375.

9 Pliny the Elder, *Natural History* 5.56; Appian, *Civil Wars* 4.61 and 108; Josephus, *Contra Apion* 60; Maehler (1983) 1–17, cannot detect complaints of heavy taxation during Kleopatra's later years.

10 Appian, *Civil Wars* 4.59; Cicero, *Ad Familiares* 12.11.

11 Appian, *Civil Wars* 4.61.

12 Appian, *Civil Wars* 5.8.

13 Plutarch, *Life of Antony* 25–6; Dio Cassius, *History of Rome* 48.24.

14 Plutarch, *Life of Antony* 28–9; Appian, *Civil Wars* 5.11.

15 Appian, *Civil Wars* 5.9.

16 Bagnall (1976) 262.

17 Dio Cassius, *History of Rome* 49.32 seems to think Antony was in Egypt at this conference. Plutarch, *Life of Antony* 36.5 says Syria, and that Antony sent for Kleopatra to attend him here; Josephus, *Antiquitates Judaicae* 15.92, for example, thinks they travelled through Syria together.

18 Josephus, *Antiquitates Judaicae* 49.32.5; Plutarch, *Life of Antony* 36.2; Josephus, *Antiquitates Judaicae* 15.94–5; *Bellum Judaicarum* 1.361.

19 Crawford (1985) 253–4, with detailed references, though he takes Plutarch's list as correct.

20 This is the title of a book by Joann Fletcher (2008), but it is an attitude implicit in most of the biographies.

21 Holbl (2001) 276, 278.

22 Josephus, *Antiquitates Judaicae* 15.96.

23 Plutarch, *Life of Antony* 36.2; Bowersock (1983) 41.

24 Holbl (2001) 242.

25 Huzar (1978) 176–9.

26 Plutarch, *Life of Antony* 51.1–2; Dio Cassius, *History of Rome* 49.31.4.

27 Huzar (1978) 145.

28 Plutarch, *Life Antony* 50.4.

29 Dio Cassius, *History of Rome* 49.40.3–41.1; Plutarch, *Life of Antony* 4.

30 Plutarch, *Life of Antony* 36.3; Dio Cassius, *History of Rome* 49.37.4.

31 Dio Cassius, *History of Rome* 49.41; Plutarch, *Life of Antony* 54.

Chapter 7: Octavian

1 Dio Cassius, *History of Rome* 51.5.5.

2 Jos. *Antiquit*ates Judaicae 15.72.

3 Dio Cassius, *History of Rome* 49.32.5; Josephus, *Antiquitates Judaicae* 15.96; *Bellum Judaicarum* 1.359–69; Seyrig (1951) 5–50, and (1954) 73–80.

4 Josephus, *Antiquitates Judaicae* 15.96; Plutarch, *Life of Antony* 36.2; discussion by Bowersock (1983) 47.

5 Josephus, *Antiquitates Judaicae* 15.107.

6 Josephus, *Antiquitates Judaicae* 15.40.

7 Josephus, *Antiquitates Judaicae* 15.41 and 52.5.

8 Josephus, *Antiquitates Judaicae* 15.64 and 75–6.

9 Richardson (1996) 262–4.

10 Discussed, e.g., by Grant (1972) 187–9, Carter (1970) 188–95, and other places – and sometimes taken seriously.

11 Josephus, *Antiquitates Judaicae* 15.108–9; Plutarch, *Life of Antony* 61.1 lists Herod as a contributor, but with no details.

12 Josephus, *Bellum Judaicarum* 1.364.

13 Josephus, *Antiquitates Judaicae* 15.111 says 'Diospolis', which is a later name for another place entirely; it is normally assumed it was a mistake for 'Dion polis'.

14 Again there is confusion over the name, which is given variously in different manuscripts. The best assumption is that it was Kanata. There is another place nearby called Kanatha, but that is further on.

15 Josephus, *Antiquitates Judaicae* 15.111–19; *Bellum Judaicarum* 1.366–9.

16 Josephus, *Antiquitates Judaicae* 15.121–2; *Bellum Judaicarum* 1.373.

17 Josephus, *Antiquitates Judaicae* 15.148–60; *Bellum Judaicarum* 1.380–5.

18 Carter (1970) 202.

19 Dio Cassius, *History of Rome* 50.2.5–7 and 6.1.

20 Dio Cassius, *History of Rome* 50.3.2; Plutarch, *Life of Antony* 57.2–3.

21 Dio Cassius, *History of Rome* 50.3.2–5; Grant (1972) 192–8.

22 Grant (1972) 204–5.

23 Dio Cassius, *History of Rome* 50.13.5.

24 Plutarch, *Moralia* 207 A.

25 Dio Cassius, *History of Rome* 50.11.3.

26 Dio Cassius, *History of Rome* 50.13.7.

27 Dio Cassius, *History of Rome* 50.14.2.

28 Dio Cassius, *History of Rome* 51.7.4.

29 Dio Cassius, *History of Rome* 51.2.2.

30 Dio Cassius, *History of Rome* 51.5.6.

31 Dio Cassius, *History of Rome* 51.7.2–6.

32 Josephus, *Antiquitates Judaicae* 15.183–93; *Bellum Judaicarum* 1.387–92.

33 Josephus, *Antiquitates Judaicae* 15.165–78.

34 Dio Cassius, *History of Rome* 51.5.4.

35 Plutarch, *Life of Antony* 69.2–3; Dio Cassius, *History of Rome* 51.7.1.

36 Dio Cassius, *History of Rome* 51.9.1–4.

37 Josephus, *Bellum Judaicarum* 1.394; *Antiquitates Judaicae* 15.199–200.

38 Josephus, *Antiquitates Judaicae* 15.344; *Bellum Judaicarum* 1.398.

39 Plutarch, *Life of Antony* 74.1; Dio Cassius, *History of Rome* 51.9.6 (blaming Kleopatra).

40 Plutarch, *Life of Antony* 74.3–76.1; Dio Cassius, *History of Rome* 51.10.1–4.

41 Plutarch, *Life of Antony* 76.2–79.3; Dio Cassius, *History of Rome* 51.10.6–14.1.

42 Dio Cassius, *History of Rome* 51.15.5; Plutarch, *Life of Antony* 81.1–82.1.

43 Sullivan (1980) 202.

44 Josephus, *Bellum Judaicarum* 1.440; Bowersock (1983) 45–6.

45 Josephus, *Bellum Judaicarum* 1.396–7; *Antiquitates Judaicae* 15.217.

46 Seyrig (1954).

47 Holbl (2001) 250.

Chapter 8: Holding Egypt: a New Roman Frontier

1   Dio Cassius, *History of Rome* 51.17.6–8.

2   Augustus, *Res Gestae Divi Augusti*, Brunt and Moore (1967) .

3   Strabo, *Geography* 17.1.12.

4   Suetonius, *Life of Augustus* 17.

5   Dio Cassius, *History of Rome* 51.18.1.

6   See the map in Alston (1995) 34.

7   Strabo, *Geography* 17.1.53; Dio Cassius, *History of Rome* 51.17.1.

8   Syme (1938) 39ff and (1939) 75; Burstein (1995) 165–73; Bouchier (1966).

9   Mond and Myers (1934).

10 Dio Cassius, *History of Rome* 51.18.1.

11 Bowman (1986) 65–8.

12 Josephus, *Bellum Judaicarum* 2.383–5; cf. Rickman (1980) 67–71 and Appendix 4.

13 Dio Cassius, *History of Rome* 51.17.4; but Strabo, *Geography* (17.1.53) emphasizes

the submissiveness of the population.

14 Strabo, *Geography* 17.1.53.

15 *OGIS* 514; *Inscriptiones Philae* II.128; the inscription is in three languages, Latin, Greek and hieroglyphic Egyptian, each slightly different. The only English translation of the Egyptian I have located is in *FHN* II.165. It is discussed in detail by Minas-Nerpel and Pfeiffer (2010) 267–98.

16 'Mile' is inaccurate and misleading, for 30 *schoinoi* is about 450 km.

17 Akinidad: Kirwan (1977) 13–31; Quper: Torok (1989–90) 171–90; neither suggestion has been taken up by others.

18 Dio Cassius, *History of Rome* 53.23.5–24.1.

19 Strabo, *Geography* 17.1.54.

20 *Inscriptiones Philae* II.159.

21 Strabo, *Geography* 17.1.54; Dio Cassius, *History of Rome* 54.5.4.

22 Welsby (1996) 25–6.

23 Pliny the Elder, *Natural History* 6.35.181.

24 Torok (1989) 49–214.

25 Pliny the Elder, *Natural History* 6.35.182; Strabo, *Geography* 17.1.54.

26 Strabo, *Geography* 17.1.54; an inscription from near Meroe seems to provide a Kushite version of these events (*FHN* II.176), but it cannot yet be read.

27 Torok (1989–90).

28 Anderson et al (1979) 125–55, with references to the excavation reports.

29 Garstang (1910) 45–52. The head is in the British Museum; the mural was destroyed in a storm in 1914; cf. Torok (1989–90).

Chapter 9: The Arabian Expedition

1 Strabo, *Geography* 17.1.46.

2 Strabo, *Geography* 16.4.22.

3 Strabo, *Geography* 16.4.22–5; Pliny the Elder, *Natural History* 6.32.160–1; Dio Cassius 53.29.3–8.

4 Strabo, *Geography* 17.1.45, mentioning the ports Berenike and Myos Hormos.

5 Thomas (1975) 121–2. Kallimachos had at least one predecessor with the same title.

6 Sidebotham (1986) 5–6, and a recent update in his (2011).

7 Strabo, *Geography* 16.4.2; Hoyland (2001) 40–1.

8 Hoyland (2001) 43–4.

9 Strabo, *Geography* 16.4.22 – 23; Jameson (1968) 71–84; Sidebotham (1986a) 590–602, and his (1986b). The most substantial discussion, which is also from the South Arabian point of view, is Pirenne (1961) chapters 2 and 3.

10 Sidebotham (1986b) 122–3.

11 Strabo, *Geography* 16.4.24.

12 There was even a version of the trireme adapted as a troop transport, with a smal-

ler crew, which could carry eighty-five soldiers; cf Casson (1986) 193. The fleet built at Kleopatris, if it was of ships of this type, could easily carry 10,000 soldiers.

13 Kirwan (1979); Cohen (2006) 329–30.

14 Brunt and Moore (1967) 26.5.

15 Pliny the Elder, *Natural History* 6.33.160.

16 Strabo, *Geography* 16.4.24; for the location of these towns and cities, see Pirenne (1961) chapter 3.

17 Strabo, *Geography* 16.4.24.

18 Costa (1977) 69–72; Bowersock (1983) appendix 1.

19 It is Bowersock's argument (previous note).

20 Strabo, *Geography* 16.4.23.

Chapter 10: The Judaean Problem

1 Pliny the Elder, *Natural History* 5.81–2; cf Jones (1971) for an analysis of Pliny's section on Syria.

2 Josephus, *Antiquitates Judaicae* 15.344.

3 Myers (2011) 32–3.

4 Josephus, *Antiquitates Judaicae* 15.343–4; *Bellum Judaicarum* 1.398.

5 Dabrowa (1998) 17–18.

6 Josephus, *Bellum Judaicarum* 1.398.

7 Strabo, *Geography* 16.7.20; Josephus, *Antiquitates Judaicae* 15.343–5.

8 Josephus, *Antiquitates Judaicae* 15.349.

9 Josephus, *Antiquitates Judaicae* 15.350–1.

10 Josephus, *Antiquitates Judaicae* 15.354–60.

11 Schurer (1973) 1.567–9.

12 Dio Cassius, *History of Rome* 54.9.2; Sullivan (1977b) and (1977a).

13 Josephus, *Antiquitates Judaicae* 15.351–2.

14 Josephus, *Antiquitates Judaicae* 15, 378–88; Roller (1998).

15 Strabo, *Geography* 16.4.21; the title is confirmed by inscriptions – Bowersock (1983) 33.

16 Josephus, *Antiquitates Judaicae* 16.20.

17 Josephus, *Antiquitates Judaicae* 16.224–5.

18 Josephus, *Antiquitates Judaicae* 16.271–5.

19 Josephus, *Antiquitates Judaicae* 16.277–85.

20 Josephus, *Antiquitates Judaicae* 16, 286–94 and 17.54–7; Strabo, *Geography* 16.4.24.

21 Josephus, *Antiquitates Judaicae* 17.23–7.

22 Josephus, *Antiquitates Judaicae* 16.355.

23 Pliny the Elder, *Natural History* 5.66–80.

24 Josephus, *Antiquitates Judaicae* 16.129, 132–5; *Bellum Judaicarum* 1.457–66.

25 Josephus, *Antiquitates Judaicae* 17.188–90; *Bellum Judaicarum* 1.664; this whole

catalogue is conveniently listed by Richardson (1996) 33–8.

26　Josephus, *Antiquitates Judaicae* 17.193–4.

27　Josephus, *Antiquitates Judaicae* 17.219–22, 224–48, 289–98.

28　Josephus, *Antiquitates Judaicae* 17.300.

29　Josephus, *Antiquitates Judaicae* 17.317–23.

Chapter 11: Kings and Governors

1　Schurer (1973) 256–7, though this is not included in Dabrowa (1998).

2　Dio Cassius, *History of Rome* 55.10.19–20 and 10a.4; Velleius Paterculus, *Roman History* 2.101–2; Syme (1980) 8–13; Romer (1979) 199–214.

3　Pliny the Elder, *Natural History* 2.168; 6.41 and 160; Bowersock (1983) 54–8.

4　Dio Cassius, *History of Rome* 55.10a.1.

5　Josephus, *Antiquitates Judaicae* 17.296.

6　Josephus, *Antiquitates Judaicae* 17.340–53; *Bellum Judaicarum* 2.111–13; Dio Cassius, *History of Rome* 55.27.6; Strabo, *Geography* 16.2.46.

7　Josephus, *Antiquitates Judaicae* 17.355 and 18.3–6; *Bellum Judaicarum* 2.117.

8　*CIL* III 6687.

9　Josephus, *Antiquitates Judaicae* 18.23; *Bellum Judaicarum* 2.118.

10　Josephus, *Antiquitates Judaicae* 18.31.

11　Schurer (1973) 1.336–53; Hoehner (1972).

12　Dio Cassius, *History of Rome* 55.9.3–4.

13　Josephus, *Bellum Judaicarum* 2.67–8.

14　Josephus, *Antiquitates Judaicae* 18.113.

15　Sullivan (1977b) 212–13 and (1977a) 782–3.

16　Josephus, *Antiquitates Judaicae* 18.53; Tacitus, *Annals* 2.42.5 and 56.4.

17　Josephus, *Antiquitates Judaicae* 18.108; Dabrowa (1998) 37–8.

18　Tacitus, *Annals* 6.31.1–3; Dio Cassius, *History of Rome* 58.26.1–4; Josephus, *Antiquitates Judaicae* 18.97–8.

19　Josephus, *Antiquitates Judaicae* 18.103–12.

20　Josephus, *Antiquitates Judaicae* 18.86–7.

21　Josephus, *Antiquitates Judaicae* 18.13–115.

22　Josephus, *Antiquitates Judaicae* 18.90.

23　Josephus, *Antiquitates Judaicae* 18.96–104, 120, 124; Suetonius, *Life of Caligula* 14.3; Dio Cassius, *History of Rome* 59.27.2.

24　Josephus, *Antiquitates Judaicae* 18.224–7; *Bellum Judaicarum* 2.181; Philo, *In Flaccum* 5–6.

25　Dio Cassius, *History of Rome* 59.8.2; 60.8.1–2.

26　Josephus, *Antiquitates Judaicae* 18.238–39, 252; *Bellum Judaicarum* 2.183.

27　Josephus, *Antiquitates Judaicae* 9.1–277; *Bellum Judaicarum* 2.204–16; Dio Cassius, *History of Rome* 6.8.2–3.

28　Bowersock (1983) 65–9.

29 Josephus, *Antiquitates Judaicae* 19.300–2; Philo, *Legatio ad Gaium*, Smallwood (1970) 248–54.

30 Josephus, *Antiquitates Judaicae* 19.326–41; *Bellum Judaicarum* 5.152–4; for the interrelationships see Sullivan's articles (note 15).

31 Josephus, *Antiquitates Judaicae* 19.354–66; *Bellum Judaicarum* 2.220.

32 Sullivan (1977c) 332–6; Schurer (1973) 1.471–3; details are unclear.

33 This period is, of course, much studied: cf Schurer (1973) 1.455–70; Goodman (1987) and (2007). Here I merely summarize.

34 Josephus, *Bellum Judaicarum* 2.266–70, 284; *Antiquitates Judaicae* 20.173–7, 183–4.

35 Josephus, *Bellum Judaicarum* 2.285–96.

36 Josephus, *Bellum Judaicarum* 2.293–332.

37 Josephus, *Bellum Judaicarum* 2.281.

38 Josephus, *Bellum Judaicarum* 2.344–440.

Chapter 12: The Jewish Rebellion: Campaigns in the Country

1 Goodman (1985) for an examination of this group.

2 Applebaum (1971) 156–70.

3 Josephus, *Bellum Judaicarum* 2.418–21 and 3.12–13.

4 Josephus, *Bellum Judaicarum* 2.422–4, 430–32, 437–40, 449–54.

5 Josephus, *Bellum Judaicarum* 2.426–8, 433–4, 441–3.

6 Josephus, *Bellum Judaicarum* 2.457–60, 466–77, and 3.12–13.

7 Josephus, *Bellum Judaicarum* 2.459, 478–80.

8 Josephus, *Bellum Judaicarum* 2.487–98; Smallwood (1981) chapter 10.

9 Josephus, *Bellum Judaicarum* 2.484–6.

10 Josephus, *Bellum Judaicarum* 2.500–2.

11 Suetonius, *Life of Nero* 19; Pliny the Elder, *Natural History* 6.15; Tacitus, *Histories* 1.6.9; Dabrowa (1998) 56–7.

12 Josephus, *Bellum Judaicarum* 2.291 and 510–12.

13 Josephus, *Bellum Judaicarum* 2.517–21.

14 Josephus, *Bellum Judaicarum* 2.528–39.

15 Josephus, *Bellum Judaicarum* 2.546–55.

16 Suetonius, *Life of Vespasian* 4; Josephus, *Bellum Judaicarum* 3.1–8; Dabrowa (1998) 57–9.

Chapter 13: The Jewish Rebellion: Vespasian's Approach

1 Josephus, *Bellum Judaicarum* 3.8 and 64; Tacitus, *Histories* 5.10.1; Levick (1999) 29.

2 Josephus, *Bellum Judaicarum* 2.503.

3 Josephus, *Bellum Judaicarum* 2.556; the date of the Christians' removal (to the Greek city of Pella) is not clear, but this was as good a time as any to leave.

4   Josephus, *Bellum Judaicarum* 2.562–4; Smallwood (1981) 298–9.

5   Kadman (1960).

6   Josephus, *Bellum Judaicarum* 2.562–8.

7   Josephus, *Bellum Judaicarum* 2.569–75.

8   Josephus, *Bellum Judaicarum* 3.9–28.

9   Josephus, *Bellum Judaicarum* 3.414–16.

10 Josephus, *Bellum Judaicarum* 3.477–584; Josephus, *Vita* 32–61, 187–9.

11 Josephus, *Bellum Judaicarum* 2.567, 585–93, 503–4, 598–632.

12 Josephus, *Bellum Judaicarum* 3.29 and 64–9; Tacitus, *Histories* 1.10.3 and 5.1.2; Suetonius, *Life of Vespasian* 4.6.

13 Josephus, *Bellum Judaicarum* 3.30–4, 59–63.

14 Josephus, *Bellum Judaicarum* 3.128–398; Smallwood (1981) 307–8.

15 Josephus, *Bellum Judaicarum* 3.399–406; Suetonius, *Life of Vespasian* 5; Dio Cassius, *History of Rome* 66.1.

16 Josephus, *Bellum Judaicarum* 3.404, 412–13, 443–5.

17 Josephus, *Bellum Judaicarum* 2.595–7; *Vita* 64–9, 112–13, 112–13 and 149–54.

18 Josephus, *Bellum Judaicarum* 3.443–61, 522–42.

19 Josephus, *Bellum Judaicarum* 4.11–120.

20 Josephus, *Bellum Judaicarum* 3.414–31.

21 Josephus, *Bellum Judaicarum* 4.130 and 444.

22 Josephus, *Bellum Judaicarum* 4.121–8, 135–317, 326–65.

23 Josephus, *Bellum Judaicarum* 4.366.

24 Josephus, *Bellum Judaicarum* 4.413, 437–9, 445–50, 486.

25 Josephus, *Bellum Judaicarum* 4.491, 497–501.

Chapter 14: The Jewish Rebellion: Jerusalem

1   A well-studied set of events. The latest account is by Morgan (2006), but see also Wellesley (1989) and Greenhalgh (1975). An account from the point of view of Vespasian is Levick (1999).

2   Josephus, *Bellum Judaicarum* 4.491, 497–502; Tacitus, *Histories* 1.10, 2.1 and 4.2; Suetonius, *Life of Titus* 5.1.

3   Tacitus, *Histories* 2.3–4; Wellesley (1989) 44.

4   Tacitus, *Histories* 2.79; Josephus, *Bellum Judaicarum* 4.616–17; Downey (1961) 202–3.

5   Tacitus, *Histories* 2.74, 78 and 81; Suetonius, *Life of Vespasian* 6.

6   Josephus, *Bellum Judaicarum* 4.389–97.

7   Josephus, *Bellum Judaicarum* 4.398–409, 503–37, 574–9; 5.5–12; Smallwood (1981) 315–16.

8   Josephus, *Bellum Judaicarum* 5.24–5.

9   Josephus, *Bellum Judaicarum* 4.550–4.

10 Morgan (2006) lists the legions and their positions and movements in his appendix 3.

11 Tacitus, *Histories* 2.82, 4.51; Suetonius, *Life of Vespasian* 6.
12 Tacitus, *Histories* 1.79.
13 Josephus, *Bellum Judaicarum* 5.41–4 and 50; Tacitus, *Histories* 5.
14 Josephus, *Bellum Judaicarum* 5.50–66, 75–105.
15 Josephus, *Bellum Judaicarum* 5.259–302, 331–42.
16 Josephus, *Bellum Judaicarum* 5.346–7, 466–85.
17 Josephus, *Bellum Judaicarum* 5.497–8, 504–8, 6.23–32, 68–80.
18 Josephus, *Bellum Judaicarum* 6.113–20.
19 Josephus, *Bellum Judaicarum* 6.150–1, 165–6, 177–92, 233–5.
20 Josephus, *Bellum Judaicarum* 6.244–53, 260–1.
21 Josephus, *Bellum Judaicarum* 6.316.
22 Josephus, *Bellum Judaicarum* 6.323–408.
23 Josephus, *Bellum Judaicarum* 7.25–6.
24 Josephus, *Bellum Judaicarum* 7.414–20.

Chapter 15: The Jewish Rebellion: Aftermath

1 Josephus, *Bellum Judaicarum* 6.238.
2 Josephus, *Bellum Judaicarum* 7.53–79.
3 Dabrowa (1998) 60–2.
4 Josephus, *Bellum Judaicarum* 6.412–13.
5 Josephus, *Bellum Judaicarum* 6.413, 7.1–2.
6 Josephus, *Bellum Judaicarum* 7.18–20.
7 Josephus, *Bellum Judaicarum* 7.23–4; Tacitus, *Histories* 2.2.
8 Cantineau (1932) 9; Bowersock (1983) 72.
9 Josephus, *Bellum Judaicarum* 7.41, 54–62, 103–4, 107–9.
10 Josephus, *Bellum Judaicarum* 7.105, 6.356–7.
11 Josephus, *Bellum Judaicarum* 7.112–15; *CIL* XVI 33.
12 Smallwood (1981) 546; Schurer (1973) 1.515.
13 Josephus, *Bellum Judaicarum* 7.116–17.
14 Josephus, *Bellum Judaicarum* 7.410; Smallwood (1981) 367.
15 Josephus, *Bellum Judaicarum* 7.117; Suetonius, *Life of Titus* 5.3.
16 Josephus, *Bellum Judaicarum* 7.411–19; Brunt (1975) 124–47.
17 Josephus, *Bellum Judaicarum* 7.437–50; Smallwood (1981) 369–71.
18 Josephus, *Bellum Judaicarum* 7.420–1, 433–5; Smallwood (1981) 367–8.
19 Josephus, *Bellum Judaicarum* 4.402–4.
20 Josephus, *Bellum Judaicarum* 4.518–19 and 7.163–4; Rocca (2008) 32–33 for a description and a plan.
21 Josephus, *Bellum Judaicarum* 7.164–208; Rocca (2008) 33; for a plan see Rollin and Streetly (1998) 175–8.
22 Josephus, *Bellum Judaicarum* 7.210–15.
23 Josephus, *Bellum Judaicarum* 7.216–17; Smallwood (1981) 371–6.

24 Josephus, *Bellum Judaicarum* 7.220–37; Sullivan (1977a) 791–4.

25 Sullivan (1977b) 218–19, and his stemma; Chad (1972) chapter 5, puts the annexation in the reign of Antoninus Pius, but can find no kings after Sohaemos.

26 Matthews (1984) 157–80; an accessible survey of Palmyran history is Stoneham (1992).

27 Dabrowa (1998) 60–8; Syme (1981) 125–44; as the father of the Emperor Trajan, Traianus is quite well known.

28 Dabrowa (1998) 65–8; van Berchem (1985) 47–87.

29 Roth (1995) 87ff.

30 Josephus, *Bellum Judaicarum* 7.280–401; Yadin (1966); Rocca (2008) 33–4.

Chapter 16: The Desert Frontier

1 Dio Cassius, *History of Rome* 68.14; Bowersock (1983) chapter 6; Kennedy (1980) 281–309; Shahid (1984) 19–21.

2 Baines and Malek (1994) 187; Parker (2009) 409–20.

3 Sidebotham (2011) chapter 8.

4 This is the basis of the '*villes mortes*' of the limestone region of Syria, north of Apamea – see Tchalenko (1953).

5 See, as a particularly vivid example of the work, Kennedy and Riley (1990); also Isaac (1992) chapter 8.

Bibliography

Abbreviations
CIL – Corpus Inscriptionem Latinarum
FHN – Fontes Historia Nubiorum
OGIS – Orientis Graecae Inscriptiones Selectae

Secondary Works
Alston, Richard (1995), *Soldier and Society in Roman Egypt*, London.

Anderson, R.D. et al (1979), 'Elegiacs by Gallus from Qasr Ibrim', *Journal of Roman Studies* 69: 125–55.

Applebaum, S. (1971), 'The Zealots: the Case for Revaluation', *Journal of Roman Studies* 61: 156–70.

Bagnall, R.S. (1976), *The Administration of the Ptolemaic Possessions Outside Egypt*, Leiden.

Bagnall, R.S. and Derow, P. (2004), *Historical Sources in Translation: The Hellenistic Period*, 2nd ed., Oxford.

Baines, J. and Malek, J. (1994), *Atlas of Ancient Egypt*, Oxford.

Ball, Warwick (2000), *Rome in the East, the Transformation of an Empire*, London.

Bouchier, P. (1996), *Caius Cornelius Gallus*, Paris.

Bowersock, G.W. (1983), *Roman Arabia*, Cambridge MA.

Bowman, Alan K. (1986), *Egypt after the Pharaohs*, London.

Brett, A.B. (1937), 'A New Kleopatra Tetradrachm of Ascalon', *American Journal of Archaeology*, 41: 452–63.

Brunt, P.A. (1971), *Italian Manpower 225 BC–AD 14*, Oxford.

Brunt, P.A. (1975), 'The Administrators of Roman Egypt', *Journal of Roman Studies*, 64: 124–47.

Brunt, P.A. and Moore, J.M. eds (1967), *Res Gestae divi Augusti. The Achievements of the Divine Augustus*, Oxford.

Burstein, S.M. (1995), 'Cornelius Gallus and Aithiopia', *Graeco-Africana, Studies in the History of Greek Relations with Egypt and Nubia*, New Rochelle NY: 165–73.

Butcher, K. (2003), *Roman Syria and the Near East*, London.

Cantineau, J. (1932), *Le Nabatéen*, vol. 2, Paris.

Carter, J.M. (1970), *The Battle of Actium*, London.

Casson, L. (1986), *Ships and Seamanship in the Ancient World*, Princeton NJ.

Chad, C. (1972), *Les Dynastes d'Emése*, Beyrouth.

Cohen, G.M. (2006), *The Hellenistic Settlements in Syria, the Red Sea Basin and North Africa*, California.

Costa, P.M. (1977), 'A Latin-Greek Inscription from the Jawf of the Yemen', *Proceedings of the Seminar for Arabian Studies*, 7: 69–72.

Crawford, M.H. (1985), *Coinage and Money under the Roman Republic*, London.

Dabrowa, Edward (1998), *The Governors of Roman Syria from Augustus to Septimius Severus*, Bonn.

Downey, G. (1951), 'The Occupation of Syria by the Romans', *Transactions of the American Philosophical Association*, 82: 149–63.

Fletcher, Joann (2008), *Cleopatra the Great*, London.

Freeman, P. and Kennedy, D.L. (1996), *The Defence of the Roman and Byzantine East*, BAR S297, Oxford.

Garstang, J. (1910), 'Preliminary Note on Excavations at Meroe in Ethiopia', *Liverpool Annals of Archaeology and Anthropology*, 3: 45–52.

Gelzer, M. (1968), *Caesar, Politician and Statesman*, trans, P. Needham, Oxford.

Goodman, M. (1987), *The Ruing Class of Judaea*, Cambridge.

Goodman, M. (2007), *Rome and Jerusalem*, London.

Grant, M. (1972), *Cleopatra*, London.

Greenhalgh, P.A.L. (1975), *The Year of the Four Emperors*, London.

Head, B.V. (1911), *Historia Numorum*, Oxford.

Hoehner, H.W. (1972), *Herod Antipas, a Contemporary of Jesus Christ*, Cambridge.

Holbl, G. (2001), *A History of the Ptolemaic Empire*, London.

Hoyland, Robert G. (2001), *Arabia and the Arabs*, London.

Huzar, E.G. (1978), *Mark Antony*, Minnesota.

Isaac, B. (1992), *The Limits of Empire*, rev. ed. Oxford.

Jameson, S. (1968), 'Chronology of the Campaigns of Aelius Gallus and C. Petronius', *Journal of Roman Studies*, 58: 71–84.

Jones, A.H.M. (1971), *Cities of the Eastern Roman Provinces*, 2nd ed., Oxford.

Kadman, L. (1960), *The Coins of the Jewish War 66–73 CE*, Jerusalem.

Kennedy, D.L. (1980), 'Legio VI Ferrata: the Annexation and Early Governors of Arabia', *Harvard Studies in Classical Philosophy*, 84: 281–309

Kennedy D.L. and Riley, D. (1990), *Rome's Desert Frontier from the Air*, London.

Kirwan, L.P. (1977), 'Rome beyond the Southern Egyptian Frontier', *Proceedings of the British Academy*, 63: 13–31.

Kirwan, L.P. (1979), 'Where to Search for the Ancient Port of Leuke Kome', in *Studies in the History of Arabia, Pre-Islamic Arabia*, Riyadh.

Levick, B. (1999), *Vespasian*, London.

McLaren, J.S. (1991), *Power and Politics in Palestine*, Sheffield: 67–79.

Maehlers, H. (1983), 'Egypt under the last Ptolemies', *Bulletin of the Institute of Cuneiform Studies* 30.

Matthews, J.E. (1984), 'The Tax Law of Palmyra, Evidence for Economic History in a City in the Roman East', *Journal of Roman Studies*, 74: 157–80.

Meuleraera, H. de (1959), 'Les strateges du nome tentyrite a la fin de l'epoque ptolemaique et au debut de l'occupation romaine', *Rivista di Studi Orientali*, 35: 1–25.

Millar, F. (1993), *The Roman Near East, 31 BC–AD 337*, Cambridge MA.

Minas-Nerpel, M. and Pfeiffer, S. (2010), 'Establishing Roman Rule in Egypt: the Trilingual Stele of C. Cornelius Gallus from Philae', in Lembke, K., Minas-Nerpel M., and Pfeiffer, S. eds, *Tradition and Transformation: Egypt under Roman Rule, Proceedings of the International Conference, Hildesheim, July 2006*, Leiden: 267–98.

Morgan, W. Gwyn (2006), *AD 69, The Year of Four Emperors*, Oxford.

Mond, R. and Myers, O.H. (1934), *The Bucheum*, London.

Myers, E.A. (2011), *The Ituraeans and the Roman Near East, Reassessing the Sources*, Cambridge.

Parker, P. (2009), *The Empire Stops Here*, London.

Pirenne, Jacques (1961), *Le Royaume Sud-Arabe de Qataban et sa Datation*, Louvain.

Pollard, N. (2000), *Soldiers, Cities and Civilians in Roman Syria*, Michigan.

Richardson, Peter (1996), *Herod, King of the Jews and Friend of the Romans*, South Carolina.

Ricketts, L.M. (1980), *The Administration of Ptolemaic Egypt under Cleopatra*, University of Minnesota PhD thesis.

Rickman, Geoffrey (1980), *The Corn Supply of Ancient Rome*, Oxford.

Rocca, S. (2008), *The Forts of Judaea 168 BC–AD 73*, Oxford.

Roller, Duane W. (1998), *The Building Programme of Herod the Great*, California.

Rollin, S. and Streetly, J. (1998), *Jordan Blue Guide*, London.

Romer, F.E. (1979), 'Gaius Caesar's Military Diplomacy in the East', *Transactions of the American Philosophical Association*, 109: 199–214.

Roth, J. (1995), 'The Length of the Siege of Masada', *Scripta Classica Israelica*, 14: 87–110.

Russell, D.S. (1967), *The Jews from Alexander to Herod*, Oxford.

Sartre, M. (2005), *The Middle East under Rome*, trans Porter, C. and Rawlings, E., Cambridge MA.

Schurer, E. (1973), *The History of the Jewish People in the Age of Jesus Christ*, vol 1, rev ed, Edinburgh.

Seyrig, H. (1950), 'Eres de quelqes villes de Syria' *Syria*, 27: 11–50.

Seyrig, H. (1954), 'Eres pompéiennes de Phénicie', *Syria*, 31: 73–80.

Shahid, I. (1984), *Rome and the Arabs*, Washington DC.

Sherwin-White, A.N. (1983), *Roman Foreign Policy in the East*, Norman Oklahoma.

Sidebotham, S.E. (1986a), 'Aelius Gallus and Arabia', *Latomus*, 45: 590–602.

Sidebotham, S.E. (1986b), *Roman Economic Policy in the Erythra Thalassa, 30 BC–AD 217*, Leiden.

Sidebotham, S.E. (2011), *Berenike and the Ancient Maritime Spice Route*, California.

Smallwood, E.M. ed. (1970), *Philonis Alexandrini, Legatio ad Gaium*, 2nd ed, Leiden.

Smallwood, E.M. (1981), *The Jews under Roman Rule from Pompey to Diocletian*, 2nd ed, Leiden.

Stoneham, Richard (1992), *Palmyra and its Empire*, Michigan.

Sullivan, D. (1980), *Near Eastern Royalty and Rome 100–30 BC*, Toronto.

Sullivan, R.D. (1977a), 'The Dynasty of Commagene', in *Aufstieg und Niedergang des Römischen Welt* II.8: 732–98.

Sullivan, R.D. (1977b), 'The Dynasty of Emesa', in *Aufstieg und Niedergang des Römischen Welt* II.8: 198–219.

Sullivan, R.D. (1977c), 'The Dynasty of Judaea', in *Aufstieg und Niedergang des Römischen Welt* II.8: 296–354.

Syme, Ronald (1938), 'The Origin of Cornelius Gallus', *Classical Quarterly*, 32: 39–44.

Syme, Ronald (1939), *The Roman Revolution*, Oxford.

Syme, R. (1980), *History in Ovid*, Oxford.

Syme, R. (1981), 'Governors Dying in Syria', *Zeitschrift für Papyrologie und Epigraphik*, 4: 125–44.

Tchalenko, G. (1953), *Villes antiques de la Syrie du nord*, Paris.

Thomas, J.D. (1975), *The Epistategos in Ptolemaic and Roman Egypt, I: The Ptolemaic Epistrategos*, Opladen.

Torok, L. (1989), 'Kush and the External World', in *Studia Meroitica 1984*, Meroitica 10: 49–214.

Torok, L. (1989–1990), 'Augustus and Meroe', *Orientalia Suecana*, 38–39: 171–90.

van Berchem, D. (1985), 'Le port de Séleucie de Piérie et l'infrastructure logistique des guerres parthiques', *Bonner Jahrbücher*, 185: 47–87.

van 't Dack, E. (1988), 'L'Armée Romaine d'Egypte de 55 a 30 av. J.-C.', in *Ptolemaica Selecta*, Louvain: 185–213.

Wellesley, Kenneth (1989), *The Long Year, AD 69*, 2nd ed., Bristol.

Welsby, D.A. (1996), *The Kingdom of Kush*, London.

Whitehorne, John (1994), *Cleopatras*, London.

Will, E. (1982), *Histoire Politique du Monde Hellénistique*, vol. 2, Nancy.

Yadin, Y. (1966), *Masada*, London.

Index